CASES AND MATERIALS ON FEDERAL CONSTITUTIONAL LAW

Volume II

Federal Executive Power and the Separation of Powers

CASES AND MATERIALS ON FEDERAL CONSTITUTIONAL LAW

Volume II
Federal Executive Power and
the Separation of Powers

THIRD EDITION

Scott W. Gaylord
Christopher R. Green
Lee J. Strang

CAROLINA ACADEMIC PRESS
Durham, North Carolina

ISBN: 978-1-5310-0838-3
eBook: 978-1-53100-839-0
LCCN: 2017960515

Carolina Academic Press, LLC
700 Kent Street
Durham, North Carolina 27701
Telephone (919) 489-7486
Fax (919) 493-5668
www.cap-press.com

Printed in the United States of America

INTRODUCTION TO THE MODULAR CASEBOOK SERIES

By now you have realized that the course materials assigned by your instructor have a very different form than traditional casebooks. The *Modular Casebook Series* is intentionally designed to break the mold. Course materials consist of one or more separate volumes selected from among a larger set of volumes. Each volume is relatively short so that an instructor may "mix and match" a suitable number of volumes for a course of varying length and focus.

Each volume is also designed to serve an instructional purpose rather than as a treatise; as a result, the *Modular Casebook Series* is published in soft cover. Publication of the separate volumes in soft cover also permits course materials to be revised more easily so that they will incorporate recent developments. Moreover, by purchasing only the assigned volumes for a given course, students are likely to recognize significant savings over the cost of a traditional casebook.

Traditional casebooks are often massive tomes, frequently exceeding 1500 pages. Traditional casebooks are lengthy because they attempt to cover the entire breadth of material that *might* be useful to an instructor for a two-semester course of six credits. Even with six credits, different instructors will cover different portions of a traditional casebook within the time available. As a consequence, traditional casebooks include a range of materials that may leave hundreds of unexplored pages in any particular six-credit class. Especially for a student in a three or four credit course, such a book is hardly an efficient means of delivering the needed materials. Students purchase much more book than they need, at great expense. And students carry large, heavy books for months at a time.

Traditional casebooks are usually hard-cover publications. It seems as though they are constructed to last as a reference work throughout decades of practice. In fact, as the presence of annual supplements to casebooks makes clear, portions of casebooks become obsolete very shortly after publication. Treatises and hornbooks are designed to serve as reference works; casebooks serve a different purpose. Once again, the traditional format of casebooks seems to impose significant added costs on students for little reason.

The form of traditional casebooks increases the probability that the content will become obsolete shortly after publication. The publication of lengthy texts in hardcover produces substantial delay between the time the author completes the final draft and the time the book reaches the hands of students. In addition, the broader scope of material addressed in a 1500 page text means that portions of the text are more likely to be superseded by later developments than any particular narrowly-tailored volume in the *Modular Casebook Series*. Because individual volumes in the *Modular Casebook Series* may be revised without requiring revision of other volumes, the materials for any particular course will be less likely to require supplementation.

Most importantly, the cases and accompanying exercises in the *Modular Casebook Series* provide students with the opportunity to learn and deploy the standard arguments in the various subject matters of constitutional law. Each case is edited to emphasize the key arguments made by the Court and justices. For instance, in many older cases, headings were added to note a new or related argument. Furthermore, the exercises following each case focus on identifying and critiquing the Court's and justices' arguments. The exercises also form the basis for rich class discussion. All of this introduces students to the most important facet of constitutional law: the deployment of standard arguments in each doctrinal context and across constitutional law doctrines.

We hope you enjoy this innovative approach to course materials.

Dedication

To Pamela and our family and to all the families who serve and
sacrifice to protect the Constitution.
S.W.G.

To Bonnie and Justice John Marshall Harlan I.
C.R.G.

To Elizabeth and Saint Thomas Aquinas.
L.J.S.

Acknowledgments

We would like to thank Tom Odom for proposing and initiating the *Modular Casebook Series*, and for inviting us to participate in the *Series*, and, for research leave and support, to the Elon University School of Law, the Jamie Lloyd Whitten Chair of Law and Government Endowment at the University of Mississippi School of Law, and the University of Toledo College of Law. Without our wives' and children's loving support, this project would not have been completed.

Preface to the Third Edition

Technological improvements permit the compilation of resources in a manner unthinkable when we were law students. Materials that permit further examination of assigned reading can be delivered in a cost-effective manner and in a format more likely to be useful in practice than reams of photocopies.

With regard to assigned reading, there is no good reason to burden students with stacks of hand-outs or expensive annual supplements. Publication through the *Modular Casebook Series* ensures that even very recent developments may be incorporated prior to publication. Moreover, if important cases are decided after publication of the latest edition of a volume, they will be included on the series website www .federalconstitutionallaw.com. Cases and materials that shed additional light on matter in the hard-copy casebook are also included on the website.

We welcome comments from readers so that we may make further improvements in the next edition of this publication.

Scott W. Gaylord
Christopher R. Green
Lee J. Strang

TECHNICAL NOTE FROM THE EDITORS

The cases and other materials excerpted in this Volume have been edited in an effort to enhance readability. Citations of multiple cases for a single proposition have been shortened in many places to reference only one or two prominent authorities. In some places, archaic language or spelling has been revised. Headings were added to some of the longer decisions to permit ease of reference to various parts of the opinion. Such headings may also assist the reader in identifying a transition from one point to another.

Cases have been edited to a suitable length. In order to achieve that result, many interesting but tangential points have been omitted. The length of some opinions also hindered the inclusion of excerpts from concurring or dissenting opinions. Where such opinions have been omitted, it is noted in the text.

In editing these cases, we have not indicated the portions of cases we deleted unless such deletion with the absence of ellipses would have been misleading. However, any time we inserted material into a case, we indicated the insertion with the use of brackets.

Scott W. Gaylord
Christopher R. Green
Lee J. Strang

TABLE OF CONTENTS

Introduction to Volume 2

The Constitution vests "[t]he executive Power" in a "President of the United States." Art. II, § 1, cl. 1. Unlike Article I, however, Article II is relatively short. For this and other reasons covered later in this Volume, there remains continuing significant debate over the scope of the President's power. In particular, one of the on-going points of debate is whether and, if so, to what extent, the President wields inherent—un-express—power. A second key facet of the debates over the scope of federal executive power is in the context of tensions between the President and Congress: where is the boundary between legislative and executive power? How and to what extent are these areas kept separate?

This volume first considers executive branch's structure—chiefly relationships between the President and others who exercise executive power—before addressing the substantive scope of executive power and the ways in which those who exercise that power are constitutionally segregated from those exercising legislative power.

A. Relationships Within the Executive Branch

Chapter 1 builds on the forms of argument you learned in Volume 1 by reviewing their use by the Supreme Court in the key cases governing the relationships between different officials exercising executive power, particularly the President's removal, appointment, and countermanding powers over other federal officers. The Chapter begins with Chief Justice Taft's magnum opus in *Myers v. United States*, 272 U.S. 52 (1926), and includes the Court's approval of the independent counsel over Justice Scalia's now-famous dissent in *Morrison v. Olson*, 487 U.S. 654 (1988).

B. The Scope of Executive Power

Chapter 2 considers what counts as executive power, beginning with the most important case on the subject, *Youngstown Sheet & Tube Co. v. Sawyer*, 343 U.S. 579 (1952), and its debate over the existence and scope of inherent and emergency presidential power. It next covers the Supreme Court's showdown with the President over executive privilege in *United States v. Nixon*, 418 U.S. 683 (1974), and several disputes over congressional versus presidential control over foreign policy, including executive agreements, war powers, and the recognition of other states.

C. Separation of Executive and Legislative Power

Chapter 3 considers the ways in which constitutional law cabins executive and legislative power away from each other. The President is excluded from lawmaking through the non-delegation doctrine, the take-care duty, and limits on the line-item veto, but may retain the ability to review legislation for constitutionality independent of the judiciary. Cases like *INS v. Chadha*, 462 U.S. 919 (1983), prevent Congress from giving itself or its components veto over actions of the executive branch.

The Constitution of the United States

We the People of the United States, in order to form a more perfect nion, establish Justice, insure domestic Tranquility, provide for the common defence, promote the general Welfare, and secure the Blessings of Liberty to ourselves and our Posterity, do ordain and establish this Constitution for the United States of America.

Article I

Section 1. All legislative Powers herein granted shall be vested in a Congress of the United States, which shall consist of a Senate and House of Representatives.

Section 2. The House of Representatives shall be composed of Members chosen every second Year by the People of the several States, and the Electors in each State shall have the Qualifications requisite for Electors of the most numerous Branch of the State Legislature.

No person shall be a Representative who shall not have attained to the Age of twenty five Years, and been seven Years a Citizen of the United States, and who shall not, when elected, be an Inhabitant of that State in which he shall be chosen.

Representatives and direct Taxes shall be apportioned among the several States which may be included within this Union, according to their respective Numbers, which shall be determined by adding to the whole Number of free Persons, including those bound to Service for a Term of Years, and excluding Indians not taxed, three fifths of all other Persons. The actual Enumeration shall be made within three Years after the first Meeting of the Congress of the United States, and within every subsequent Term of ten Years, in such Manner as they shall by Law direct. The Number of Representatives shall not exceed one for every thirty Thousand, but each State shall have at Least one Representative; and until such enumeration shall be made, the State of New Hampshire shall be entitled to chuse three, Massachusetts eight, Rhode-Island and Providence Plantations one, Connecticut five, New-York six, New Jersey four, Pennsylvania eight, Delaware one, Maryland six, Virginia ten, North Carolina five, South Carolina five, and Georgia three.

When vacancies happen in the Representation from any State, the Executive Authority thereof shall issue Writs of Election to fill such Vacancies.

The House of Representatives shall chuse their Speaker and other Officers; and shall have the sole Power of Impeachment.

Section 3. The Senate of the United States shall be composed of two Senators from each State, chosen by the Legislature thereof, for six Years; and each Senator shall have one Vote.

Immediately after they shall be assembled in Consequence of the first Election, they shall be divided as equally as may be into three Classes. The Seats of the Senators of the first Class shall be vacated at the Expiration of the second Year, of the second Class at the Expiration of the fourth Year, and of the third Class at the Expiration of the sixth Year, so that one third may be chosen every second Year; and if Vacancies happen by Resignation, or otherwise, during the Recess of the Legislature of any

State, the Executive thereof may make temporary Appointments until the next Meeting of the Legislature, which shall then fill such Vacancies.

No Person shall be a Senator who shall not have attained to the Age of thirty Years, and been nine Years a Citizen of the United States, and who shall not, when elected, be an Inhabitant of that State for which he shall be chosen.

The Vice President of the United States shall be President of the Senate, but shall have no Vote, unless they be equally divided.

The Senate shall choose their other Officers, and also a President pro tempore, in the Absence of the Vice President, or when he shall exercise the Office of President of the United States.

The Senate shall have the sole Power to try all Impeachments. When sitting for that Purpose, they shall be on Oath or Affirmation. When the President of the United States is tried, the Chief Justice shall preside: and no Person shall be convicted without the Concurrence of two thirds of the Members present.

Judgment in Cases of Impeachment shall not extend further than to removal from Office, and disqualification to hold and enjoy any Office of honor, Trust or Profit under the United States: but the Party convicted shall nevertheless be liable and subject to Indictment, Trial, Judgment and Punishment, according to Law.

Section 4. The Times, Places and Manner of holding Elections for Senators and Representatives, shall be prescribed in each State by the Legislature thereof; but the Congress may at any time by Law make or alter such Regulations, except as to the Places of chusing Senators.

The Congress shall assemble at least once in every Year, and such Meeting shall be on the first Monday in December, unless they shall by Law appoint a different Day.

Section 5. Each House shall be the Judge of the Elections, Returns and Qualifications of its own Members, and a Majority of each shall constitute a Quorum to do Business; but a smaller Number may adjourn from day to day, and may be authorized to compel the Attendance of absent Members, in such Manner, and under such Penalties as each House may provide.

Each House may determine the Rules of its Proceedings, punish its Members for disorderly Behaviour, and, with the Concurrence of two thirds, expel a Member.

Each House shall keep a Journal of its Proceedings, and from time to time publish the same, excepting such Parts as may in their Judgment require Secrecy; and the Yeas and Nays of the Members of either House on any question shall, at the Desire of one fifth of those Present, be entered on the Journal.

Section 6. The Senators and Representatives shall receive a Compensation for their Services, to be ascertained by Law, and paid out of the Treasury of the United States. They shall in all Cases, except Treason, Felony and Breach of the Peace, be privileged from Arrest during their Attendance at the Session of their respective Houses, and in going to and returning from the same; and for any Speech or Debate in either House, they shall not be questioned in any other Place.

No Senator or Representative shall, during the Time for which he was elected, be appointed to any civil Office under the Authority of the United States, which shall have been created, or the Emoluments whereof shall have been encreased during such time; and no Person holding any Office under the United States, shall be a Member of either House during his Continuance in Office.

Section 7. All Bills for raising Revenue shall originate in the House of Representatives; but the Senate may propose or concur with Amendments as on other Bills.

Every Bill which shall have passed the House of Representatives and the Senate, shall, before it become a Law, be presented to the President of the United States; If he approve he shall sign it, but if not he shall return it, with his Objections to that House in which it shall have originated, who shall enter the Objections at large on their Journal, and proceed to reconsider it. If after such Reconsideration two thirds of that House shall agree to pass the Bill, it shall be sent, together with the Objections, to the other House, by which it shall likewise be reconsidered, and if approved by two thirds of that House, it shall become a Law. But in all such Cases the Votes of both Houses shall be determined by yeas and Nays, and the Names of the Persons voting for and against the Bill shall be entered on the Journal of each House respectively. If any Bill shall not be returned by the President within ten days (Sundays excepted) after it shall have been presented to him, the Same shall be a Law, in like Manner as if he had signed it, unless the Congress by their Adjournment prevent its Return in which Case it shall not be a Law.

Every Order, Resolution, or Vote to which the Concurrence of the Senate and House of Representatives may be necessary (except on a question of Adjournment) shall be presented to the President of the United States; and before the Same shall take Effect, shall be approved by him, or being disapproved by him, shall be repassed by two thirds of the Senate and House of Representatives, according to the Rules and Limitations prescribed in the Case of a Bill.

Section 8. The Congress shall have Power To lay and collect Taxes, Duties, Imposts and Excises, to pay the Debts and provide for the common Defence and general Welfare of the United States; but all Duties, Imposts and Excises shall be uniform throughout the United States;

To borrow Money on the credit of the United States;

To regulate Commerce with foreign Nations, and among the several States, and with the Indian Tribes;

To establish an uniform Rule of Naturalization, and uniform Laws on the subject of Bankruptcies throughout the United States;

To coin Money, regulate the Value thereof, and foreign Coin, and fix the Standard of Weights and Measures;

To provide for the Punishment of counterfeiting the Securities and current Coin of the United States;

To establish Post Offices and post Roads;

To promote the Progress of Science and useful Arts, by securing for limited Times to Authors and Inventors the exclusive Right to their respective Writings and Discoveries;

To constitute Tribunals inferior to the supreme Court;

To define and punish Piracies and Felonies committed on the high Seas, and Offences against the Law of Nations;

To declare War, grant Letters of Marque and Reprisal, and make Rules concerning Captures on Land and Water;

To raise and support Armies, but no Appropriation of Money to that Use shall be for a longer Term than two Years;

To provide and maintain a Navy;

To make Rules for the Government and Regulation of the land and naval Forces;

To provide for calling forth the Militia to execute the Laws of the Union, suppress Insurrections and repel Invasions;

To provide for organizing, arming, and disciplining, the Militia, and for governing such Part of them as may be employed in the Service of the United States, reserving to the States respectively, the Appointment of the Officers, and the Authority of training the Militia according to the discipline prescribed by Congress;

To exercise exclusive Legislation in all Cases whatsoever, over such District (not exceeding ten Miles square) as may, by Cession of particular States, and the Acceptance of Congress, become the Seat of the Government of the United States, and to exercise like Authority over all Places purchased by the Consent of the Legislature of the State in which the Same shall be, for the Erection of Forts, Magazines, Arsenals, dock-Yards, and other needful Buildings;—And

To make all Laws which shall be necessary and proper for carrying into Execution the foregoing Powers, and all other Powers vested by this Constitution in the Government of the United States, or in any Department or Officer thereof.

Section 9. The Migration or Importation of such Persons as any of the States now existing shall think proper to admit, shall not be prohibited by the Congress prior to the Year one thousand eight hundred and eight, but a Tax or duty may be imposed on such Importation, not exceeding ten dollars for each Person.

The Privilege of the Writ of Habeas Corpus shall not be suspended, unless when in Cases of Rebellion or Invasion the public Safety may require it.

No Bill of Attainder or ex post facto Law shall be passed.

No Capitation, or other direct, Tax shall be laid, unless in Proportion to the Census or Enumeration herein before directed to be taken.

No Tax or Duty shall be laid on Articles exported from any State.

No Preference shall be given by any Regulation of Commerce or Revenue to the Ports of one State over those of another; nor shall Vessels bound to, or from, one State, be obliged to enter, clear, or pay Duties in another.

No Money shall be drawn from the Treasury, but in Consequence of Appropriations made by Law; and a regular Statement and Account of the Receipts and Expenditures of all public Money shall be published from time to time.

No Title of Nobility shall be granted by the United States: And no Person holding any Office of Profit or Trust under them, shall, without the Consent of the Congress, accept of any present, Emolument, Office, or Title, of any kind whatever, from any King, Prince, or foreign State.

Section 10. No State shall enter into any Treaty, Alliance, or Confederation; grant Letters of Marque and Reprisal; coin Money; emit Bills of Credit; make any Thing but gold and silver Coin a Tender in Payment of Debts; pass any Bill of Attainder, ex post facto Law, or Law impairing the Obligation of Contracts, or grant any Title of Nobility.

No State shall, without the Consent of the Congress, lay any Imposts or Duties on Imports or Exports, except what may be absolutely necessary for executing it's inspection Laws: and the net Produce of all Duties and Imposts, laid by any State on Imports or Exports, shall be for the Use of the Treasury of the United. States; and all such Laws shall be subject to the Revision and Controul of the Congress.

No State shall, without the Consent of Congress, lay any Duty of Tonnage, keep Troops, or Ships of War in time of Peace, enter into any Agreement or Compact with another State, or with a foreign Power, or engage in War, unless actually invaded, or in such imminent Danger as will not admit of delay.

Article II

Section 1. The executive Power shall be vested in a President of the United States of America. He shall hold his Office during the Term of four Years, and, together with the Vice President, chosen for the same Term, be elected as follows

Each State shall appoint, in such Manner as the Legislature thereof may direct, a Number of Electors, equal to the whole Number of Senators and Representatives to which the State may be entitled in the Congress: but no Senator or Representative, or Person holding an Office of Trust or Profit under the United States, shall be appointed an Elector.

The Electors shall meet in their respective States, and vote by Ballot for two Persons, of whom one at least shall not be an Inhabitant of the same State with themselves. And they shall make a List of all the Persons voted for, and of the Number of Votes for each; which List they shall sign and certify, and transmit sealed to the Seat of the Government of the United States, directed to the President of the Senate. The President of the Senate shall, in the Presence of the Senate and House of Representatives, open all the Certificates, and the Votes shall then be counted. The Person having the greatest Number of Votes shall be the President, if such Number be a Majority of the whole Number of Electors appointed; and if there be more than one who have such Majority, and have an equal Number of Votes, then the House of Representatives shall immediately chuse by Ballot one of them for President; and if no Person have a Majority, then from the five highest on the List the said House shall in like Manner chuse the President. But in chusing the President, the Votes shall be taken by States, the Representation from each State having one Vote; A quorum for this Purpose shall consist of a Member or Members from two thirds of the States, and a Majority of all the States shall be necessary to a Choice. In every Case, after the Choice of the President, the Person having the greatest Number of Votes of the Electors shall be the Vice President. But if there should remain two or more who have equal Votes, the Senate shall chuse from them by Ballot the Vice President.

The Congress may determine the Time of chusing the Electors, and the Day on which they shall give their Votes; which Day shall be the same throughout the United States.

No Person except a natural born Citizen, or a Citizen of the United States, at the time of the Adoption of this Constitution, shall be eligible to the Office of President; neither shall any Person be eligible to that Office who shall not have attained to the Age of thirty five Years, and been fourteen Years a Resident within the United States.

In the Case of the Removal of the President from Office, or of his Death, Resignation, or Inability to discharge the Powers and Duties of the said Office, the Same shall devolve on the Vice President, and the Congress may by Law provide for the Case of Removal, Death, Resignation or Inability, both of the President and Vice President, declaring what Officer shall then act as President, and such Officer shall act accordingly, until the Disability be removed, or a President shall be elected.

The President shall, at stated Times, receive for his Services, a Compensation, which shall neither be encreased nor diminished during the Period for which he shall have been elected, and he shall not receive within that Period any other Emolument from the United States, or any of them.

Before he enter on the Execution of his Office, he shall take the following Oath or Affirmation: — "I do solemnly swear (or affirm) that I will faithfully execute the Office of the President of the United States, and will to the best of my Ability, preserve, protect and defend the Constitution of the United States."

Section 2. The President shall be the Commander in Chief of the Army and Navy of the United States, and of the Militia of the several States, when called into the actual service of the United States; he may require the Opinion, in writing, of the principal Officer in each of the executive Departments, upon any Subject relating to the Duties of their respective Offices, and he shall have Power to grant Reprieves and Pardons for Offenses against the United States, except in Cases of Impeachment.

He shall have Power, by and with the Advice and Consent of the Senate, to make Treaties, provided two thirds of the Senators present concur; and he shall nominate, and by and with the Advice and Consent of the Senate, shall appoint Ambassadors, other public Ministers and Consuls, Judges of the supreme Court, and all other Officers of the United States, whose Appointments are not herein otherwise provided for, and which shall be established by Law but the Congress may by Law vest the Appointment of such inferior Officers, as they think proper, in the President alone, in the Courts of Law, or in the Heads of Departments.

The President shall have Power to fill up all Vacancies that may happen during the Recess of the Senate, by granting Commissions which shall expire at the End of their next Session.

Section 3. He shall from time to time give to the Congress Information of the State of the Union, and recommend to their Consideration such Measures as he shall judge necessary and expedient; he may, on extraordinary Occasions, convene both Houses, or either of them, and in Case of Disagreement between them, with Respect to the Time of Adjournment, he may adjourn them to such Time as he shall think proper; he shall receive Ambassadors and other public Ministers; he shall take Care that the Laws be faithfully executed, and shall Commission all the Officers of the United States.

Section 4. The President, Vice President and all civil Officers of the United States, shall be removed from Office on Impeachment for, and Conviction of, Treason, Bribery, or other high Crimes and Misdemeanors.

Article III

Section 1. The judicial Power of the United States, shall be vested in one supreme Court, and in such inferior Courts as the Congress may from time to time ordain and establish. The Judges, both of the supreme and inferior Courts, shall hold their Offices during good Behaviour, and shall, at stated Times, receive for their Services, a Compensation, which shall not be diminished during their Continuance in Office.

Section 2. The judicial Power shall extend to all Cases, in Law and Equity, arising under this Constitution, the Laws of the United States, and Treaties made, or which shall be made, under their Authority;—to all Cases affecting Ambassadors, other public Ministers and Consuls;—to all Cases of admiralty and maritime Jurisdiction;—to Controversies to which the United States shall be a Party;—to Controversies between two or more States;—between a State and Citizens of another State;—between Citizens of different States;—between Citizens of the same State claiming Lands under Grants of different States, and between a State, or the Citizens thereof, and foreign States, Citizens or Subjects.

In all cases affecting Ambassadors, other public Ministers and Consuls, and those in which a State shall be a Party, the supreme Court shall have original Jurisdiction. In all the other Cases before mentioned, the supreme Court shall have appellate Jurisdiction, both as to Law and Fact, with such Exceptions, and under such Regulations as the Congress shall make.

The Trial of all Crimes, except in Cases of Impeachment, shall be by Jury; and such Trial shall be held in the State where the said Crimes shall have been committed; but when not committed within any State, the Trial shall be at such Place or Places as the Congress may by Law have directed.

Section 3. Treason against the United States, shall consist only in levying War against them, or in adhering to their Enemies, giving them Aid or Comfort. No Person shall be convicted of Treason unless on the Testimony of two Witnesses to the same overt Act, or on Confession in open Court.

The Congress shall have Power to declare the Punishment of Treason, but no Attainder of Treason shall work Corruption of Blood, or Forfeiture except during the Life of the Person attainted.

Article IV

Section 1. Full Faith and Credit shall be given in each State to the public Acts, Records, and judicial Proceedings of every other State. And the Congress may by general Laws prescribe the Manner in which such Acts, Records and Proceedings shall be proved, and the Effect thereof.

Section 2. The Citizens of each State shall be entitled to all Privileges and Immunities of Citizens in the several States.

A Person charged in any State with Treason, Felony, or other Crime, who shall flee from Justice, and be found in another State, shall on Demand of the executive Authority of the State from which he fled, be delivered up, to be removed to the State having Jurisdiction of the Crime.

No Person held to Service or Labour in one State, under the Laws thereof, escaping into another, shall, in Consequence of any Law or Regulation therein, be discharged from such Service or Labour, but shall be delivered up on Claim of the Party to whom such Service or Labour may be due.

Section 3. New States may be admitted by the Congress into this Union; but no new State shall be formed or erected within the Jurisdiction of any other State; nor any State be formed by the Junction of two or more States, or Parts of States, without the Consent of the Legislatures of the States concerned as well as of the Congress.

The Congress shall have Power to dispose of and make all needful Rules and Regulations respecting the Territory or other Property belonging to the United States; and nothing in this Constitution shall be so construed to Prejudice any Claims of the United States, or of any particular State.

Section 4. The United States shall guarantee to every State in this Union a Republican Form of Government, and shall protect each of them against Invasion; and on Application of the Legislature, or of the Executive (when the Legislature cannot be convened) against domestic Violence.

Article V

The Congress, whenever two thirds of both Houses shall deem it necessary, shall propose Amendments to this Constitution, or, on the Application of the Legislatures of two thirds of the several States, shall call a Convention for proposing Amendments, which, in either Case, shall be valid to all Intents and Purposes, as Part of this Constitution, when ratified by the Legislatures of three fourths of the several States, or by Conventions in three fourths thereof, as the one or the other Mode of Ratification may be proposed by the Congress; provided that no Amendment which may be made prior to the Year One thousand eight hundred and eight shall in any Manner affect the first and fourth Clauses in the Ninth Section of the first Article;

and that no State, without its Consent, shall be deprived of its equal Suffrage in the Senate.

Article VI

All Debts contracted and Engagements entered into, before the adoption of this Constitution, shall be as valid against the United States under this Constitution, as under the Confederation.

This Constitution, and the Laws of the United States which shall be made in Pursuance thereof; and all Treaties made, or which shall be made, under the Authority of the United States, shall be the supreme Law of the Land; and the Judges in every State shall be bound thereby, any Thing in the Constitution or Laws of any State to the Contrary notwithstanding.

The Senators and Representatives before mentioned, and the members of the several State Legislatures, and all executive and judicial Officers, both of the United States and of the several States, shall be bound by Oath or Affirmation, to support this Constitution; but no religious Test shall ever be required as a Qualification to any Office or public Trust under the United States.

Article VII

The Ratification of the Conventions of nine States, shall be sufficient for the Establishment of this Constitution between the States so ratifying the Same.

Go. Washington—Presidt.

And deputy from Virginia

New Hampshire
John Langdon
Nicholas Gilman

Massachusetts
Nathaniel Gorham
Rufus King

Connecticut
Wm. Saml. Johnson
Roger Sherman

New Jersey
Wil: Livingston
David Brearley
Wm. Paterson
Jona: Dayton

Pennsylvania
B Franklin

Thomas Mifflin
Robt. Morris
Geo. Clymer
Thos. Fitzsimons
Jared Ingersoll

New York
Alexander Hamilton

Delaware
Geo: Read
Cunning Bedford jun
John Dickinson
Richard Bassett

Maryland
James McHenry
Dan of St. Thos. Jenifer
Danl. Carroll

Virginia
John Blair
James Madison Jr.
James Wilson
Gouv Morris

North Carolina
Wm: Blount.
Richd. Dobbs Spaight
Hu Williamson
Jaco: Broom

South Carolina
J. Rutledge
Charles Cotesworth Pinckney
Pierce Butler

Georgia
William Few
Abr Baldwin

The Bill of Rights
(1791)

Amendment I

Congress shall make no law respecting an establishment of religion, or prohibiting the free exercise thereof; or abridging the freedom of speech, or of the press; or the right of the people peaceably to assemble, and to petition the government for a redress of grievances.

Amendment II

A well regulated militia, being necessary to the security of a free state, the right of the people to keep and bear arms, shall not be infringed.

Amendment III

No soldier shall, in time of peace be quartered in any house, without the consent of the owner, nor in time of war, but in a manner to be prescribed by law.

Amendment IV

The right of the people to be secure in their persons, houses, papers, and effects, against unreasonable searches and seizures, shall not be violated, and no warrants shall issue, but upon probable cause, supported by oath or affirmation, and particularly describing the place to be searched, and the persons or things to be seized.

Amendment V

No person shall be held to answer for a capital, or otherwise infamous crime, unless on a presentment or indictment of a grand jury, except in cases arising in the land or naval forces, or in the militia, when in actual service in time of war or public danger; nor shall any person be subject for the same offense to be twice put in jeopardy of life or limb; nor shall be compelled in any criminal case to be a witness against himself, nor be deprived of life, liberty, or property, without due process of law; nor shall private property be taken for public use, without just compensation.

Amendment VI

In all criminal prosecutions, the accused shall enjoy the right to a speedy and public trial, by an impartial jury of the state and district wherein the crime shall have been committed, which district shall have been previously ascertained by law, and to be informed of the nature and cause of the accusation; to be confronted with the witnesses against him; to have compulsory process for obtaining witnesses in his favor, and to have the assistance of counsel for his defense.

Amendment VII

In suits at common law, where the value in controversy shall exceed twenty dollars, the right of trial by jury shall be preserved, and no fact tried by a jury, shall be otherwise reexamined in any court of the United States, then according to the rules of the common law.

Amendment VIII

Excessive bail shall not be required, nor excessive fines imposed, nor cruel and unusual punishments inflicted.

Amendment IX

The enumeration in the Constitution, of certain rights, shall not be construed to deny or disparage others retained by the people.

Amendment X

The powers not delegated to the United States by the Constitution, nor prohibited by it to the states, are reserved to the states respectively, or to the people.

Later Amendments

Amendment XI

(1798)

The judicial power of the United States shall not be construed to extend to any suit in law or equity, commenced or prosecuted against one of the United States by Citizens of another State, or by Citizens or Subjects of any Foreign State.

Amendment XII

(1804)

The Electors shall meet in their respective states and vote by ballot for President and Vice-President, one of whom, at least, shall not be an inhabitant of the same state with themselves; they shall name in their ballots the person voted for as President, and in distinct ballots the person voted for as Vice-President, and they shall make distinct lists of all persons voted for as President, and of all persons voted for as Vice-President, and of the number of votes for each, which lists they shall sign and certify, and transmit sealed to the seat of the government of the United States, directed to the President of the Senate;—The President of the Senate shall, in the presence of the Senate and House of Representatives, open all the certificates and the votes shall then be counted;—the person having the greatest number of votes for President, shall be the President, if such number be a majority of the whole number of Electors appointed; and if no person have such majority, then from the persons having the highest numbers not exceeding three on the list of those voted for as President, the House of Representatives shall choose immediately, by ballot, the President. But in choosing the President, the votes shall be taken by states, the representation from each state having one vote; a quorum for this purpose shall consist of a member or members from two-thirds of the states, and a majority of all the states shall be necessary to a choice. And if the House of Representatives shall not choose a President whenever the right of choice shall devolve upon them, before the fourth day of March next following, then the Vice-President shall act as President, as in the case of the death or other constitutional disability of the President. The person having the greatest number of votes as Vice-President, shall be the Vice-President, if such number be a majority of the whole number of Electors appointed, and if no person have a majority, then from the two highest numbers on the list, the Senate shall choose the Vice-President; a quorum for the purpose shall consist of two-thirds of the whole number of Senators, and a majority of the whole number shall be necessary to a choice. But no person constitutionally ineligible to the office of President shall be eligible to that of Vice-President of the United States.

Amendment XIII

(1865)

Section 1. Neither slavery nor involuntary servitude, except as a punishment for crime whereof the party shall have been duly convicted, shall exist within the United States, or any place subject to their jurisdiction.

Section 2. Congress shall have power to enforce this article by appropriate legislation.

Amendment XIV

(1868)

Section 1. All persons born or naturalized in the United States, and subject to the jurisdiction thereof, are citizens of the United States and of the State wherein they reside. No State shall make or enforce any law which shall abridge the privileges or immunities of citizens of the United States; nor shall any State deprive any person of life, liberty, or property, without due process of law; nor deny to any person within its jurisdiction the equal protection of the laws.

Section 2. Representatives shall be apportioned among the several States according to their respective numbers, counting the whole number of persons in each State, excluding Indians not taxed. But when the right to vote at any election for the choice of electors for President and Vice President of the United States, Representatives in Congress, the Executive and Judicial.officers of a State, or the members of the Legislature thereof, is denied to any of the male inhabitants of such State, being twenty-one years of age, and citizens of the United States, or in any way abridged, except for participation in rebellion, or other crime, the basis of representation therein shall be reduced in the proportion which the number of such male citizens shall bear to the whole number of male citizens twenty-one years of age in such State.

Section 3. No person shall be a Senator or Representative in Congress, or elector of President and Vice President, or hold any office, civil or military, under the United States, or under any State, who, having previously taken an oath, as a member of Congress, or as an officer of the United States, or as a member of any State legislature, or as an executive or judicial officer of any State, to support the Constitution of the United States, shall have engaged in insurrection or rebellion against the same, or given aid or comfort to the enemies thereof. But Congress may by a vote of two-thirds of each House, remove such disability.

Section 4. The validity of the public debt of the United States, authorized by law, including debts incurred for payment of pensions and bounties for services in suppressing insurrection or rebellion, shall not be questioned. But neither the United States nor any State shall assume or pay any debt or obligation incurred in aid of insurrection or rebellion against the United States, or any claim for the loss or emancipation of any slave; but all such debts, obligations and claims shall be held illegal and void.

Section 5. The Congress shall have power to enforce, by appropriate legislation, the provisions of this article.

Amendment XV

(1870)

Section 1. The right of citizens of the United States to vote shall not be denied or abridged by the United States or by any State on account of race, color, or previous condition of servitude.

Section 2. The Congress shall have power to enforce this article by appropriate legislation.

Amendment XVI

(1913)

The Congress shall have power to lay and collect taxes on incomes, from whatever source derived, without apportionment among the several States, and without regard to any census or enumeration.

Amendment XVII

(1913)

The Senate of the United States shall be composed of two Senators from each State, elected by the people thereof, for six years; and each Senator shall have one vote. The electors in each State shall have the qualifications requisite for electors of the most numerous branch of the State legislature.

When vacancies happen in the representation of any State in the Senate, the executive authority of such State shall issue writs of election to fill such vacancies: *Provided*, That the legislature of any State may empower the executive thereof to make temporary appointments until the people fill the vacancies by election as the legislature may direct.

This amendment shall not be so construed as to effect the election or term of any Senator chosen before it becomes valid as part of the Constitution.

Amendment XVIII

(1919)

Section 1. After one year from the ratification of this article the manufacture, sale, or transportation of intoxicating liquors within, the importation thereof into, or the exportation thereof from the United States and all territory subject to the jurisdiction thereof for beverage purposes is hereby prohibited.

Section 2. The Congress and the several States shall have concurrent power to enforce this article by appropriate legislation.

Section 3. This article shall be inoperative unless it shall have been ratified as an amendment to the Constitution by the legislatures of the several States, as provided in the Constitution, within seven years from the date of the submission hereof to the States by the Congress.

Amendment XIX

(1920)

The right of citizens of the United States to vote shall not be denied or abridged by the United States or by any State on account of sex.

Congress shall have power to enforce this article by appropriate legislation.

Amendment XX

(1933)

Section 1. The terms of the President and Vice President shall end at noon on the 20th day of January, and the terms of Senators and Representatives at noon on the 3d day of January, of the years in which such terms would have ended if this article had not been ratified; and the terms of their successors shall then begin.

Section 2. The Congress shall assemble at least once in every year, and such meeting shall begin at noon on the 3d day of January, unless they shall by law appoint a different day.

Section 3. If, at the time fixed for the beginning of the term of the President, the President elect shall have died, the Vice President elect shall become President. If a President shall not have been chosen before the time fixed for the beginning of his term, or if the President elect shall have failed to qualify, then the Vice President elect shall act as President until a President shall have qualified; and the Congress may by law provide for the case wherein neither a President elect nor a Vice President elect shall have qualified, declaring who shall then act as President, or the manner in which one who is to act shall be selected, and such person shall act accordingly until a President or Vice President shall have qualified.

Section 4. The Congress may by law provide for the case of the death of any of the persons from whom the House of Representatives may choose a President whenever the right of choice shall have devolved upon them, and for the case of the death of any of the persons from whom the Senate may choose a Vice President whenever the right of choice shall have devolved upon them.

Section 5. Sections 1 and 2 shall take effect on the 15th day of October following the ratification of this article.

Section 6. This article shall be inoperative unless it shall have been ratified as an amendment to the Constitution by the legislatures of three-fourths of the several States within seven years from the date of its submission.

Amendment XXI

(1933)

Section 1. The eighteenth article of amendment to the Constitution of the United States is hereby repealed.

Section 2. The transportation or importation into any State, territory, or possession of the United States for delivery or use therein of intoxicating liquors, in violation of the laws thereof, is hereby prohibited.

Section 3. This article shall be inoperative unless it shall have been ratified as an amendment to the Constitution by conventions in the several States, as provided in the Constitution, within seven years from the date of the submission hereof to the States by the Congress.

Amendment XXII

(1951)

Section 1. No person shall be elected to the office of the President more than twice, and no person who has held the office of President, or acted as President, for more than two years of a term to which some other person was elected President shall be elected to the office of the President more than once. But this article shall not apply to any person holding the office of President when this article was proposed by the Congress, and shall not prevent any person who may be holding the office of President, or acting as President, during the term within which this article becomes operative from holding the office of President or acting as President during the remainder of such term.

Section 2. This article shall be inoperative unless it shall have been ratified as an amendment to the Constitution by the legislatures of three-fourths of the several States within seven years from the date of its submission to the States by the Congress.

Amendment XXIII

(1961)

Section 1. The District constituting the seat of government of the United States shall appoint in such manner as the Congress may direct:

A number of electors of President and Vice President equal to the whole number of Senators and Representatives in Congress to which the District would be entitled if it were a State, but in no event more than the least populous State; they shall be in addition to those appointed by the States, but they shall be considered, for the purposes of the election of the President and Vice President, to be electors appointed by a State; and they shall meet in the District and perform such duties as provided by the twelfth article of amendment.

Section 2. The Congress shall have power to enforce this article by appropriate legislation.

Amendment XXIV

(1964)

Section 1. The right of citizens of the United States to vote in any primary or other election for President or Vice President, for electors for President or Vice President, or for Senator or Representative in Congress, shall not be denied or abridged by the United States or any State by reason of failure to pay any poll tax or other tax.

Section 2. The Congress shall have the power to enforce this article by appropriate legislation.

Amendment XXV

(1967)

Section 1. In case of the removal of the President from office or his death or resignation, the Vice President shall become President.

Section 2. Whenever there is a vacancy in the office of the Vice President, the President shall nominate a Vice President who shall take office upon confirmation by a majority vote of both Houses of Congress.

Section 3. Whenever the President transmits to the President pro tempore of the Senate and the Speaker of the House of Representatives his written declaration that he is unable to discharge the powers and duties of his office, and until he transmits to them a written declaration to the contrary, such powers and duties shall be discharged by the Vice President as Acting President.

Section 4. Whenever the Vice President and a majority of either the principal officers of the executive departments or such other body as Congress may by law provide, transmit to the President pro tempore of the Senate and the Speaker of the House of Representatives their written declaration that the President is unable to discharge the powers and duties of his office, the Vice President shall immediately assume the powers and duties of the office as Acting President.

Thereafter, when the President transmits to the President pro tempore of the Senate and the Speaker of the House of Representatives his written declaration that no inability exists, he shall resume the powers and duties of his office unless the Vice President and a majority of either the principal officers of the executive department or of such other body as Congress may by law provide, transmit within four days to the President pro tempore of the Senate and the Speaker of the House of Representatives their written declaration that the President is unable to discharge the powers and duties of his office. Thereupon Congress shall decide the issue, assembling within forty-eight hours for that purpose if not in session. If the Congress, within twenty-one days after receipt of the latter written declaration, or, if Congress is not in session, within twenty-one days after Congress is required to assemble, determine by two-thirds vote of both Houses that the President is unable to discharge the powers and duties of his office, the Vice President shall continue to discharge the same as Acting President; otherwise, the President shall resume the powers and duties of his office.

Amendment XXVI

(1971)

Section 1. The right of citizens of the United States, who are 18 years of age or older, to vote, shall not be denied or abridged by the United States or any State on account of age.

Section 2. The Congress shall have the power to enforce this article by appropriate legislation.

Amendment XXVII

(1992)

No law varying the compensation for the services of the Senators and Representatives shall take effect until an election of Representatives shall have intervened.

CASES AND MATERIALS ON FEDERAL CONSTITUTIONAL LAW

Chapter 1

RELATIONSHIPS WITHIN THE EXECUTIVE BRANCH

A. INTRODUCTION

Volume 1 in this series introduced five commonly-accepted forms of argument used in constitutional interpretation: (1) the Constitution's own *structure* and the structure of the government established by the Constitution, (2) the *historical setting* from which the Constitution emerged, in particular the ratification process and early implementation, (3) the *text* of the Constitution itself, (4) the *tradition* or historical precedent of understanding the Constitution, and (5) the weight of *judicial precedent* in light of the doctrine of stare decisis. Those forms of argument were introduced through materials primarily directed to the structure and power of the federal judiciary. All the same forms of argument are available to address other questions of constitutional law.

Each of the five forms of argument were introduced in Volume 1 with materials selected to support the different forms of argument, including ratification debates, legislation from the First Congress, letters illustrating early interpretations of the Constitution, and early judicial precedents. The next step, beyond understanding the various forms of argument, is the identification and use of source material to support one or more arguments. This Chapter will therefore focus on one key facet of executive power—the way that executive power is structured internally through the president's removal, appointment, and control of federal officers—before turning to the broader question of the scope of executive power in Chapter 2 and how that power is kept separate from legislative power in Chapter 3. Below, you will see how the five forms of argument were marshaled by the Supreme Court to support its interpretation of the Constitution's text governing executive power.

EXERCISE 1:

Apply the first four forms of argument to questions regarding the scope of the executive power, particularly with respect to the power to appoint officers and to remove them from office.

1. If Volume 1 was assigned prior to this Volume, re-read the description you prepared in Volume 1, Exercise 1. Regardless of whether you previously performed that

exercise, consider what the *structure* of the Constitution and federal government suggests is the scope of the President's power of appointment and removal. Conversely, what does the structure of the federal government suggest about the power of Congress to limit the President's ability to appoint or remove officers? What role, if any, does Congress have in the appointment and removal of officers?

2. (Re)read the U.S. Constitution. What does the *text* of the Constitution provide as to the scope of the President's power of appointment and removal? Conversely, what does the text suggest about the power of Congress to limit the President's ability to appoint or remove officers? What role, if any, does Congress have in the appointment and removal of officers?

3. (Re)read the statutes enacted by the First Congress creating executive departments and establishing the judiciary. Excerpts of these materials appear in Volume 1, **Chapter 2.** (The full text of those statutes is included on the case book website.) What does the text of these post-ratification *historical* sources reveal regarding the scope of the President's power of appointment and removal, as derived from the Constitution directly rather than from legislation? Conversely, what do these sources suggest about the power of Congress to limit the President's ability to appoint or remove officers? (Re)read the Act Concerning the District of Columbia and consider whether it changes your view. An excerpt of that Act appears in Volume 1 in connection with *Marbury v. Madison*, and the full text of that statute is included on the case book website.

4. The website associated with these printed materials contains additional "Tools for Textualists" that may permit you to frame additional textual arguments. You may want to examine the partial concordance or a dictionary that defines terms that may have been more-familiar to those who drafted and ratified the Constitution. If you do so, does the additional information change your view?

5. The website contains additional "Tools for Originalists" including the text of many essays written to influence the decision of whether to ratify the Constitution. You may want to examine those materials to support an argument regarding the shared public understanding of the Constitution. If you do so, does the additional information change your view?

6. The website contains additional "Tools for Traditionalists" including the full text of multiple early treatises on the Constitution. St. George Tucker taught law at William and Mary in the 1790s. He adapted his notes from his course in constitutional law into his *View of the Constitution*, published in 1803. Henry Baldwin, as Associate Justice of the U.S. Supreme Court, published his one volume treatise on constitutional law in 1837. Joseph Story, an associate justice of the U.S. Supreme Court, first published his multi-volume treatise on constitutional law in 1833. You may want to examine one or more of those treatises to ascertain the traditional understanding of the appointment and removal powers prior to the controversies addressed in the case law later in this Chapter.

7. While this volume will not consider questions about presidential selection, what do you make of the fact that the Constitution consistently uses male pronouns to refer to the President? Is that a good argument that women cannot be president? At the confirmation hearings for Neil Gorsuch's nomination to the Supreme Court, Senator Amy Klobuchar asked him whether women could be president under an originalist interpretation, and nominee Gorsuch gruffly replied that they could. He did not, however, give a rationale. Can you construct one? Read the Sixth Amendment carefully for one possible source of support. If we were to interpret the Constitution according to the meaning that its text has *today*, rather than its meaning at the time of the Framing, what would happen if "he" came to be used universally (as it is used in certain academic circles) only to refer to men? Can you see an argument *for* originalism in the neighborhood here? For one attempt to construct one, see goo.gl/Dc8uBp.

B. PRESIDENTIAL REMOVAL AUTHORITY

1. The Rise

MYERS v. UNITED STATES

272 U.S. 52 (1926)

CHIEF JUSTICE TAFT delivered the opinion of the Court.

This case presents the question whether under the Constitution the President has the exclusive power of removing executive officers of the United States whom he has appointed by and with the advice and consent of the Senate.

[I]

[Frank S.] Myers was on July 21, 1917, appointed by the President, by and with the advice and consent of the Senate, to be a postmaster of the first class at Portland, Or[egon], for a term of four years. On January 20, 1920, Myers' resignation was demanded. He refused the demand. On February 2, 1920, he was removed from office by order of the Postmaster General, acting by direction of the President. He protested to the department against his removal, and continued to do so until the end of his term. On April 21, 1921, he brought this suit in the Court of Claims for his salary from the date of his removal, $8,838.71. In August, 1920, the President made a recess appointment of one Jones, who took office September 19, 1920. The Court of Claims gave judgment against Myers and this is an appeal from that judgment.

By the sixth section of the Act of Congress of July 12, 1876, ch. 179, 19 Stat. 80, 81, under which Myers was appointed with the advice and consent of the Senate as a first-class postmaster, it is provided that:

> Postmasters of the first, second, and third classes shall be appointed and may
> be removed by the President by and with the advice and consent of the

Senate, and shall hold their offices for four years unless sooner removed or suspended according to law.

The Senate did not consent to the President's removal of Myers during his term. If this statute in its requirement that his term should be four years unless sooner removed by the President by and with the advice and consent of the Senate is valid, the appellant, Myers' administratrix, is entitled to recover his unpaid salary for his full term and the judgment of the Court of Claims must be reversed. The government maintains that the requirement is invalid, for the reason that under Article II of the Constitution the President's power of removal of executive officers appointed by him with the advice and consent of the Senate is full and complete without consent of the Senate. If this view is sound, the removal of Myers by the President without the Senate's consent was legal, and the judgment of the Court of Claims against the appellant was correct, and must be affirmed, though for a different reason from [that] given by that court. We are therefore confronted by the constitutional question and cannot avoid it.

[II]

[A]

[The Court's quotation of Article II and Article III, section 1, of the Constitution are omitted.]

The question where the power of removal of executive officers appointed by the President by and with the advice and consent of the Senate was vested, was presented early in the first session of the First Congress. There is no express provision respecting removals in the Constitution, except for removal from office by impeachment. The subject was not discussed in the Constitutional Convention. Under the Articles of Confederation, Congress was given the power of appointing certain executive officers of the Confederation, and during the Revolution and while the articles were given effect, Congress exercised the power of removal.

[B]

Consideration of the executive power was initiated in the Constitutional Convention by the seventh resolution in the Virginia Plan introduced by Edmund Randolph. MAX FARRAND, RECORDS OF THE FEDERAL CONVENTION OF 1787, p. 21 (1911). It gave to the executive "all the executive powers of Congress under the Confederation," which would seem therefore to have intended to include the power of removal which had been exercised by that body as incident to the power of appointment. As modified by the committee of the whole this resolution declared for a national executive of one person to be elected by the Legislature, with the power to carry into execution the national laws and to appoint to offices in cases not otherwise provided for. It was referred to the committee on detail, which recommended that the executive powers should be vested in a single person to be styled the President of the United States, that he should take care that the laws of the United States be duly and faithfully executed, and that he should commission all the officers of the United States and appoint officers in all cases not otherwise provided by the Constitution.

The committee further recommended that the Senate be given power to make treaties, and to appoint ambassadors, and judges of the Supreme Court.

After the great compromises of the convention—the one giving the states equality of representation in the Senate, and the other placing the election of the President, not in Congress, as once voted, but in an electoral college, in which the influence of larger states in the selection would be more nearly in proportion to their population— the smaller states led by Roger Sherman, fearing that under the second compromise the President would constantly be chosen from one of the larger states, secured a change by which the appointment of all officers, which theretofore had been left to the President without restriction, was made subject to the Senate's advice and consent, and the making of treaties and the appointments of ambassadors, public ministers, consuls, and judges of the Supreme Court were transferred to the President, but made subject to the advice and consent of the Senate. Although adopted finally without objection by any state in the last days of the convention, members from the larger states, like [James] Wilson and others, criticized this limitation of the President's power of appointment of executive officers and the resulting increase of the power of the Senate.

[C]

[1]

In the House of Representatives of the First Congress, on Tuesday, May 18, 1789, Mr. Madison moved in the committee of the whole that there should be established three executive departments, one of Foreign Affairs, another of the Treasury, and a third of War, at the head of each of which there should be a Secretary, to be appointed by the President by and with the advice and consent of the Senate, and to be removable by the President. The committee agreed to the establishment of a Department of Foreign Affairs, but a discussion ensued as to making the Secretary removable by the President. "The question was now taken and carried, by a considerable majority, in favor of declaring the power of removal to be in the President."

On June 16, 1789, the House resolved itself into a committee of the whole on a bill proposed by Mr. Madison for establishing an executive department to be denominated the Department of Foreign Affairs, in which the first clause, after stating the title of the officer and describing his duties, had these words "to be removable from office by the President of the United States." 1 ANNALS OF CONGRESS 455. After a very full discussion the question was put; Shall the words "to be removable by the President" be struck out? It was determined in the negative—yeas, 20, nays 34.

On June 22, in the renewal of the discussion:

> Mr. Benson moved to amend the bill, by altering the second clause, so as to imply the power of removal to be in the President alone. The clause enacted that there should be a chief clerk, to be appointed by the Secretary of Foreign Affairs, and employed as he thought proper, and who, in case of vacancy, should have the charge and custody of all records, books, and papers appertaining to the department. The amendment proposed that the chief clerk,

"whenever the said principal officer shall be removed from office by the President of the United States, or in any other case of vacancy," should during such vacancy, have the charge and custody of all records, books, and papers appertaining to the department.

Mr. Benson stated that his objection to the clause "to be removable by the President" arose from an idea that the power of removal by the President hereafter might appear to be exercised by virtue of a legislative grant only, and consequently be subjected to legislative instability, when he was well satisfied in his own mind that it was fixed by a fair legislative construction of the Constitution.

Mr. Benson declared, if he succeeded in this amendment, he would move to strike out the words in the first clause, "to be removable by the President," which appeared somewhat like a grant. Now the mode he took would evade that point and establish a legislative construction of the Constitution. He also hoped his amendment would succeed in reconciling both sides of the House to the decision, and quieting the minds of gentlemen.

Mr. Madison admitted the objection made by the gentleman near him (Mr. Benson) to the words of the bill. He said:

They certainly may be construed to imply a legislative grant of power. He wished everything like ambiguity expunged, and the sense of the House explicitly declared, and therefore seconded the motion. Gentlemen have all along proceeded on the idea that the Constitution vests the power in the President, and what arguments were brought forward respecting the convenience or inconvenience of such disposition of the power were intended only to throw light upon what was meant by the compilers of the Constitution. Now, as the words proposed by the gentleman from New York expressed to his mind the meaning of the Constitution, he should be in favor of them, and would agree to strike out those agreed to in the committee.

Mr. Benson's first amendment to alter the second clause by the insertion of the italicized words, made that clause read as follows:

That there shall be in the State Department an inferior officer to be appointed by the said principal officer, and to be employed therein as he shall deem proper, to be called the chief clerk in the Department of Foreign Affairs, *and who, whenever the principal officers shall be removed from office by the President of the United States*, or in any other case of vacancy, shall, during such vacancy, have charge and custody of all records, books and papers appertaining to said department.

The first amendment was then approved by a vote of 30 to 18. Mr. Benson then moved to strike out in the first clause the words "to be removable by the President," in pursuance of the purpose he had already declared, and this second motion of his was carried by a vote of 31 to 19.

The bill as amended was ordered to be engrossed, and read the third time the next day, June 24, 1789, and was then passed by a vote of 29 to 22, and the clerk was directed to carry the bill to the Senate and desire their concurrence.

It is very clear from this history that the exact question which the House voted upon was whether it should recognize and declare the power of the President under the Constitution to remove the Secretary of Foreign Affairs without the advice and consent of the Senate. [U]ntil the Johnson impeachment trial in 1868 its meaning was not doubted, even by those who questioned its soundness.

The discussion was a very full one. Fourteen out of the 29 who voted for the passage of the bill and 11 of the 22 who voted against the bill took part in the discussion. Of the members of the House, 8 had been in the Constitutional Convention, and of these 6 voted with the majority, and 2, Roger Sherman and Elbridge Gerry, the latter of whom had refused to sign the Constitution, voted in the minority. After the bill as amended had passed the House, it was sent to the Senate, where it was discussed in secret session, without report. The critical vote there was upon the striking out of the clause recognizing and affirming the unrestricted power of the President to remove. The Senate divided, requiring the deciding vote of the Vice President, John Adams, who voted against striking out, and in favor of the passage of the bill as it had left the House. The bill, having passed as it came from the House, was signed by President Washington and became a law. Act of July 27, 1789, ch. 4, 1 Stat. 28.

[2]

It is convenient in the course of our discussion of this case to review the reasons advanced by Mr. Madison and his associates for their conclusion, supplementing them, so far as may be, by additional considerations which lead this court to concur therein.

[a]

First. Mr. Madison insisted that Article II by vesting the executive power in the President was intended to grant him the power of appointment and removal of executive officers except as thereafter expressly provided in that Article. He pointed out that one of the chief purposes of the convention was to separate the legislative from the executive functions. He said:

> If there is a principle in our Constitution, indeed in any free Constitution more sacred than another, it is that which separates the legislative, executive and judicial powers. If there is any point in which the separation of the legislative and executive powers ought to be maintained with great caution, it is that which relates to officers and offices.

Their union under the Confederation had not worked well, as the members of the convention knew. Montesquieu's view that the maintenance of independence, as between the legislative, the executive and the judicial branches, was a security for the people had their full approval. 2 MAX FARRAND, *supra*, at 56 (statement of James Madison). Accordingly the Constitution was so framed as to vest in the Congress all legislative powers therein granted, to vest in the President the executive power, and to vest in one Supreme Court and such inferior courts as Congress might establish the judicial power. From this division on principle, the reasonable construction of the Constitution must be that the branches should be kept separate in all cases in which they were not expressly blended, and the Constitution should be expounded to blend them no more than it affirmatively requires. 1 ANNALS OF CONGRESS 497 (statement of James Madison).

The debates in the Constitutional Convention indicated the intention to create a strong executive, and after a controversial discussion the executive power of the government was vested in one person and many of his important functions were specified so as to avoid the humiliating weakness of the Congress during the Revolution and under the Articles of Confederation. 1 MAX FARRAND, *supra*, at 66–67.

Mr. Madison and his associates in the discussion in the House dwelt at length upon the necessity there was for construing Article II to give the President the sole power of removal in his responsibility for the conduct of the executive branch, and enforced this by emphasizing his duty expressly declared in the third section of the Article to "take care that the laws be faithfully executed." 1 ANNALS OF CONGRESS 496, 497 (statement of James Madison).

The vesting of the executive power in the President was essentially a grant of the power to execute the laws. But the President alone and unaided could not execute the laws. He must execute them by the assistance of subordinates. This view has since been repeatedly reaffirmed by this court. As he is charged specifically to take care that they be faithfully executed, the reasonable implication, even in the absence of express words, was that as part of his executive power he should select those who were to act for him under his direction in the execution of the laws. The further implication must be, in the absence of any express limitation respecting removals, that as his selection of administrative officers is essential to the execution of the laws by him, so must be his power of removing those for whom he cannot continue to be responsible. It was urged that the natural meaning of the term "executive power" granted the President included the appointment and removal of executive subordinates. If such appointments and removals were not an exercise of executive power, what were they? They certainly were not the exercise of legislative or judicial power in government as usually understood. In the British system, the crown, which was the executive, had the power of appointment and removal of executive officers, and it was natural, therefore, for those who framed our Constitution to regard the words "executive power" as including both.

The requirement of the second section of Article II that the Senate should advise and consent to the presidential appointments, was to be strictly construed. The words of section 2, following the general grant of executive power under section 1, were either an enumeration and emphasis of specific functions of the executive, not all inclusive, or were limitations upon the general grant of the executive power, and as such, being limitations, should not be enlarged beyond the words used. 1 ANNALS OF CONGRESS 462, 463, 464 (statement of James Madison). The executive power was given in general terms strengthened by specific terms where emphasis was regarded as appropriate, and was limited by direct expressions where limitation was needed, and the fact that no express limit was placed on the power of removal by the executive was convincing indication that none was intended. This is the same construction of Article II as that of Alexander Hamilton quoted *infra*.

[b]

Second. The view of Mr. Madison and his associates was that not only did the grant of executive power to the President in the first section of Article II carry with it the power of removal, but the express recognition of the power of appointment in the second section enforced this view on the well-approved principle of constitutional and statutory construction that the power of removal of executive officers was incident to the power of appointment. It was agreed by the opponents of the bill, with only one or two exceptions, that as a constitutional principle the power of appointment carried with it the power of removal. The reason for the principle is that those in charge of and responsible for administering functions of government, who select their executive subordinates, need in meeting their responsibility to have the power to remove those whom they appoint.

Under section 2 of Article II, however, the power of appointment by the executive is restricted in its exercise by the provision that the Senate, a part of the legislative branch of the government, may check the action of the executive by rejecting the officers he selects. Does this make the Senate part of the removing power? And this, after the whole discussion in the House is read attentively, is the real point which was considered and decided in the negative by the vote already given.

The history of the clause by which the Senate was given a check upon the President's power of appointment makes it clear that it was not prompted by any desire to limit removals. This was made apparent by the remarks of Abraham Baldwin, of Georgia, in the debate in the First Congress. He had been a member of the Constitutional Convention. In opposing the construction which would extend the Senate's power to check appointments to removals from office, he said:

> I am well authorized to say that the mingling of the powers of the President and Senate was strongly opposed in the convention which had the honor to submit to the consideration of the United States and the different States the present system for the government of the Union. Some gentlemen opposed it to the last, and finally it was the principal ground on which they refused to give it their signature and assent.

Madison said:

> Perhaps there was no argument urged with more success or more plausibly grounded against the Constitution under which we are now deliberating than that founded on the mingling of the executive and legislative branches of the government in one body.

The Senate has full power to reject newly proposed appointees whenever the President shall remove the incumbents. Such a check enables the Senate to prevent the filling of offices with bad or incompetent men, or with those against whom there is tenable objection.

The power to prevent the removal of an officer who has served under the President is different from the authority to consent to or reject his appointment. When a nomination is made, it may be presumed that the Senate is, or may become, as well advised as to the fitness of the nominee as the President, but in the nature of things the defects in ability or intelligence or loyalty in the administration of the laws of one who has served as an officer under the President are facts as to which the President, or his trusted subordinates, must be better informed than the Senate, and the power to remove him may therefore be regarded as confined for very sound and practical reasons, to the governmental authority which has administrative control.

Oliver Ellsworth was a member of the Senate of the First Congress, and was active in securing the imposition of the Senate restriction upon appointments by the President. He was the author of the Judiciary Act in that Congress and subsequently Chief Justice of the United States. His view as to the meaning of this Article of the Constitution, upon the point as to whether the advice of the Senate was necessary to removal, like that of Madison, formed and expressed almost in the very atmosphere of the convention, was entitled to great weight. What he said in the discussion in the Senate was reported by Senator William Patterson, as follows:

> The three distinct powers, legislative, judicial and executive should be placed in different hands. To turn a man out of office is an exercise neither of legislative nor judicial power; it is like a tree growing upon land that has been granted. The advice of the Senate does not make the appointment. The President appoints. There are certain restrictions in certain cases, but the restriction is as to the appointment, and not as to the removal.

2 George Bancroft, History of the Constitution of the United States 192 [(1882)].

Another argument advanced in the First Congress against implying the power of removal in the President alone from its necessity in the proper administration of the executive power was that all embarrassment in this respect could be avoided by the President's power of suspension of officers, disloyal or incompetent, until the Senate could act.

To this, Mr. Benson said:

> Surely gentlemen do not pretend that the President has the power of suspension granted expressly by the Constitution. If they are willing to allow a power of suspending, it must be because they construe some part of the Constitution in favor of such a grant. The construction in this case must be equally unwarrantable.

Mr. Vining said:

> The gentlemen say the President may suspend. They were asked if the Constitution gave him this power any more than the other? Do they contend the one to be a more inherent power than the other? If they do not, why shall it be objected to us that we are making a Legislative construction of the Constitution, when they are contending for the same thing?

In the case before us, the same suggestion has been made for the same purpose, and we think it is well answered in the foregoing. The implication of removal by the President alone is no more a strained construction of the Constitution than that of suspension by him alone and the broader power is much more needed and more strongly to be implied.

[c]

Third. Another argument urged against the constitutional power of the President alone to remove executive officers appointed by him with the consent of the Senate is that, in the absence of an express power of removal granted to the President, power to make provision for removal of all such officers is vested in the Congress by section 8 of Article I.

[i]

Mr. Madison, mistakenly thinking that an argument like this was advanced by Roger Sherman, took it up and answered it as follows:

> He seems to think (if I understand him rightly) that the power of displacing from office is subject to legislative discretion, because, it having a right to create, it may limit or modify as it thinks proper. I shall not say but at first view this doctrine may seem to have some plausibility. But when I consider that the Constitution clearly intended to maintain a marked distinction between the legislative, executive and judicial powers of government, and when I consider that, if the Legislature has a power such as is contended for, they may subject and transfer at discretion powers from one department of our government to another, they may, on that principle, exclude the President altogether from exercising any authority in the removal of officers, they may give to the Senate alone, or the President and Senate combined, they may vest it in the whole Congress, or they may reserve it to be exercised by this House. When I consider the consequences of this doctrine, and compare them with the true principles of the Constitution, I own that I cannot subscribe to it.

[ii]

The constitutional construction that excludes Congress from legislative power to provide for the removal of superior officers finds support in the second section of Article II. By it the appointment of all officers, whether superior or inferior, by the President is declared to be subject to the advice and consent of the Senate. In the absence of any specific provision to the contrary, the power of appointment to executive office carries with it, as a necessary incident, the power of removal. Whether the Senate must concur in the removal is aside from the point we now are considering. That point is that by the specific constitutional provision for appointment of executive officers with its necessary incident of removal, the power of appointment and removal is clearly provided for by the Constitution, and the legislative power of Congress in respect to both is excluded save by the specific exception as to inferior officers in the clause that follows. This is "but the Congress may by law vest the appointment of such inferior officers, as they think proper, in the President alone, in the Courts of Law, or in the Heads of Departments." These words, it has been held by this Court, give to Congress the power to limit and regulate removal of such inferior officers by heads of departments when it exercises its constitutional power to lodge the power of appointment with them. *United States v. Perkins*, 116 U.S. 483 (1886). Here then is an express provision introduced in words of exception for the exercise by Congress of legislative power in the matter of appointments and removals in the case of inferior executive officers. The phrase, "But Congress may by law vest," is equivalent to "excepting that Congress may by law vest." By the plainest implication it excludes congressional dealing with appointments or removals of executive officers not falling within the exception and leaves unaffected the executive power of the President to appoint and remove them.

A reference of the whole power of removal to general legislation by Congress is quite out of keeping with the plan of government devised by the framers of the Constitution. It could never have been intended to leave to Congress unlimited discretion to vary fundamentally the operation of the great independent executive branch of government and thus most seriously to weaken it.

[iii]

It is reasonable to suppose also that had it been intended to give Congress power to regulate or control removals in the manner suggested, it would have been included among the specifically enumerated legislative powers in Article I, or in the specified limitations on the executive power in Article II. The difference between the grant of legislative power under Article I to Congress which is limited to the powers therein enumerated, and the more general grant of executive power to the President under Article II is significant. The fact that the executive power is given in general terms strengthened by specific terms where emphasis is appropriate, and limited by direct expressions where limitation is needed, and that no express limit is placed on the power of removal by the executive is a convincing indication that none was intended.

[iv]

It is argued that the denial of the legislative power to regulate removals in some way involves the denial of power to prescribe qualifications for office, or reasonable classification for promotion, and yet that has been often exercised. We see no conflict between the latter power and that of appointment and removal, provided of course that the qualifications do not so limit selection and so trench upon executive choice as to be in effect legislative designation. As Mr. Madison said in the First Congress:

> The powers relative to offices are partly legislative and partly executive. The Legislature creates the office, defines the powers, limits its duration, and annexes a compensation. This done, the legislative power ceases. They ought to have nothing to do with designating the man to fill the office. That I conceive to be of an executive nature.

The legislative power here referred to by Mr. Madison is the legislative power of Congress under the Constitution, not legislative power independently of it. Article II expressly and by implication withholds from Congress power to determine who shall appoint and who shall remove except as to inferior offices. To Congress under its legislative power is given the establishment of offices, the determination of their functions and jurisdiction, the prescribing of reasonable and relevant qualifications and rules of eligibility of appointees, and the fixing of the term for which they are to be appointed and their compensation—all except as otherwise provided by the Constitution.

[v]

An argument in favor of full congressional power to make or withhold provision for removals of all appointed by the President is sought to be found in an asserted analogy between such a power in Congress and its power in the establishment of inferior federal courts. It is clear that the mere establishment of a federal inferior court does not vest that court with all the judicial power of the United States as conferred in the second section of Article III, but only that conferred by Congress specifically on the particular court. It must be limited territorially and in the classes of cases to be heard, and the mere creation of the courts does not confer jurisdiction except as it is conferred in the law of its creation or its amendments. It is said that similarly in the case of the executive power, which is "vested in the President," the power of appointment and removal cannot arise until Congress creates the office and its duties and powers, and must accordingly be exercised and limited only as Congress shall in the creation of the office prescribe.

We think there is little or no analogy between the two legislative functions of Congress in the cases suggested. The duty of Congress to make provision for the vesting of the whole federal judicial power in federal courts, were it held to exist, would be one of imperfect obligation and unenforceable. On the other hand, the moment an office and its powers and duties are created, the power of appointment and removal, as limited by the Constitution, vests in the executive. The functions of distributing jurisdiction to courts and the exercise of it when distributed and vested are not at all parallel to the creation of an office, and the mere right of appointment to, and of removal from, the office which at once attaches to the executive by virtue of the Constitution.

[d]

Fourth. Mr. Madison and his associates pointed out with great force the unreasonable character of the view that the convention intended to give to Congress or the Senate the means of thwarting the executive in the exercise of his great powers by fastening upon him, as subordinate executive officers, men who by their inefficient service under him, by their lack of loyalty to the service, or by their different views of policy might make his taking care that the laws be faithfully executed most difficult or impossible.

As Mr. Madison said in the debate in the First Congress:

> Vest this power in the Senate jointly with the President, and you abolish at once that great principle of unity and responsibility in the executive department, which was intended for the security of liberty and the public good. If the President should possess alone the power of removal from office, those who are employed in the execution of the law will be in their proper situation, and the chain of dependence be preserved; the lowest officers, the middle grade, and the highest will depend, as they ought, on the President, and the President on the community.

Mr. Boudinot of New Jersey said upon the same point:

> Does not this set the Senate over the head of the President? But suppose they shall decide in favor of the officer, what a situation is the President then in, surrounded by officers with whom, by his situation, he is compelled to act, but in whom he can have no confidence?

Made responsible under the Constitution for the effective enforcement of the law, the President needs as an indispensable aid to meet it the disciplinary influence upon those who act under him of a reserve power of removal. But it is contended that executive officers appointed by the President with the consent of the Senate are bound by the statutory law, and are not to do his will. Each head of a department is and must be the President's alter ego in the matters of that department where the President is required by law to exercise authority.

In all such cases, the discretion to be exercised is that of the President in determining the national public interest and in directing the action to be taken by his executive subordinates to protect it. In this field his cabinet officers must do his will. He must place in each member of his official family, and his chief executive subordinates, implicit faith. The moment that he loses confidence in the intelligence, ability, judgment, or loyalty of any one of them, he must have the power to remove him without delay.

But this is not to say that there are not strong reasons why the President should have a like power to remove his appointees charged with other duties than those above described. Laws are often passed with specific provisions for adoption of regulations by a department or bureau head to make the law workable and effective. The ability and judgment manifested by the official thus empowered, as well as his energy and stimulation of his subordinates, are subjects which the President must consider and supervise in his administrative control. Finding such officers to be negligent and inefficient, the President should have the power to remove them. Of course there may be duties so peculiarly and specifically committed to the discretion of a particular officer as to raise a question whether the President may overrule or revise the officer's interpretation of his statutory duty in a particular instance. Then there may be duties of a *quasi*-judicial character imposed on executive officers and members of executive tribunals whose decisions after hearing affect interests of individuals, the discharge of which the President cannot in a particular case properly influence or control. But even in such a case he may consider the decision after its rendition as a reason for removing the officer, on the ground that the discretion regularly entrusted to that officer by statute has not been on the whole intelligently or wisely exercised. Otherwise he does not discharge his own constitutional duty of seeing that the laws be faithfully executed.

[3]

We have devoted much space to this discussion and decision of the question of the presidential power of removal in the First Congress, not because a congressional conclusion on a constitutional issue is conclusive, but first because of our agreement with the reasons upon which it was avowedly based, second because this was the decision of the First Congress on a question of primary importance in the organization of the government made within two years after the Constitutional Convention and within a much shorter time after its ratification, and third because that Congress numbered among its leaders those who had been members of the convention. It must necessarily constitute a precedent upon which many future laws supplying the machinery of the new government would be based and, if erroneous, would be likely to evoke dissent and departure in future Congresses. [I]t was soon accepted as a final decision of the question by all branches of the government.

[a]

A typical case of such acquiescence was that of Alexander Hamilton. In this discussion in the House of Representatives in 1789, Mr. White and others cited the opinion of Mr. Hamilton in respect to the necessity for the consent of the Senate to the removals.

> It has been mentioned as one of the advantages to be expected from the cooperation of the Senate in the business of appointments, that it would contribute to the stability of the administration. The consent of that body would be necessary to displace as well as to appoint. A change of the Chief Magistrate, therefore, would not occasion so violent or so general a revolution in the officers of the government as might be expected if he were the sole disposer of offices.

1 ANNALS OF CONGRESS 456 (quoting FEDERALIST No. 77 (Alexander Hamilton)).

Hamilton changed his view of this matter during his incumbency as Secretary of the Treasury in Washington's Cabinet, as is shown by his view of Washington's first proclamation of neutrality in the war between France and Great Britain. That proclamation was at first criticized as an abuse of executive authority. [Hamilton defended the Administration and based his argument on] Article II of the Constitution and followed exactly the reasoning of Madison and his associates as to the executive power upon which the legislative decision of the First Congress as to Presidential removal depends, and he cites it as authority. He said:

> [Article II] of the Constitution of the United States, section first, establishes this general proposition, that 'the Executive Power shall be vested in a President of the United States of America.' The same Article, in a succeeding section, proceeds to delineate particular cases of executive power.
>
> It would not consist with the rules of sound construction, to consider this enumeration of particular authorities as derogating from the more comprehensive grant in the general clause, further than as it may be coupled with express restrictions or limitations, as in regard to the co-operation of the Senate in the appointment of officers and the making of treaties. The difficulty of a complete enumeration of all the cases of executive authority would naturally dictate the use of general terms, and would render it improbable that a specification of certain particulars was designed as a substitute for those terms, when antecedently used. The different mode of expression employed in the Constitution, in regard to the two powers, the legislative and the executive, serves to confirm this inference. In the Article which gives the legislative powers of the government, the expressions are 'All legislative powers herein granted shall be vested in a congress of the United States.' In that which grants the executive power, the expressions are 'The executive power shall be vested in a President of the United States.'
>
> The enumeration ought therefore to be considered, as intended merely to specify the principle articles implied in the definition of executive power; leaving the rest to flow from the general grant of that power, interpreted in conformity with other parts of the Constitution, and with the principles of free government. The general doctrine of our Constitution then is that the executive power of the nation is vested in the President, subject only to the exceptions and qualifications, which are expressed in the instrument.

7 J.C. Hamilton, Works of Hamilton 80, 81 (1851).

[b]

The words of a second great constitutional authority quoted as in conflict with the congressional decision are those of Chief Justice Marshall. They were used by him in *Marbury v. Madison*, 5 U.S. 137 (1803). The judgment in that case is one of the great landmarks in the history of the construction of the Constitution of the United States, and is of supreme authority first in respect to the power and duty of the Supreme Court and other courts to consider and pass upon the validity of acts of Congress enacted in violation of the limitations of the Constitution. But it is not to be regarded as such authority in respect of the power of the President to remove officials appointed by the advice and consent of the Senate, for that question was not before the court.

[i]

The rule was discharged by the Supreme Court, for the reason that the court had no jurisdiction in such a case to issue a writ of mandamus. [T]he opinion assumed that in the case of a removable office the writ would fail on the presumption that there was in such a case discretion of the appointing power to withhold the commission. And so the Chief Justice proceeded to express an opinion on the question whether the appointee was removable by the President.

There was no answer by Madison to the rule issued in the case. The case went by default. It would seem to have been quite consistent with the case as shown that this was merely an arbitrary refusal by the Secretary to perform his ministerial function, and therefore that the expression of opinion that the officer was not removable by the President was necessary, even to the conclusion that a writ in a proper case could issue. [T]he whole statement was certainly *obiter dictum* with reference to the judgment actually reached. The question whether the officer was removable was not argued to the court by any counsel contending for that view. Counsel for [Marbury], who made the only argument, contended that the officer was not removable by the President, because he held a judicial office and under the Constitution could not be deprived of his office for the five years of his term by presidential action. The opinion contains no wider discussion of the question than that quoted above.

In such a case we may well recur to the Chief Justice's own language in *Cohens v. Virginia*, 19 U.S. 264 (1821), in which, in declining to yield to the force of his previous language in *Marbury v. Madison*, which was unnecessary to the judgment in that case and was *obiter dictum* [explained that such statements are not binding].

[ii]

The weight of this *dictum* of the Chief Justice as to presidential removal in *Marbury v. Madison*, was considered by this Court in *Parsons v. United States*, 167 U.S. 324 (1897). It was a suit by Parsons against the United States for the payment of the balance due for his salary and fees as United States district attorney for Alabama. He had been commissioned as such under the statute for the term of four years from the date of the commission, subject to the conditions prescribed by law. There was no express power of removal provided. Before the end of the four years he was removed by the President. He was denied recovery.

The language of the court in *Marbury v. Madison*, already referred to, was pressed upon this court to show that Parsons was entitled, against the presidential action of removal, to continue in office. If it was authoritative, and stated the law as to an executive office, it ended the case; but this court did not recognize it as such, for the reason that the Chief Justice's language relied on was not germane to the point decided in *Marbury v. Madison*. If his language was more than a dictum and a decision, then *Parsons'* case overrules it.

[iii]

If the Chief Justice in *Marbury v. Madison* intended to express an opinion for the court inconsistent with the legislative decision of 1789, it is enough to observe that he changed his mind, for otherwise it is inconceivable that he should have written and printed his full account of the discussion and decision in the First Congress and his acquiescence to it [in the biography of George Washington that he authored]. He concluded his account as follows:

> To obviate any misunderstanding of the principle on which the question had been decided, Mr. Benson (later) moved in the House, when the report of the committee of the whole was taken up, to amend the second clause in the bill so as clearly to imply the power of removal to be solely in the President. As the bill passed into a law, it has ever been considered as a full expression of the sense of the Legislature on this important part of the American Constitution.

5 JOHN MARSHALL, THE LIFE OF GEORGE WASHINGTON 192–200 (1805–07). This language was first published in 1807, four years after the judgment in *Marbury v. Madison*, and the edition was revised by the Chief Justice in 1832.

[D]

[1]

Congress in a number of acts followed and enforced the legislative decision of 1789 for 74 years. In the act of the First Congress, which adapted to the Constitution the ordinance of 1787 for the government of the Northwest Territory, which had provided for the appointment and removal of executive territorial officers by the Congress under the Articles of Confederation, it was said

> in all cases where the United States in Congress assembled, might, by the said ordinance, revoke any commission or remove from any office, the President is hereby declared to have the same powers of revocation and removal.

This was approved 11 days after the act establishing the Department of Foreign Affairs and was evidently in form a declaration in accord with the constitutional construction of the latter act. In the provision for the Treasury and War Departments, the same formula was used as occurred in the act creating the Department of Foreign Affairs.

Occasionally we find that Congress thought it wiser to make express what would have been understood. Thus in the Judiciary Act of 1789 we find it provided in section 27:

> That a marshall shall be appointed in and for each district for the term of four years, but shall be removable . . . at pleasure, whose duty it shall be to attend the District and Circuit Courts.

That act became a law on September 24. It was formulated by a Senate committee of which Oliver Ellsworth was chairman and which presumably was engaged in drafting it during the time of the congressional debate on removals. Section 35 of the same act provided for the appointment of an attorney for the United States to prosecute crimes and conduct civil actions on behalf of the United States, but nothing was said as to his term of office or of his removal. The difference in the two cases was evidently to avoid any inference from the fixing of the term that a conflict with the legislative decision of 1789 was intended.

In the Act of May 15, 1820, Ch. 102, 3 Stat. 582, Congress provided that thereafter all district attorneys, collectors of customs [and numerous other specified officers], to be appointed under the laws of the United States shall be appointed for the term of four years, but shall be removable from office at pleasure. It is argued that these express provisions for removal at pleasure indicate that without them no such power would exist in the President. We cannot accede to this view. Indeed the conclusion that they were adopted to show conformity to the legislative decision of 1789 is authoritatively settled by a specific decision of this court.

In *Parsons v. United States*, 167 U.S. 324 (1897), [t]his court held that the [1820 Act] should be construed as having been passed in light of the acquiescence of Congress in the decision of 1789, and therefore included the power of removal by the President, even though the clause for removal was omitted. This reasoning was essential to the conclusion reached and makes the construction by this court of the act of 1820 authoritative.

> The provision for a removal from office at pleasure was not necessary for the exercise of that power by the President, because of the fact that he was then regarded as being clothed with such power in any event. Considering the construction of the Constitution in this regard as given by the Congress of 1789, and having in mind the constant and uniform practice of the Government in harmony with such construction, we must construe this act as providing absolutely for the expiration of the term of office at the end of four years, and not as giving a term that shall last, at all events, for that time, and we think the provision that the officials were removable from office at pleasure was but a recognition of the construction thus almost universally adhered to and acquiesced in as to the power of the President to remove.

In the Act of July 17, 1862, ch. 200, § 17, 12 Stat. 596, Congress actually requested the President to make removals in the following language:

> The President of the United States be, and hereby is, authorized and requested to dismiss and discharge from the military service . . . any officer for any cause which, in his judgment, either renders such officer unsuitable for, or whose dismiss[al] would promote, the public service.

Attorney General Devens (15 Op. A.G. 421) said of this act that, so far as it gave authority to the President, it was simply declaratory of the long-established law; that the force of the act was to be found in the word "requested," by which it was intended to re-enforce strongly this power in the hands of the President at a great crisis of the state—a comment by the Attorney General which was expressly approved by this court in *Blake v. United States*, 103 U.S. 227, 234 (1881).

The acquiescence in the legislative decision of 1789 for nearly three-quarters of a century by all branches of the government has been affirmed by this court in unmistakable terms. In *Parsons v. United States* this court said:

> Many distinguished lawyers originally had very different opinions in regard to this power from the one arrived at by this Congress, but when the question was alluded to in after years they recognized that the decision of Congress in 1789, and the universal practice of the Government under it, had settled the question beyond any power of alteration.

[2]

We find this confirmed by Chancellor Kent's and Mr. Justice Story's comments.

In his Commentaries, referring to this question, the Chancellor said:

> This question has never been made the subject of judicial decision; and the construction given to the Constitution in 1789 has continued to rest on this loose, incidental, declaratory opinion of Congress, and the sense and practice of government since that time. It may now be considered as firmly and definitely settled, and there is good sense and practical utility in the construction.

1 JAMES KENT, COMMENTARIES ON AMERICAN LAW 310 (1830).

[Justice Story, in his treatise published in 1833, found] that until the administration of President Jackson, the power of unrestricted removal had been exercised by all the Presidents, but that moderation and forbearance had been shown; that under President Jackson, however, an opposite course had been pursued extensively and brought again the executive power of removal to a severe scrutiny. The learned author then says:

> If there has been any aberration from the true constitutional exposition of the power of removal (which the reader must decide for himself), it will be difficult, and perhaps impracticable, after 40 years' experience, to recall the practice to correct theory. But, at all events, it will be a consolation to those who love the Union, and honor a devotion to the patriotic discharge of duty, that in regard to 'inferior officers' (which appellation probably includes ninety-nine out of a hundred of the lucrative offices in the government), the remedy for any permanent abuse is still within the power of Congress, by the simple expedient of requiring the consent of the Senate to removals in such cases.

2 JOSEPH STORY, COMMENTARIES ON THE CONSTITUTION OF THE UNITED STATES § 1544.

[3]

The legislative decision of 1789 and this court's recognition of it was followed in 1842 by Attorney General Legare in the administration of President Tyler (4 Op. A.G. 1), in 1847 by Attorney General Clifford in the administration of President Polk (4 Op. A.G. 603), by Attorney General Crittenden in the administration of President Fillmore (5 Op. A.G. 288), and by Attorney General Cushing in the Administration of President Buchanan (6 Op. A.G. 4), all of whom delivered opinions of a similar tenor.

[E]

We come now to consider an argument that this case concerns only the removal of an inferior officer, and that such an office was not included within the legislative decision of 1789, which related only to superior officers to be appointed by the President by and with the advice and consent of the Senate.

The very heated discussions during General Jackson's administration related to the distribution of offices, which were most of them inferior offices, and it was the operation of the legislative decision of 1789 upon the power of removal of incumbents of such offices that led the General to refuse to comply with the request of the Senate that he give his reasons for the removals therefrom. It was to such inferior offices that Chancellor Kent's commentaries on the decision of 1789 [applied, specifically] with reference to the removal of United States marshals. It was such inferior offices that Mr. Justice Story conceded to be covered by the legislative decision in his treatise on the Constitution. It was with reference to removals from such inferior offices that the already cited opinions of the Attorneys General, in which the legislative decision of 1789 was referred to as controlling authority, were delivered. Finally, *Parsons'* case, where it was the point in judgment, conclusively establishes for this court that the legislative decision of 1789 applied to a United States attorney, an inferior officer.

It is further pressed on us that, even though the legislative decision of 1789 included inferior officers, yet under the legislative power given Congress with respect to such officers it might directly legislate as to the method of their removal without changing their method of appointment by the President with the consent of the Senate. We do not think the language of the Constitution justifies such a contention.

In *United States v. Perkins*, 116 U.S. 483 (1886), a cadet engineer, a graduate of the Naval Academy, brought suit to recover his salary for the period after his removal by the Secretary of the Navy. It was decided that his right was established. The Court of Claims said:

> Whether or not Congress can restrict the power of removal incident to the power of appointment of those officers who are appointed by the President does not arise in this case and need not be considered. We have no doubt that, when Congress by law vests the appointment of inferior officers in the heads of departments it may limit and restrict the power of removal as it deems best for the public interest. The head of a department has no constitutional prerogative of appointment to offices independently of the legislation of Congress, and by such legislation he must be governed, not only in making appointments, but in all that is incident thereto.

This language of the Court of Claims was approved by this court and the judgment was affirmed.

The authority of Congress given by the excepting clause to vest the appointment of such inferior officers in the heads of departments carries with it authority incidentally to invest the heads of departments with power to remove. It has been the practice of Congress to do so and this court has recognized that power. The court also has recognized in the *Perkins* case that Congress, in committing the appointment of such inferior officers to the heads of departments, may prescribe incidental regulations controlling and restricting the latter in the exercise of the power of removal.

Assuming, then, the power of Congress to regulate removals as incidental to the exercise of its constitutional power to vest appointments of inferior officers in the heads of departments, certainly so long as Congress does not exercise that power, the power of removal must remain where the Constitution places it, with the President, as part of the executive power.

[F]

[1]

We come now to a period in the history of the government when both houses of Congress attempted to reverse this constitutional construction, and to subject the power of removing executive officers appointed by the President and confirmed by the Senate to the control of the Senate, indeed finally to the assumed power in Congress to place the removal of such officers anywhere in the government.

This reversal grew out of the serious political difference between Congress and President [Andrew] Johnson. There was a two-thirds majority of the republican party, in control of each house of Congress, which resented what it feared would be Mr. Johnson's obstructive course in the enforcement of the reconstruction measures in respect to the states whose people had lately been at war against the national government. This led the two houses to enact legislation to curtail the then acknowledged powers of the President. [T]he chief legislation in support of the reconstruction policy of Congress was the Tenure of Office Act of March 2, 1867, providing that all officers appointed by and with the consent of the Senate should hold their offices until their successors should have in like manner been appointed and qualified; that certain heads of departments, including the Secretary of War, should hold their offices during the term of the President by whom appointed and one month thereafter, subject to removal by consent of the Senate. The Tenure of Office Act was vetoed, but it was passed over the veto. The House of Representatives preferred articles of impeachment against President Johnson for refusal to comply with, and for conspiracy to defeat, the legislation above referred to, but he was acquitted for lack of a two-thirds vote for conviction in the Senate.

The extreme provisions of all this legislation were a full justification for the considerations, so strongly advanced by Mr. Madison and his associates in the First Congress, for insisting that the power of removal of executive officers by the President alone was essential in the division of powers between the executive and legislative bodies. It exhibited in a clear degree the paralysis to which a partisan Senate and Congress could subject the executive arm, and destroy the principle of executive responsibility, and separation of the powers sought for by the framers of our government, if the President had no power of removal save by consent of the Senate. It was an attempt to redistribute the powers and minimize those of the President.

[2]

After President Johnson's term ended, the injury and invalidity of the Tenure of Office Act in its radical innovation were immediately recognized by the executive and objected to. General Grant, succeeding Mr. Johnson in the presidency, earnestly recommended in his first message the total repeal of the act.

While in response to this a bill for repeal of that act passed the House, it failed in the Senate, and, though the law was changed, it still limited the presidential power of removal. The feeling growing out of the controversy with President Johnson retained the act on the statute book until 1887, when it was repealed. During this interval, on June 8, 1872, Congress passed an act reorganizing and consolidating the Post Office Department, and provided that the Postmaster General and his three assistants should be appointed by the President by and with the advice and consent of the Senate, and might be removed in the same manner. In 1876 the act here under discussion was passed, making the consent of the Senate necessary both to the appointment and removal of first, second, and third class postmasters.

In the same interval, in March, 1886, President Cleveland, in discussing the requests which the Senate had made for his reasons for removing officials, and the assumption that the Senate had the right to pass upon those removals and thus to limit the power of the President, said:

> I believe the power to remove or suspend such officials is vested in the President alone by the Constitution, which in express terms provides that "the executive power shall be vested in a President of the United States of America," and that "he shall take care that the laws be faithfully executed."

> When the Constitution by express provision superadded to its legislative duties the right to advise and consent to appointments to office and to sit as a court of impeachment, it conferred upon that body all the control and regulation of executive action supposed to be necessary for the safety of the people; and this express and special grant of such extraordinary powers should be held, under a familiar maxim of construction, to exclude every other right of interference with executive functions.

[3]

[a]

The attitude of the Presidents on this subject has been unchanged and uniform to the present day whenever an issue has clearly been raised. [President Wilson in

1920 and President Coolidge in 1924 both reaffirmed Presidential power of removal in formal messages to Congress.]

[b]

In spite of the foregoing presidential declarations, it is contended that, since the passage of the Tenure of Office Act, there has been general acquiescence by the executive in the power of Congress to forbid the President alone to remove executive officers, an acquiescence which has changed any formerly accepted constitutional construction to the contrary. Instances are cited of the signed approval by President Grant and other Presidents of legislation in derogation of such construction. We think these are all to be explained, not by acquiescence therein, but by reason of the otherwise valuable effect of the legislation approved. Such is doubtless the explanation of the executive approval of the act of 1876, which we are considering, for it was an appropriation act on which the section here in question was imposed as a rider.

[i]

In the use of congressional legislation to support or change a particular construction of the Constitution by acquiescence, its weight for the purpose must depend not only upon the nature of the question, but also upon the attitude of the executive and judicial branches of the government, as well as upon the number of instances in the execution of the law in which opportunity for objection in the courts or elsewhere is afforded. When instances which actually involve the question are rare or have not in fact occurred, the weight of the mere presence of acts on the statute book for a considerable time as showing general acquiescence in the legislative assertion of a questioned power is minimized. No instance is cited to us where any question has arisen respecting a removal of a Postmaster General or one of his assistants. The President's request for resignation of such offices is generally complied with. The same thing is true of the postmasters. There have been many executive removals of them and but few protests or objections. Even when there has been a refusal by a postmaster to resign, removal by the President has been followed by a nomination of a successor and the Senate's confirmation has made unimportant the inquiry as to the necessity for the Senate's consent to the removal.

[ii]

Other acts of Congress are referred to which contain provisions said to be inconsistent with the 1789 decision. Since the provision for an Interstate Commerce Commission in 1887, many administrative boards have been created whose members are appointed by the President, by and with the advice and consent of the Senate, and in the statutes creating them have been provisions for the removal of the members for specified causes. Such provisions are claimed to be inconsistent with the independent power of removal by the President. This, however, is shown to be unfounded by the case of *Shurtleff v. United States*, 189 U.S. 311 (1903). That concerned an act creating a board of general appraisers and provided for their removal for inefficiency, neglect of duty, or malfeasance in office. The President removed an appraiser without notice or hearing. It was forcibly contended that the affirmative language of the statute implied the negative of the power to remove except for cause and after a hearing. [T]he court held that, in the absence of constitutional or statutory provision otherwise, the President could by virtue of his general power of appointment remove an officer notwithstanding specific provisions for his removal for cause, on the ground that the power of removal inhered in the power to appoint. This is an indication that many of the statutes cited are to be reconciled to the unrestricted power of the President to remove, if he chooses to exercise his power.

[G]

The fact seems to be that all departments of the government have constantly had in mind, since the passage of the Tenure of Office Act, that the question of power of removal by the President of officers appointed by him with the Senate's consent has not been settled adversely to the legislative action of 1789, but, in spite of congressional action, has remained open until the conflict should be subjected to judicial investigation and decision.

The actions of this court cannot be said to constitute assent to a departure from the legislative decision of 1789, when the *Parsons* and *Shurtleff* cases, one decided in 1897, and the other in 1903, are considered for they certainly leave the question open. Those cases indicate no tendency to depart from the view of the First Congress. This court has since the Tenure of Office Act manifested an earnest desire to avoid a final settlement of the question until it should be inevitably presented, as it is here.

This court has repeatedly laid down the principle that a contemporaneous legislative exposition of the Constitution, when the founders of our government and framers of our Constitution were actively participating in public affairs, acquiesced in for a long term of years, fixes the construction to be given its provisions. *See Stuart v. Laird*, 5 U.S. [1 Cranch] 299 (1803); *Cohens v. Virginia*, 19 U.S. [6 Wheat.] 264 (1821). We are now asked to set aside this construction thus buttressed and adopt an adverse view, because the Congress of the United States did so during a heated political difference of opinion between the then President and the majority leaders of Congress over the reconstruction measures adopted as a means of restoring to their proper status the states which attempted to withdraw from the Union at the time of the Civil War. The extremes to which the majority in both Houses carried legislative measures in that matter are now recognized by all. Without animadverting on the character of the measures taken, we are certainly justified in saying that they should not be given the weight affecting proper constitutional construction to be accorded to that reached by the First Congress during a political calm and acquiesced in by the whole government for three-quarters of a century, especially when the new construction contended for has never been acquiesced in by either the executive or the judicial departments.

For the reasons given, we must therefore hold that the provisions of the law of 1876 by which the unrestricted power of removal of first-class postmasters is denied to the President is in violation of the Constitution and invalid. This leads to an affirmance of the judgment of the Court of Claims.

Judgment affirmed.

[The dissenting opinions of Justices McReynolds, Brandeis, and Holmes are omitted.]

EXERCISE 2:

Consider how the Court in *Myers v. United States* resolves questions regarding the scope of the executive power, particularly with respect to the power to appoint officers and to remove them from office. In addition to the doctrinal answers, note the forms of argument and supporting sources the Court found persuasive. Specifically, consider:

1. What is the Court's holding? To what extent, if any, may Congress limit the President's power to remove federal officers?

2. In Part II(A), the Supreme Court asserted that the Constitution contains no express provision governing removals from office other than the provision for impeachment. Is that correct? What inference regarding removal should be drawn based upon the impeachment provision? Are there any other textual provisions that support an inference regarding the removability of officers (other than judges appointed to Article III courts)?

3. In Part II(B), the Supreme Court addressed the drafting history of Article II of the Constitution. What light, if any, does the drafting history shed on the meaning of the President's powers and the authority of Congress to limit those powers? What weight should be given to the drafting history?

4. In Part II(C)(1), the Supreme Court reviewed the actions of the First Congress in establishing the first executive department and the first principal officer of an executive department. Is it clear that Congress declared its interpretation of the Constitution as vesting in the President the unilateral and unlimited power to remove the Secretary of Foreign Affairs? Or, is there some other explanation for the historical materials? If the First Congress did so express its understanding of the Constitution, should that view fix the meaning of the Constitution for all time? Why or why not?

5. Assume that when, in September 1789, Congress expanded the duties of the Secretary of Foreign Affairs and his executive department—which resulted in the more-appropriate name "State" being substituted for "Foreign Affairs"—Congress expressly provided that the Secretary would "serve in office for a period of two years unless previously removed by the President with the concurrence of the Senate." If several years later, President Adams unilaterally removed from office his Secretary of State, Timothy Pickering, less than two years into Pickering's term, would Pickering have a claim to his salary for the unexpired term?

6. Does the answer to the previous question depend at all on whether President Washington signed the legislation rather than it being passed over his veto? Why or why not?

7. According to the historical materials summarized by the Court in Parts II(C) (2)(a)–(b) of its opinion, did the Framers (or, at least, the Framers as understood by

the First Congress) draw any pertinent distinction between the President's power uni-laterally to remove the Secretary of State and:

a. any other principal, executive officer?

b. any other principal officer (other than judges appointed to Article III courts)?

c. any inferior, executive officer?

8. In Part II(C)(2)(a) of its opinion, the Court asserted that "the reasonable con-struction of the Constitution must be that the branches should be kept separate in all cases in which they were not expressly blended, and the Constitution should be expounded to blend them no more than it affirmatively requires." Do you agree with that principle of construction?

9. In the final paragraph of Part II(C)(2)(a), the Supreme Court referenced James Madison's explanation in the First Congress of the meaning of the first sentence of Article II in conjunction with more specific provisions in subsequent sections of that Article. What are the implications of that explanation for whether the President has unenumerated or "inherent" powers?

10. In Part II(C)(2)(c) of its opinion, the Supreme Court addressed the argument that the "greater power" to create an office implies the "lesser power" to prescribe conditions for removal from office. Is the lesser power implied? If so, does it not equally follow that the power to dictate the mode of appointment flows from the power to create the office? Under that reasoning, could Congress create the office of Commissioner of the Internal Revenue and vest appointment to that office in the Speaker of the House of Representatives? Why or why not?

11. Does the "greater power" to create an office imply the "lesser power" to pre-scribe qualifications for the office? Could Congress create the office of Attorney Gen-eral and require that only individuals admitted to the practice of law for twenty years be eligible to fill the office? If so, could Congress create a group of offices (for example, all the judgeships for the U.S. Supreme Court) and, in order to "moderate" the partisan influence in selecting officers, require that the President name no more than a bare majority of nominees of the same political party? Or, to limit geographic concentration of power, could Congress require that no two of the group of officers reside in the same State? Would it make any difference if the offices were not in the Article III judiciary?

12. In Part II(C)(2)(c)(ii) of its opinion, the Court drew a distinction between the power of Congress to limit removal of inferior officers appointed by the President with Senate confirmation and the power of Congress to limit removal of inferior offi-cers the appointment of whom Congress vested in the "Heads of Departments." Does that distinction follow from the constitutional text? Does that distinction find support in the views of the Framers and/or the views of the First Congress?

13. Based on the rationale of Part II(C)(2)(c)(ii) of the Court's opinion, would Congress have the authority to limit the removal of inferior officers appointed by the President alone, without Senate confirmation? Why or why not?

14. In Part II(C)(2)(c)(iv) of its opinion, the Court quoted Madison regarding the power of Congress to play a role in selecting the individual to fill an office it creates. Assume Congress enacted legislation prohibiting the President from appointing to any office a member of his own family, expressly defining the relations so disqualified. Should the Court enforce such a prohibition?

15. In Part II(C)(2)(d) of its opinion, the Court explored some policy reasons articulated by Madison (and others) for finding unlimited and unilateral power of removal in the President. Do those reasons support any pertinent distinction between the President's power unilaterally to remove the Secretary of State and:

a. any other principal, executive officer?

b. any other principal officer (other than judges appointed to Article III courts)?

c. any inferior, executive officer?

16. Do the reasons considered in Question 15 support any pertinent distinction between inferior officers appointed by the President with the advice and consent of the Senate and:

a. inferior officers appointed by the President alone?

b. inferior officers appointed by the Heads of Departments?

17. In Part II(C)(3)(a) of its opinion, the Court quoted a statement of Alexander Hamilton in THE FEDERALIST to the effect that Senate approval would be required for a President to remove officers. Should that source receive more or less weight than the debates in the Constitutional Convention, discussed in Part II(A) of the Court's opinion? Why?

18. In Part II(C)(3)(a) of its opinion, the Court quoted Alexander Hamilton's defense of President Washington's action in proclaiming neutrality in the war between France and Great Britain. Why should a matter subsequent to ratification of the Constitution be considered in interpreting the meaning of its terms?

19. In Part II(C)(3)(b) of its opinion, the Court addressed the precedent established by *Marbury v. Madison*. Did the Court fairly characterize the holding of *Marbury*? Should *Marbury* be viewed as applicable precedent to the issue before the Court?

20. In Part II(D)(2) of its opinion, the Court quoted Justice Story—who simultaneously served on the U.S. Supreme Court and held an appointment as a law professor at Harvard and published leading treatises and expositions of the law—as believing that the historical precedent of 1789 did not limit Congress with respect to inferior officers. Was Justice Story correct?

21. In Part II(E) of its opinion, the Court addressed the argument that the congressional interpretation of the Constitution recognizing unlimited presidential power of removal applied only to principal officers. Did the Court convincingly

demonstrate a historical understanding that inferior officers were subject to presidential removal?

22. In Part II(E) of its opinion, the Court described its precedent in *United States v. Perkins*. In what way did that case modify the doctrine regarding the power of Congress to limit the removability of non-judicial officers? What are the textual and historical bases for the interpretation adopted in *Perkins*?

23. In Part II(F) of its opinion, the Court detailed legislation through which Congress sought to limit the President's power to remove non-judicial officers. At the time it was enacted, did the Tenure of Office Act violate the text and/or historical understanding of the Constitution? At the time it was enacted, did the Tenure of Office Act violate any Supreme Court precedent?

24. Some of the legislation addressed in Part II(F) of the Court's opinion was enacted with presidential approval while other legislation was enacted over presidential veto. Should judicial determination of whether legislation limiting presidential authority is constitutional consider whether the legislation was approved by the President? Why or why not?

25. In Part II(F)(3)(b)(i) of its opinion, the Court suggested some criteria by which one might determine which legislative precedents (or, perhaps, historical precedents more broadly) properly fix the meaning of the Constitution. Do these criteria establish meaningful and appropriate principles? If so, in a case where the criteria are satisfied, should the Court adhere to legislative precedent despite contrary constitutional text or ascertainable views of the Framers? What if *both* constitutional text and the views of the Framers are opposed to the legislative precedent?

26. In Part II(F)(3)(b)(ii) of its opinion, the Court addressed the Interstate Commerce Act of 1887 and other subsequent legislation which created various modern federal administrative agencies. The Court acknowledged that those statutes purported to provide the officers who head those agencies with tenure for fixed terms of years subject to earlier removal by the President only for specified causes, usually limited to "inefficiency, neglect of duty, or malfeasance in office." Assume that in such a statute, Congress clearly expressed its intent to limit the President's power to remove an officer (other than a judge of an Article III court) who had been appointed by the President with the advice and consent of the Senate. If the Supreme Court could not avoid the constitutional issue through any other interpretation of the statute, does *Myers* (and/or the judicial precedents discussed therein) hold that the President nonetheless retains unlimited power of removal?

27. Did the *Myers* Court rule that Article II determinately gave to the President the power to removal federal officers? Or, did the Court rule that the Constitution was indeterminate on that point, and that the Decision of 1789 cleared up that ambiguity, and thereby determined that the President possessed the removal power?

28. How might the fact that Chief Justice Taft was previously President have influenced his decision? Is there any evidence in the opinion to support your conclusion?

29. Should the Supreme Court have taken this case? Or, should the Court have allowed the political branches to "fight it out" under the political question doctrine?

———————

The story of the removal power is long and rich. Professors Steven G. Calabresi and Christopher S. Yoo, in their book on Presidential power, THE UNITARY EXECUTIVE: PRESIDENTIAL POWER FROM WASHINGTON TO BUSH (2008), observed that the matter is not limited to historical battles that shaped our Constitution. Rather the removal power presents "one of the biggest issues of our time" because it concerns "how to establish better control over big, unresponsive government bureaucracies." *Id.* at 6.

Professors Calabresi's and Yoo's extensive compilation provided "a comprehensive historical chronicle of the struggles between the president and Congress over control of execution of federal law." *Id.* at 14. As such, it is an important resource for arguments in this field premised upon tradition as distinguished from text, structure, and ratification history. One important caveat is that the authors expressly limit their presentation to "*presidential claims* about the unitary executive debate." *Id.* at 18 (emphasis added). (To counterbalance the self-interest of the Executive in such matters, it will be appropriate to consult scholarship addressing congressional efforts to limit Executive power.)

In the course of their work, Professors Calabresi and Yoo addressed the various historical episodes referenced in the *Myers* opinion, including:

- The preratification origins of the Unitary Executive debate and the Decision of 1789, *see id.* at 30–36;
- President Jackson's aggressive use of the removal power, *see id.* at 99–104, and the controversy over his removal of the Treasury Secretary, *see id.* at 105–12;
- The Tenure of Office Act and the impeachment of President Andrew Johnson, *see id.* at 179–87; and
- President Wilson's instruction of the removal of Frank S. Myers, *see id.* at 255–56.

They also addressed President Franklin D. Roosevelt's attempted removal of William E. Humphrey and the litigation it prompted. *See id.* at 283–88. Other historians and political scientists have covered the same ground as well. See, e.g., J. DAVID ALVIS, JEREMY D. BAILEY, & F. FLAGG TAYLOR IV, THE CONTESTED REMOVAL POWER, 1789–2010 (2013).

2. The Fall

One might be forgiven—based on the length of the opinion, depth of research displayed, and robustness of arguments utilized—for thinking that *Myers* settled, once and for all, the question of whether Congress could limit the President's removal power of presidential appointees. However, less than a decade later, the Supreme Court modified its course. As you read *Humphrey's Executor*, think about what may have caused the Court to "trim its sails."

HUMPHREY'S EXECUTOR v. UNITED STATES
295 U.S. 602 (1935)

JUSTICE SUTHERLAND delivered the opinion of the Court.

Plaintiff brought suit in the Court of Claims against the United States to recover a sum of money alleged to be due the deceased as salary as a Federal Trade Commissioner from October 8, 1933, when the President undertook to remove him from office, to the time of his death on February 14, 1934.

William E. Humphrey, the decedent, on December 10, 1931, was nominated by President Hoover as a member of the Federal Trade Commission, and he was confirmed by the United States Senate. He was duly commissioned for a term of seven years, expiring September 25, 1938; and, after taking the required oath of office, entered upon his duties. On July 25, 1933, President Roosevelt addressed a letter to the commissioner asking for his resignation, on the ground "that the aims and purposes of the Administration with respect to the work of the Commission can be carried out most effectively with personnel of my own selection," but disclaiming any reflection upon the commissioner or upon his services.

The commissioner declined to resign; and on October 7, 1933, the President wrote him: "Effective as of this date you are hereby removed from the office of Commissioner of the Federal Trade Commission." Humphrey never acquiesced in this action, but continued thereafter to insist that he was still a member of the commission, entitled to perform its duties and receive the compensation provided by law at the rate of $10,000 per annum.

The Federal Trade Commission Act creates a commission of five members to be appointed by the President by and with the advice and consent of the Senate, and section 1 provides:

> Not more than three of the commissioners shall be members of the same political party. The first commissioners . . . but their successors shall be appointed for terms of seven years. Any commissioner may be removed by the President for inefficiency, neglect of duty, or malfeasance in office.

[I]

The question first to be considered is whether, by the provisions of section 1 of the Federal Trade Commission Act already quoted, the President's power is limited to removal for the specific causes enumerated therein. The negative contention of the government is based principally upon the decision of this court in *Shurtleff v. United States*, 189 U.S. 311 (1903). [The 1890 statute at issue in that case provided that the President could remove from office a general appraiser of merchandise for "inefficiency, neglect of duty, or malfeasance in office."] That opinion, after saying that no term of office was fixed by the act and that, with the exception of judicial officers provided for by the Constitution, [observed that] no civil officers had ever held office by life tenure since the foundation of the government.

In the face of the unbroken precedent against life tenure, except in the case of the judiciary, the conclusion that Congress intended that, from among all other civil officers, appraisers alone should be selected to hold office for life was so extreme as to forbid, in the opinion of the court, any ruling which would produce that result if it reasonably could be avoided.

The situation here presented is plainly and wholly different. The statute fixes a term of office. The words of the act are definite and unambiguous. [T]he fixing of a definite term subject to removal for cause, unless there be some countervailing provision or circumstance indicating the contrary, which here we are unable to find, is enough to establish the legislative intent that the term is not to be curtailed in the absence of such cause.

The commission is to be nonpartisan; and it must, from the very nature of its duties, act with entire impartiality. Its duties are neither political nor executive, but predominantly *quasi*-judicial and *quasi*-legislative. Like the Interstate Commerce Commission, its members are called upon to exercise the trained judgment of a body of experts "appointed by law and informed by experience." The legislative reports in both houses of Congress clearly reflect the view that a fixed term was necessary to the effective and fair administration of the law.

Thus, the language of the act, the legislative reports, and the general purposes of the legislation as reflected in the debates, all combine to demonstrate the congressional intent to create a body of experts who shall gain experience by length of service; a body which shall be independent of executive authority, except in its selection, and free to exercise its judgment without the leave or hindrance of any other official or any department of the government. To the accomplishment of these purposes, it is clear that Congress was of opinion that length and certainty of tenure would vitally contribute.

We conclude that the intent of the act is to limit the executive power of removal to the causes enumerated, the existence of none of which is claimed here.

[II]

To support its contention that the removal provision of section 1 is an unconstitutional interference with the executive power of the President, the government's chief reliance is *Myers v. United States*, 272 U.S. 52 (1926). That case has been so recently decided, and the prevailing and dissenting opinions so fully review the general subject of the power of executive removal, that further discussion would add little of value to the wealth of material there collected. These opinions examine at length the historical, legislative, and judicial data bearing upon the question, beginning with what is called "the decision of 1789" in the first Congress and coming down almost to the day when the opinions were delivered. They occupy 243 pages of the volume in which they are printed. Nevertheless, the narrow point actually decided was only that the President had power to remove a postmaster of the first class, without the advice and consent of the Senate as required by act of Congress. In the course of the opinion of the court, expressions occur which tend to sustain the government's contention, but those are beyond the point involved and, therefore, do not come within the rule of stare decisis. In so far as they are out of harmony with the views here set forth, these expressions are disapproved. A like situation was presented in the case of *Cohens v. Virginia*, 19 U.S. [6 Wheat.] 264 (1821), in respect of certain general expressions in the opinion in *Marbury v. Madison*, 5 U.S. [1 Cranch] 137 (1803).

The office of a postmaster is so essentially unlike the office now involved that the decision in the *Myers* case cannot be accepted as controlling our decision here. A postmaster is an executive officer restricted to the performance of executive functions. He is charged with no duty at all related to either the legislative or judicial power. The actual decision in the *Myers* case finds support in the theory that such an officer is merely one of the units in the executive department and, hence, inherently subject to the exclusive and illimitable power of removal by the Chief Executive, whose subordinate and aid he is. Putting aside *dicta*, which may be followed if sufficiently persuasive but which are not controlling, the necessary reach of the decision goes far enough to include all purely executive officers. It goes no farther; much less does it include an officer who occupies no place in the executive department and who exercises no part of the executive power vested by the Constitution in the President.

The Federal Trade Commission is an administrative body created by Congress to carry into effect legislative policies embodied in the statute in accordance with the legislative standard therein prescribed, and to perform other specified duties as a legislative or as a judicial aid. Such a body cannot in any proper sense be characterized as an arm or an eye of the executive. Its duties are performed without executive leave and, in the contemplation of the statute, must be free from executive control. In administering the provisions of the statute in respect of "unfair methods of competition," that is to say, in filling in and administering the details embodied by that general standard, the commission acts in part *quasi*-legislatively and in part *quasi*-judicially. In making investigations and reports thereon for the information of Congress under section 6, in aid of the legislative power, it acts as a legislative agency. Under section 7, which authorizes the commission to act as a master in chancery under rules prescribed by the court, it acts as an agency of the judiciary. To the extent that it exercises any executive function, as distinguished from executive power in the constitutional sense, it does so in the discharge and effectuation of its *quasi*-legislative or *quasi*-judicial powers, or as an agency of the legislative or judicial departments of the government.

If Congress is without authority to prescribe causes for removal of members of the trade commission and limit executive power of removal accordingly, that power at once becomes practically all-inclusive in respect of civil officers with the exception of the judiciary provided for by the Constitution. The Solicitor General, at the bar, apparently recognizing this to be true, with commendable candor, agreed that his view in respect of the removability of members of the Federal Trade Commission necessitated a like view in respect of the Interstate Commerce Commission and the Court of Claims. We are thus confronted with the serious question whether not only the members of these *quasi*-legislative and *quasi*-judicial bodies, but the judges of the legislative Court of Claims, exercising judicial power continue in office only at the pleasure of the President.

We think it plain under the Constitution that illimitable power of removal is not possessed by the President in respect of officers of the character of those just named. The authority of Congress, in creating *quasi*-legislative or *quasi*-judicial agencies, to require them to act in discharge of their duties independently of executive control cannot well be doubted; and that authority includes, as an appropriate incident, power to fix the period during which they shall continue, and to forbid their removal except for cause in the meantime. For it is quite evident that one who holds his office only during the pleasure of another cannot be depended upon to maintain an attitude of independence against the latter's will.

The fundamental necessity of maintaining each of the three general departments of government entirely free from the control or coercive influence, direct or indirect, of either of the others, has often been stressed and is hardly open to serious question. So much is implied in the very fact of the separation of powers of these departments by the Constitution; and in the rule which recognizes their essential coequality. The sound application of a principle that makes one master in his own house precludes him from imposing his control in the house of another who is master there. James Wilson, one of the Framers of the Constitution and a former justice of this court, said that the independence of each department required that its proceedings "should be free from the remotest influence, direct or indirect, of either of the other two powers." JAMES DEWITT ANDREWS, 1 THE WORKS OF JAMES WILSON 367 (1896).

The power of removal here claimed for the President falls within this principle, since its coercive influence threatens the independence of a commission, which is not only wholly disconnected from the executive department, but which, as already fully appears, was created by Congress as a means of carrying into operation legislative and judicial powers, and as an agency of the legislative and judicial departments.

In light of the question now under consideration, we have re-examined the precedents referred to in the *Myers* case, and find nothing in them to justify a conclusion contrary to that which we have reached. The so-called "decision of 1789" had relation to a bill proposed by Mr. Madison to establish an executive Department of Foreign Affairs. The bill provided that the principal officer was "to be removable from office by the President of the United States." This clause was changed to read "whenever the principal officer shall be removed from office by the President of the United States," certain things would follow, thereby, in connection with the debates, recognizing and confirming, as the court thought in the *Myers* case, the sole power of the President in the matter. We shall not discuss the subject further, since it is so fully covered by the opinions in the *Myers* case, except to say that the office under consideration by Congress was not only purely executive, but the officer one who was responsible to the President, and to him alone, in a very definite sense. A reading of the debates shows that the President's illimitable power of removal was not considered in respect of other than executive officers.

In *Marbury v. Madison*, 5 U.S. at 162, 165–66, it is made clear that Chief Justice Marshall was of opinion that a justice of the peace for the District of Columbia was not removable at the will of the President; and that there was a distinction between such an officer and officers appointed to aid the President in the performance of his constitutional duties. In the latter case, the distinction he saw was that "their acts are his acts" and his will, therefore, controls; and, by way of illustration, he adverted to the act establishing the Department of Foreign Affairs, which was the subject of the "decision of 1789."

The result of what we now have said is this: Whether the power of the President to remove an officer shall prevail over the authority of Congress to condition the power by fixing a definite term and precluding a removal except for cause will depend upon the character of the office; the *Myers* decision, affirming the power of the President alone to make the removal, is confined to purely executive officers; and as to officers of the kind here under consideration, we hold that no removal can be made during the prescribed term for which the officer is appointed, except for one or more of the causes named in the applicable statute.

JUSTICE McREYNOLDS, concurring in the judgement. [Omitted.]

EXERCISE 3:

Consider the following questions in connection with *Humphrey's Executor v. United States*:

1. *Humphrey's Executor* is a key case making the modern administrative state possible. How did *Humphrey's Executor* legitimate the administrative state?

2. Was the *Humphrey's Executor* Court faithful to *Myers*?

3. Was *Humphrey's Executor* faithful to the Decision of 1789?

4. Was Humphreys really a "purely executive" official, as the Court described him? What characteristics of his office made him purely executive?

5. The Court recited that, in creating the Federal Trade Commission, Congress purported to require the President to select Commissioners on the basis of partisan political affiliation. Is that limitation on the President's appointment authority consistent with pertinent constitutional text and/or the views of the Framers (discussed at length in *Myers*) and/or the views expressed by a majority in the First Congress (also discussed at length in *Myers*)?

6. Is this purported limitation on the President's appointment power consistent with any legislative precedent referenced in *Myers*?

7. Are Commissioners of the Federal Trade Commission "principal" or "inferior" officers? Does that make any difference to the Court's analysis in *Myers* or any of

the judicial precedents discussed therein? Does the Court in *Humphrey's Executor* place any significance on such classification?

8. The Court recited that in enacting the Federal Trade Commission Act, Congress purported to limit the President's authority to remove Commissioners before expiration of a term of office. In light of the fact that Congress required that the Commissioners be appointed with Senate confirmation, what, if anything, would *Myers* indicate regarding whether that limitation was constitutional? Which, if any, of the following matters supports or rejects the constitutionality of the limitation:

a. the text of the Constitution (itself or as viewed by the majority in *Myers*);

b. the views of the Framers (discussed at length in *Myers*);

c. the views expressed by a majority in the First Congress (also discussed at length in *Myers*)?

9. In Part I of its opinion, the Court discussed its precedent, *Shurtleff v. United States*. Was the Court's view of the case consistent with the characterization of that precedent in *Myers*?

10. In Part I of its opinion, the Court asserted that Congress intended that the FTC "be nonpartisan," that the FTC's duties "are neither political nor executive," and that Congress designed the FTC to be "independent of executive authority, except in its selection." Assuming that the Court correctly discerned the intent of Congress, does Congress have constitutional authority to create offices other than (1) legislative officers, like the Speaker of the House or the President pro tempore of the Senate (*see* Art. I, § 2, ¶ 5; Art. I, § 3, ¶ 5); (2) judges, clerks, and marshals of the federal courts contemplated by Article III (*see* Art. I, § 8, cl. 9); (3) military officers (*see* Art. I, § 8, cls.12–14); (4) officers for the District of Columbia, like justices of the peace, and other land within states purchased by the federal government, like park police (*see* Art. I, § 8, cl.17); (5) officers "in each of the executive Departments" (*see* Art. II, § 2, ¶ 1), including "Ambassadors . . . and Consuls" (*see* Art. II, § 2, ¶ 2); and (6) territorial officers for lands within the jurisdiction of the United States but not located within any state, such as the governor of the Northwest Territories (*see* Art. IV, § 3, ¶ 2)? If so, what is the textual basis for that authority?

11. In the view of the Framers (discussed at length in *Myers*), were federal civil (not military) officers exercising nationwide authority (not limited to the territories or other federal enclaves), to be exclusively divided into legislative, executive, and judicial departments? If so, what purposes were to be served by such division?

12. In Part II of its opinion, the Court acknowledged that *Myers* constituted the primary precedent upon which the President relied for his removal authority. *Myers* had been decided in 1926, just nine years prior to the decision in *Humphrey's Executor*. In *Myers*, the Court ruled, by a 6–3 margin, that the President had removal authority. In *Humphrey's Executor*, the Court ruled 9–0 against the President's removal authority and "disapproved" any portion of *Myers* inconsistent with its decision. If the Court in *Humphrey's Executor* determined that *Myers* was incorrectly decided,

would stare decisis favor following *Myers*? Why or why not? In answering this question, utilize the factors articulated by the Supreme Court in *Casey*, discussed in Volume 1.

13. In Part II of its opinion, the Court asserted that, in *Myers*, "the narrow point actually decided was only that the President had the power to remove a postmaster of the first class, without the advice and consent of the Senate as required by act of Congress." If Humphrey had been a postmaster of the second class, rather than a Commissioner of the Federal Trade Commission, would *Myers* have constituted controlling precedent? Why or why not? If Humphrey had been a non-postmaster, inferior officer serving in the State Department, who had been appointed by the President with Senate confirmation, would *Myers* have constituted controlling precedent? Why or why not?

14. In Part II of its opinion, the Court distinguished between the office from which Myers was removed and the office from which Humphrey was removed. In terms of promoting the policy of the President, which of the two officers does the President most need to control?

15. In Part II of its decision, the Court asserted that "the necessary reach of" its prior decision in *Myers* "goes far enough to include *all* purely executive officers." Does that mean that an inferior, "purely executive" officer must be subject to unlimited power of Presidential removal even if the officer was appointed without Senate confirmation? If so, is the Civil Service Act of 1883 (discussed in *Myers*) subject to constitutional attack?

16. The same quote from Part II of the Court's decision raises the question whether there are any "purely" executive officers. Do all executive officers wield some incidental quasi-legislative or quasi-judicial powers? When the Secretary of State promulgates regulations regarding procedures for applications for a passport, is he engaged in quasi-legislative activities? When the Secretary of State decides whether to issue a travel advisory regarding a foreign nation or selects among competing contractors to operate a facility, is he engaged in quasi-judicial activities?

17. The Supreme Court stated that Humphrey "occupies no place in the executive department." Then where, in the federal government, was Humphrey located? Section 3 of the Act creating the FTC indicated that the Commission replaced an earlier agency—the Bureau of Corporations—which had been subject to the supervision of the Secretary of Commerce. "All pending investigations and proceedings of the Bureau" were transferred to the Commission as were the clerks and employees, the records and papers and property, and appropriations and unexpended funds. Does the Constitution permit such an office as Humphrey's?

18. Does the oath in Article VI tell us anything about the universe of governmental power, according to the Constitution? Would quasi-legislative, quasi-judicial officers be required to take the oath? Would that make any sense?

19. In Part II of its decision, the Court distinguished *Myers* because, it said, this case involved an officer "who exercises no part of the executive power vested by the

Constitution in the President." Is it true that the Federal Trade Commission exercises no "executive power"? The Court acknowledged that the FTC did exercise some "executive function[s]" but asserted that those functions did not constitute "executive power in the constitutional sense" and such functions were merely ancillary to the FTC's quasi-legislative or quasi-judicial activities. Section 5 of the Act creating the FTC indicates that the Commission had the authority to draft and file a "complaint stating its charges" that the named party was using "any unfair method of competition in commerce," which would then initiate adjudicatory proceedings. Is the decision whether and when to bring a complaint a function of the executive (as distinguished from the legislature or judiciary)? In the criminal context, are the prosecutor's duties ancillary to the legislature's criminalization of certain conduct and/or the judiciary's trial of the defendant? Or, is prosecution a core function of the executive that the Framers would have separated from legislative and judicial power? How, if at all, is the FTC's role in identifying parties and charges different from that of a prosecutor?

20. In Part II of its decision, the Court asserted that, if Congress was not permitted to limit the President's power to remove Commissioners of the FTC, the President's constitutional power of removal "at once becomes practically all-inclusive in respect of civil officers with the exception of the judiciary." Is there no limiting principle available? Would a ruling that President Roosevelt had constitutional authority to remove Humphrey from office necessarily require that the President have unlimited authority to remove inferior officers appointed by the heads of executive departments?

21. With respect to the asserted lack of a limiting principle, the Court stated that, if President Roosevelt had constitutional authority to remove Humphrey from office, that would logically require that he had unlimited authority to remove Commissioners of the Interstate Commerce Commission and "judges" of the Court of Claims (which is not a "court" within the meaning of Article III). Is there, in fact, any basis to distinguish among those officers?

22. Assuming the Court in *Humphrey's Executor* perceived no readily-apparent limiting principle, how should that fact influence the Court's decision? Should the Court decide the fate of Humphrey's claim in the shadow of a hypothetical presidential removal of a judge of the Court of Claims? Or, should the Court ignore the potential broader consequences of its ruling and consider only the specific circumstance of Humphrey's removal?

23. In Part II of its decision, the Court asserted that, when the First Congress established its interpretation of the Constitution with respect to the President's power to remove officers, it addressed only the context of executive officers. If the only officers contemplated by the Framers were those in classes identified in the constitutional text—referenced above in Question 10—does the failure to consider officers like Humphrey represent the intent to exempt such officers from "the decision of 1789" or doubt that such officers were constitutionally permitted?

24. Assuming the administration had foreseen the result in *Humphrey's Executor*, how might President Roosevelt, acting unilaterally, have obtained an FTC populated

with officers of his own selection without establishing adverse judicial precedent? President Roosevelt came into office with majorities of his own party in both Houses of Congress. Working together with Congress, how might President Roosevelt have obtained his goal without setting an adverse Supreme Court precedent?

3. The Recharacterization

In 1988, the Court upheld the independent counsel statute against attacks related both to the independent counsel's appointment—which we will consider below in Section C—and to the independent counsel's insulation from removal, which we consider here. *Humphrey's Executor*'s distinction between "executive" and "quasi-legislative, quasi-judicial" officers was replaced with a new standard for presidential removability.

MORRISON v. OLSON
487 U.S. 654 (1988)

CHIEF JUSTICE REHNQUIST delivered the opinion of the Court.

This case presents us with a challenge to the independent counsel provisions of the Ethics in Government Act of 1978. We hold today that these provisions of the Act do not . . . impermissibly interfere with the President's authority under Article II in violation of the constitutional principle of separation of powers.

I

Briefly stated, Title VI of the Ethics in Government Act (Title VI or the Act), 28 U.S.C. §§ 591–599, allows for the appointment of an "independent counsel" to investigate and, if appropriate, prosecute certain high-ranking Government officials for violations of federal criminal laws. The Act requires the Attorney General, upon receipt of information that he determines is "sufficient to constitute grounds to investigate whether any person [covered by the Act] may have violated any Federal criminal law," to conduct a preliminary investigation of the matter. When the Attorney General has completed this investigation, or 90 days has elapsed, he is required to report to a special court (the Special Division) created by the Act "for the purpose of appointing independent counsels." If the Attorney General determines that "there are no reasonable grounds to believe that further investigation is warranted," then he must notify the Special Division of this result. In such a case, "the division of the court shall have no power to appoint an independent counsel." If, however, the Attorney General has determined that there are "reasonable grounds to believe that further investigation or prosecution is warranted," then he "shall apply to the division of the court for the appointment of an independent counsel." Upon receiving this application, the Special Division "shall appoint an appropriate independent counsel and shall define that independent counsel's prosecutorial jurisdiction."

With respect to all matters within the independent counsel's jurisdiction, the Act grants the counsel "full power and independent authority to exercise all investigative and prosecutorial functions and powers of the Department of Justice, the Attorney General, and any other officer or employee of the Department of Justice." The functions of the independent counsel include conducting grand jury proceedings and other investigations, participating in civil and criminal court proceedings and litigation, and appealing any decision in any case in which the counsel participates in an official capacity. The Act also states that an independent counsel "shall, except where not possible, comply with the written or other established policies of the Department of Justice respecting enforcement of the criminal laws." An independent counsel has "full authority to dismiss matters within [his or her] prosecutorial jurisdiction without conducting an investigation or at any subsequent time before prosecution, if to do so would be consistent" with Department of Justice policy.

Two statutory provisions govern the length of an independent counsel's tenure in office. The first defines the procedure for removing an independent counsel. Section 596(a)(1) provides:

> An independent counsel appointed under this chapter may be removed from office, other than by impeachment and conviction, only by the personal action of the Attorney General and only for good cause, physical disability, mental incapacity, or any other condition that substantially impairs the performance of such independent counsel's duties.

The other provision governing the tenure of the independent counsel defines the procedures for "terminating" the counsel's office. [T]he office of an independent counsel terminates when he or she notifies the Attorney General that he or she has completed or substantially completed any investigations or prosecutions undertaken pursuant to the Act. In addition, the Special Division, acting either on its own or on the suggestion of the Attorney General, may terminate the office of an independent counsel at any time if it finds that "the investigation of all matters within the prosecutorial jurisdiction of such independent counsel . . . have been completed or so substantially completed that it would be appropriate for the Department of Justice to complete such investigations and prosecutions." Finally, the Act provides for congressional oversight of the activities of independent counsel.

The proceedings in this case provide an example of how the Act works in practice. In 1982, two Subcommittees of the House of Representatives issued subpoenas directing the Environmental Protection Agency (EPA) to produce certain documents. At that time, appellee Olson was the Assistant Attorney General for the Office of Legal Counsel (OLC). Acting on the advice of the Justice Department, the President ordered the Administrator of EPA to invoke executive privilege to withhold certain of the documents on the ground that they contained "enforcement sensitive information." The Administrator obeyed this order and withheld the documents. In response, the House voted to hold the Administrator in contempt, after which the Administrator and the United States together filed a lawsuit against the House. The conflict abated in March 1983, when the administration agreed to give the House Subcommittees limited access to the documents.

The following year, the House Judiciary Committee began an investigation into the Justice Department's role in the controversy over the EPA documents. During this investigation, appellee Olson testified before a House Subcommittee on March 10, 1983. Both before and after that testimony, the Department complied with several Committee requests to produce certain documents. Other documents were at first withheld, although these documents were eventually disclosed by the Department after the Committee learned of their existence. In 1985, the majority members of the Judiciary Committee published a lengthy report on the Committee's investigation. The report not only criticized various [DOJ] officials for their role in the EPA executive privilege dispute, but it also suggested that appellee Olson had given false and misleading testimony to the Subcommittee on March 10, 1983 thus obstructing the Committee's investigation. The Chairman of the Judiciary Committee forwarded a copy of the report to the Attorney General with a request that he seek the appointment of an independent counsel to investigate the allegations against Olson.

The Attorney General directed the Public Integrity Section of the Criminal Division to conduct a preliminary investigation. The Section's report concluded that the appointment of an independent counsel was warranted to investigate the Committee's allegations. [T]he Attorney General chose to apply to the Special Division for the appointment of an independent counsel solely with respect to appellee Olson. The Attorney General also requested that the independent counsel have authority to investigate "any other matter related to that allegation."

On April 23, 1986, the Special Division appointed [an] independent counsel to investigate "whether the testimony of . . . Olson and his revision of such testimony on March 10, 1983, violated . . . federal law." The court also ordered that the independent counsel

> shall have jurisdiction to investigate any other allegation of evidence of violation of any Federal criminal law by Theodore Olson developed during investigations, by the Independent Counsel, referred to above, and connected with or arising out of that investigation, and Independent Counsel shall have jurisdiction to prosecute for any such violation.

[I]n May and June 1987, appellant caused a grand jury to issue and serve subpoenas *ad testificandum* and *duces tecum* on appellees. All three appellees moved to quash the subpoenas, claiming, among other things, that the independent counsel provisions of the Act were unconstitutional and that appellant accordingly had no authority to proceed. On July 20, 1987, the District Court upheld the constitutionality of the Act and denied the motions to quash. The court subsequently ordered that appellees be held in contempt for continuing to refuse to comply with the subpoenas. The court stayed the effect of its contempt orders pending expedited appeal.

A divided Court of Appeals reversed. Appellant then sought review by this Court, and we noted probable jurisdiction. We now reverse.

* * *

V

We now turn to consider whether the Act is invalid under the constitutional principle of separation of powers. Two related issues must be addressed: The first is whether the provision of the Act restricting the Attorney General's power to remove the independent counsel to only those instances in which he can show "good cause," taken by itself, impermissibly interferes with the President's exercise of his constitutionally appointed functions. The second is whether, taken as a whole, the Act violates the separation of powers by reducing the President's ability to control the prosecutorial powers wielded by the independent counsel.

A

Two Terms ago we had occasion to consider whether it was consistent with the separation of powers for Congress to pass a statute that authorized a Government official who is removable only by Congress to participate in what we found to be "executive powers." *Bowsher v. Synar*, 478 U.S. 714, 730 (1986). Unlike both *Bowsher* and *Myers*, this case does not involve an attempt by Congress itself to gain a role in the removal of executive officials other than its established powers of impeachment and conviction. The Act instead puts the removal power squarely in the hands of the Executive Branch; an independent counsel may be removed from office, "only by the personal action of the Attorney General, and only for good cause." § 596(a)(1). There is no requirement of congressional approval of the Attorney General's removal decision, though the decision is subject to judicial review. § 596(a)(3). In our view, the removal provisions of the Act make this case more analogous to *Humphrey's Executor v. United States*, 295 U.S. 602 (1935), and *Wiener v. United States*, 357 U.S. 349 (1958), than to *Myers* or *Bowsher*.

In *Humphrey's Executor*, the issue was whether a statute restricting the President's power to remove the Commissioners of the Federal Trade Commission (FTC) only for "inefficiency, neglect of duty, or malfeasance in office" was consistent with the Constitution. 295 U.S. at 619. We stated that whether Congress can "condition the [President's power of removal] by fixing a definite term and precluding a removal except for cause, will depend upon the character of the office." *Id.* at 631. Contrary to the implication of some *dicta* in *Myers*, the President's power to remove Government officials simply was not "all-inclusive in respect of civil officers with the exception of the judiciary provided for by the Constitution." 295 U.S. at 629. At least in regard to "quasi-legislative" and "quasi-judicial" agencies such as the FTC, "[t]he authority of Congress, in creating [such] agencies, to require them to act in discharge of their duties independently of executive control . . . includes, as an appropriate incident, power to fix the period during which they shall continue in office, and to forbid their removal except for cause in the meantime." *Id.* In *Humphrey's Executor*, we found it "plain" that the Constitution did not give the President "illimitable power of removal" over the officers of independent agencies. *Id.*

Similarly, in *Wiener* . . . .

Appellees contend that *Humphrey's Executor* and *Wiener* are distinguishable from this case because they did not involve officials who performed a "core executive function." They argue that our decision in *Humphrey's Executor* rests on a distinction between "purely executive" officials and officials who exercise "quasi-legislative" and "quasi-judicial" powers. In their view, when a "purely executive" official is involved, the governing precedent is *Myers*, not *Humphrey's Executor*. And, under *Myers*, the President must have absolute discretion to discharge "purely" executive officials at will. *See Myers*, 272 U.S. at 132–34.

We undoubtedly did rely on the terms "quasi-legislative" and "quasi-judicial" to distinguish the officials involved in *Humphrey's Executor* and *Wiener* from those in *Myers*, but our present considered view is that the determination of whether the Constitution allows Congress to impose a "good cause"-type restriction on the President's power to remove an official cannot be made to turn on whether or not that official is classified as "purely executive." The analysis contained in our removal cases is designed not to define rigid categories of those officials who may or may not be removed at will by the President, but to ensure that Congress does not interfere with the President's exercise of the "executive power" and his constitutionally appointed duty to "take care that the laws be faithfully executed" under Article II. *Myers* was undoubtedly correct in its holding, and in its broader suggestion that there are some "purely executive" officials who must be removable by the President at will if he is to be able to accomplish his constitutional role. *See* 272 U.S. at 132–34. But as the Court noted in *Wiener*:

> The assumption was short-lived that the *Myers* case recognized the President's inherent constitutional power to remove officials no matter what the relation of the executive to the discharge of their duties and no matter what restrictions Congress may have imposed regarding the nature of their tenure.

357 U.S. at 352.

At the other end of the spectrum from *Myers*, the characterization of the agencies in *Humphrey's Executor* and *Wiener* as "quasi-legislative" or "quasi-judicial" in large part reflected our judgment that it was not essential to the President's proper execution of his Article II powers that these agencies be headed up by individuals who were removable at will. We do not mean to suggest that an analysis of the functions served by the officials at issue is irrelevant. But the real question is whether the removal restrictions are of such a nature that they impede the President's ability to perform his constitutional duty, and the functions of the officials in question must be analyzed in that light.

Considering for the moment the "good cause" removal provision in isolation from the other parts of the Act at issue in this case, we cannot say that the imposition of a "good cause" standard for removal by itself unduly trammels on executive authority. There is no real dispute that the functions performed by the independent counsel are "executive" in the sense that they are law enforcement functions that typically have been undertaken by officials within the Executive Branch. As we noted above, however, the independent counsel is an inferior officer under the Appointments Clause, with limited jurisdiction and tenure and lacking policymaking or significant administrative authority. Although the counsel exercises no small amount of discretion and judgment in deciding how to carry out his or her duties under the Act, we simply do not see how the President's need to control the exercise of that discretion is so central to the functioning of the Executive Branch as to require as a matter of constitutional law that the counsel be terminable at will by the President. . . .

JUSTICE SCALIA, dissenting.

* * *

IV

There is, of course, no provision in the Constitution stating who may remove executive officers, except the provisions for removal by impeachment. Before the present decision it was established, however, (1) that the President's power to remove principal officers who exercise purely executive powers could not be restricted, *see Myers v. United States,* 272 U.S. 52, 127, (1926), and (2) that his power to remove inferior officers who exercise purely executive powers, and whose appointment Congress had removed from the usual procedure of Presidential appointment with Senate consent, could be restricted, at least where the appointment had been made by an officer of the Executive Branch, *see id.; United States v. Perkins,* 116 U.S. 483, 485 (1886).

The Court could have resolved the removal power issue in this case by simply relying upon its erroneous conclusion that the independent counsel was an inferior officer, and then extending our holding that the removal of inferior officers appointed by the Executive can be restricted, to a new holding that even the removal of inferior officers appointed by the courts can be restricted. That would in my view be a considerable and unjustified extension, giving the Executive full discretion in *neither* the selection *nor* the removal of a purely executive officer.

Since our 1935 decision in *Humphrey's Executor v. United States*—which was considered by many at the time the product of an activist, anti-New Deal Court bent on reducing the power of President Franklin Roosevelt—it has been established that the line of permissible restriction upon removal of principal officers lies at the point at which the powers exercised by those officers are no longer purely executive. Thus, removal restrictions have been generally regarded as lawful for so-called "independent regulatory agencies," such as the Federal Trade Commission, the Interstate Commerce Commission, and the Consumer Product Safety Commission, which engage substantially in what has been called the "quasi-legislative activity" of rulemaking, and for members of Article I courts, such as the Court of Military Appeals, who engage in the "quasi-judicial" function of adjudication. It has often been observed, correctly in my view, that the line between "purely executive" functions and "quasi-legislative" or "quasi-judicial" functions is not a clear one or even a rational one. But at least it permitted the identification of certain officers, and certain agencies, whose functions were entirely within the control of the President. Congress had to be aware of that restriction in its legislation. Today, however, *Humphrey's Executor* is swept into the dustbin of repudiated constitutional principles. "[O]ur present considered view," the Court says, "is that the determination of whether the Constitution allows Congress to impose a 'good cause'—type restriction on the President's power to remove an official cannot be made to turn on whether or not that official is classified as 'purely executive.'" What *Humphrey's Executor* (and presumably *Myers*) really means, we are now told, is not that there are any "rigid categories of those officials who may or may not be removed at will by the President," but simply that Congress cannot "interfere with the President's exercise of the 'executive power' and his constitutionally appointed duty to 'take care that the laws be faithfully executed.'"

One can hardly grieve for the shoddy treatment given today to *Humphrey's Executor*, which, after all, accorded the same indignity (with much less justification) to Chief Justice Taft's opinion 10 years earlier in *Myers v. United States*—gutting, in six quick pages devoid of textual or historical precedent for the novel principle it set forth, a carefully researched and reasoned 70-page opinion. But one must grieve for the Constitution. *Humphrey's Executor* at least had the decency formally to observe the constitutional principle that the President had to be the repository of all executive power, *see* 295 U.S. at 627–28, which, as *Myers* carefully explained, necessarily means that he must be able to discharge those who do not perform executive functions according to his liking. As far as I can discern from the Court's opinion, it is now open season upon the President's removal power for all executive officers, with not even the superficially principled restriction of *Humphrey's Executor* as cover. The Court essentially says to the President: "Trust us. We will make sure that you are able to accomplish your constitutional role." I think the Constitution gives the President—and the people—more protection than that.

EXERCISE 4:

1. Under the *Morrison* analysis, could Congress provide that all United States Attorneys—the chief federal prosecutor for each federal district—would be subject to removal only for cause for the first five years following appointment? Could Congress provide similar protection for any or all of the following officers: the Solicitor General, the Administrator of the Environmental Protection Agency, and the Secretary of Commerce?

2. In dissent, Justice Scalia asserted that prosecution is a "quintessentially executive activity." Do you agree? Is there a basis to distinguish the authority to investigate and prosecute placed in the hands of the independent counsel from that placed in the hands of the FTC?

3. In dissent, Justice Scalia asserted that the majority "replaced the clear constitutional prescription that the executive power belongs to the President with a 'balancing test.'" Is that a fair characterization of the majority's position? Why or why not?

4. In dissent, Justice Scalia asserted that the majority's analysis provided no criteria to guide future decisions of which officers, who are not subject to removal by the

President at will, may be vested with executive powers. Is that a fair criticism of the majority's approach?

5. In dissent, Justice Scalia asserted that the independent counsel provisions will "reduce the zeal" of the President's staff and erode the President's "public support," thereby weakening the President in head-to-head confrontations with Congress. Does the history of independent counsel investigations and prosecutions, before and after *Morrison*, support those observations?

6. In dissent, Justice Scalia summarized the Court's precedents in *Myers v. United States* and *United States v. Perkins* (discussed in *Myers*). Did he fairly state the doctrine as it existed prior to *Morrison*?

7. In dissent, Justice Scalia addressed the historical setting of *Humphrey's Executor v. United States*. Does that context help explain the Court's departure from its then-less-than-decade-old precedent in *Myers*? Were there any other significant doctrinal shifts at the same time?

8. Separation-of-powers cases have sometimes been seen as a long battle between "formalism" and "functionalism." *See, e.g.*, Peter L. Strauss, *Formal and Functional Approaches to Separation-of-Powers Questions: A Foolish Inconsistency?*, 72 CORNELL L REV. 488 (1987). Formalists aim for clear rules and sharp boundaries between the three branches, while functionalists consider the relationships between the branches at a higher level of generality, allowing for more flexibility when they see the basic goals of the separation of powers not to be threatened. Which opinions are formalist or functionalist? Explain your answer.

9. Congress permitted the Independent Counsel Act to lapse in 1999. Some scholars have characterized that development as follows:

> Democrats and Republicans alike came to agree that the law was both unconstitutional and unwise. Indeed, the eventual bipartisan consensus against the use of independent counsels underscores the extent to which the presidential support for the unitary executive is less a reflection of partisan politics, as some have claimed, and more the result of fundamental questions about the allocation of power within the federal government.

STEVEN S. CALABRESI & CHRISTOPHER S. YOO, THE UNITARY EXECUTIVE: PRESIDENTIAL POWER FROM WASHINGTON TO BUSH 11 (2008). For a case study of the impeachment of President Clinton and the demise of the Independent Counsel Act, see *id.* at 400–04. What influence should later political reaction have on the force of *Morrison* as a precedent? Adrian Vermeule has tweeted that *Morrison* is now "fake law." See https://twitter.com/avermeule/status/873333410672119808. Justice Elena Kagan, who was clerking for Justice Thurgood Marshall at the time, has described Justice Scalia's *Morrison* dissent as "one of the best dissents ever written and every year it gets better," a statement which a panel of the D.C. Circuit has used to read *Morrison* narrowly. *See PHH Corp. v. CFPB*, 839 F.3d 1, 20 (D.C. Cir. 2016), *rehearing en banc granted* (Feb. 16, 2017). Is this a proper way for lower courts to use justices' off-the-bench statements?

4. The Rise Again

FREE ENTERPRISE FUND v. PUBLIC COMPANY ACCOUNTING OVERSIGHT BOARD

561 U.S. 477 (2010)

CHIEF JUSTICE ROBERTS delivered the opinion of the Court.

Our Constitution divided the "powers of the new Federal Government into three defined categories, Legislative, Executive, and Judicial." *INS v. Chadha*, 462 U.S. 919, 951 (1983). Article II vests "[t]he executive Power . . . in a President of the United States of America," who must "take Care that the Laws be faithfully executed." Art. II, § 1, cl. 1; *id.*, § 3.

Since 1789, the Constitution has been understood to empower the President to keep these officers accountable — by removing them from office, if necessary. See generally *Myers v. United States*, 272 U.S. 52 (1926). This Court has determined, however, that this authority is not without limit. In *Humphrey's Executor v. United States*, 295 U.S. 602 (1935), we held that Congress can, under certain circumstances, create independent agencies run by principal officers appointed by the President, whom the President may not remove at will but only for good cause. Likewise, in *United States v. Perkins*, 116 U.S. 483 (1886), and *Morrison v. Olson*, 487 U.S. 654 (1988), the Court sustained similar restrictions on the power of principal executive officers — themselves responsible to the President — to remove their own inferiors. The parties do not ask us to reexamine any of these precedents, and we do not do so.

We are asked, however, to consider a new situation not yet encountered by the Court. The question is whether these separate layers of protection may be combined. May the President be restricted in his ability to remove a principal officer, who is in turn restricted in his ability to remove an inferior officer, even though that inferior officer determines the policy and enforces the laws of the United States?

We hold that such multilevel protection from removal is contrary to Article II's vesting of the executive power in the President. The President cannot "take Care that the Laws be faithfully executed" if he cannot oversee the faithfulness of the officers who execute them. Here the President cannot remove an officer who enjoys more than one level of good-cause protection, even if the President determines that the officer is neglecting his duties or discharging them improperly. That judgment is instead committed to another officer, who may or may not agree with the President's determination, and whom the President cannot remove simply because that officer disagrees with him. This contravenes the President's "constitutional obligation to ensure the faithful execution of the laws."

I

A

After a series of celebrated accounting debacles, Congress enacted the Sarbanes-Oxley Act of 2002 (or Act). Among other measures, the Act introduced tighter regulation of the accounting industry under a new Public Company Accounting Oversight Board. The Board is composed of five members, appointed to staggered 5-year terms by the Securities and Exchange Commission. The Board is charged with enforcing the Sarbanes-Oxley Act, the securities laws, the Commission's rules, its own rules, and professional accounting standards.

The Board promulgates auditing and ethics standards, performs routine inspections of all accounting firms, demands documents and testimony, and initiates formal investigations and disciplinary proceedings. The willful violation of any Board rule is treated as a willful violation of the Securities Exchange Act of 1934, a federal crime punishable by up to 20 years' imprisonment or $25 million in fines ($5 million for a natural person). And the Board itself can issue severe sanctions in its disciplinary proceedings, up to and including the permanent revocation of a firm's registration, a permanent ban on a person's associating with any registered firm, and money penalties of $15 million ($750,000 for a natural person). [T]he parties agree that the Board is "part of the Government" for constitutional purposes, and that its members are " 'Officers of the United States' " who "exercis[e] significant authority pursuant to the laws of the United States," *Buckley v. Valeo*, 424 U.S. 1, 125–126 (1976) (*per curiam*) (quoting Art. II, § 2, cl. 2); cf. Brief for Petitioners 9, n. 1; Brief for United States 29, n. 8.

The Act places the Board under the SEC's oversight, particularly with respect to the issuance of rules or the imposition of sanctions (both of which are subject to Commission approval and alteration). But the individual members of the Board are substantially insulated from the Commission's control. The Commission cannot remove Board members at will, but only "for good cause shown," "in accordance with" certain procedures. § 7211(e)(6). Those procedures require a Commission finding, "on the record" and "after notice and opportunity for a hearing," that the Board member

> (A) has willfully violated any provision of th[e] Act, the rules of the Board, or the securities laws; (B) has willfully abused the authority of that member; or (C) without reasonable justification or excuse, has failed to enforce compliance with any such provision or rule, or any professional standard by any registered public accounting firm or any associated person thereof.

The parties agree that the Commissioners cannot themselves be removed by the President except under the *Humphrey's Executor* standard of "inefficiency, neglect of duty, or malfeasance in office," 295 U.S., at 620.

B

Free Enterprise Fund, a nonprofit organization, sued the Board and its members, seeking (among other things) a declaratory judgment that the Board is unconstitutional and an injunction preventing the Board from exercising its powers. [T]he District Court granted summary judgment to respondents. A divided Court of Appeals affirmed. We granted certiorari.

III

We hold that the dual for-cause limitations on the removal of Board members contravene the Constitution's separation of powers.

A

The Constitution provides that "[t]he executive Power shall be vested in a President of the United States of America." Art. II, § 1, cl. 1. As Madison stated on the floor of the First Congress, "if any power whatsoever is in its nature Executive, it is the power of appointing, overseeing, and controlling those who execute the laws." 1 Annals of Cong. 463 (1789).

The removal of executive officers was discussed extensively in Congress when the first executive departments were created. The view that "prevailed, as most consonant to the text of the Constitution" and "to the requisite responsibility and harmony in the Executive Department," was that the executive power included a power to oversee executive officers through removal; because that traditional executive power was not "expressly taken away, it remained with the President." Letter from James Madison to Thomas Jefferson (June 30, 1789). "This Decision of 1789 provides contemporaneous and weighty evidence of the Constitution's meaning since many of the Members of the First Congress had taken part in framing that instrument." *Bowsher v. Synar*, 478 U.S. 714, 723–724 (1986).

The landmark case of *Myers v. United States* reaffirmed the principle that Article II confers on the President "the general administrative control of those executing the laws." 272 U.S., at 164. It is *his* responsibility to take care that the laws be faithfully executed. As we explained in *Myers*, the President therefore must have some "power of removing those for whom he can not continue to be responsible." *Id.*, at 117.

Nearly a decade later in *Humphrey's Executor*, this Court held that *Myers* did not prevent Congress from conferring good-cause tenure on the principal officers of certain independent agencies. In *Perkins*, a naval cadet-engineer was honorably discharged from the Navy because his services were no longer required. This Court adopted verbatim the reasoning of the Court of Claims, which had held that when Congress "vests the appointment of inferior officers in the heads of Departments[,] it may limit and restrict the power of removal as it deems best for the public interest." *Morrison* concerned the Ethics in Government Act. We recognized that the independent counsel was undoubtedly an executive officer, rather than "'quasi-legislative'" or "'quasi-judicial,'" but we stated as "our present considered view" that Congress had power to impose good-cause restrictions on her removal. *Morrison* did not, however, address the consequences of more than one level of good-cause tenure—leaving the issue "a question of first impression" in this Court.

B

As explained, we have previously upheld limited restrictions on the President's removal power. In those cases, however, only one level of protected tenure separated the President from an officer exercising executive power. It was the President — or a subordinate he could remove at will — who decided whether the officer's conduct merited removal under the good-cause standard.

The Act before us does something quite different. It not only protects Board members from removal except for good cause, but withdraws from the President any decision on whether that good cause exists. That decision is vested instead in other tenured officers — the Commissioners — none of whom is subject to the President's direct control. The result is a Board that is not accountable to the President, and a President who is not responsible for the Board.

The added layer of tenure protection makes a difference. Without a layer of insulation between the Commission and the Board, the Commission could remove a Board member at any time, and therefore would be fully responsible for what the Board does. The President could then hold the Commission to account for its supervision of the Board, to the same extent that he may hold the Commission to account for everything else it does.

A second level of tenure protection changes the nature of the President's review. Now the Commission cannot remove a Board member at will. The President therefore cannot hold the Commission fully accountable for the Board's conduct, to the same extent that he may hold the Commission accountable for everything else that it does. The Commissioners are not responsible for the Board's actions. They are only responsible for their own determination of whether the Act's rigorous good-cause standard is met. And even if the President disagrees with their determination, he is powerless to intervene — unless that determination is so unreasonable as to constitute "inefficiency, neglect of duty, or malfeasance in office." *Humphrey's Executor*, 295 U.S., at 620.

This novel structure does not merely add to the Board's independence, but transforms it. Neither the President, nor anyone directly responsible to him, nor even an officer whose conduct he may review only for good cause, has full control over the Board. The President is stripped of the power our precedents have preserved, and his ability to execute the laws — by holding his subordinates accountable for their conduct — is impaired.

That arrangement is contrary to Article II's vesting of the executive power in the President. Without the ability to oversee the Board, or to attribute the Board's failings to those whom he *can* oversee, the President is no longer the judge of the Board's conduct. He is not the one who decides whether Board members are abusing their offices or neglecting their duties. He can neither ensure that the laws are faithfully executed, nor be held responsible for a Board member's breach of faith. This violates the basic principle that the President "cannot delegate ultimate responsibility or the active obligation to supervise that goes with it," because Article II "makes a single President responsible for the actions of the Executive Branch."[4]

---

4. Contrary to the dissent's suggestion, the second layer of tenure protection does compromise the President's ability to remove a Board member the Commission wants to retain. Without a

Indeed, if allowed to stand, this dispersion of responsibility could be multiplied. If Congress can shelter the bureaucracy behind two layers of good-cause tenure, why not a third? At oral argument, the Government was unwilling to concede that even *five* layers between the President and the Board would be too many. Tr. of Oral Arg. 47–48. The officers of such an agency—safely encased within a Matryoshka doll of tenure protections—would be immune from Presidential oversight, even as they exercised power in the people's name.

[T]he separation of powers does not depend on the views of individual Presidents, nor on whether "the encroached-upon branch approves the encroachment," *New York v. United States*, 505 U.S. 144, 182 (1992). The President can always choose to restrain himself in his dealings with subordinates. He cannot, however, choose to bind his successors by diminishing their powers, nor can he escape responsibility for his choices by pretending that they are not his own.

The diffusion of power carries with it a diffusion of accountability. The people do not vote for the "Officers of the United States." Art. II, §2, cl. 2. They instead look to the President to guide the "assistants or deputies . . . subject to his superintendence." THE FEDERALIST No. 72, p. 487 (J. Cooke ed.1961) (A. Hamilton). Without a clear and effective chain of command, the public cannot "determine on whom the blame or the punishment of a pernicious measure, or series of pernicious measures ought really to fall." *Id.*, No. 70, at 476 (same). That is why the Framers sought to ensure that "those who are employed in the execution of the law will be in their proper situation, and the chain of dependence be preserved; the lowest officers, the middle grade, and the highest, will depend, as they ought, on the President, and the President on the community." 1 Annals of Cong., at 499 (J. Madison).

By granting the Board executive power without the Executive's oversight, this Act subverts the President's ability to ensure that the laws are faithfully executed—as well as the public's ability to pass judgment on his efforts. The Act's restrictions are incompatible with the Constitution's separation of powers.

C

Respondents and the dissent resist this conclusion, portraying the Board as "the kind of practical accommodation between the Legislature and the Executive that should be permitted in a 'workable government.'" No one doubts Congress's power to create a vast and varied federal bureaucracy. But where, in all this, is the role for oversight by an elected President? The Constitution requires that a President chosen by the entire Nation oversee the execution of the laws. And the "'fact that a given law or procedure is efficient, convenient, and useful in facilitating functions of government, standing alone, will not save it if it is contrary to the Constitution,'" for

---

second layer of protection, the Commission has no excuse for retaining an officer who is not faithfully executing the law. With the second layer in place, the Commission can shield its decision from Presidential review by finding that good cause is absent—a finding that, given the Commission's own protected tenure, the President cannot easily overturn.

"'[c]onvenience and efficiency are not the primary objectives—or the hallmarks—of democratic government.'" *Bowsher*, 478 U.S., at 736 (quoting *Chadha*, 462 U.S., at 944).

One can have a government that functions without being ruled by functionaries, and a government that benefits from expertise without being ruled by experts. Our Constitution was adopted to enable the people to govern themselves, through their elected leaders. The growth of the Executive Branch, which now wields vast power and touches almost every aspect of daily life, heightens the concern that it may slip from the Executive's control, and thus from that of the people. This concern is largely absent from the dissent's paean to the administrative state.

For example, the dissent dismisses the importance of removal as a tool of supervision, concluding that the President's "power to get something done" more often depends on "who controls the agency's budget requests and funding, the relationships between one agency or department and another, . . . purely political factors (including Congress' ability to assert influence)," and indeed whether particular *unelected* officials support or "resist" the President's policies. The Framers did not rest our liberties on such bureaucratic minutiae. As we said in *Bowsher*, *supra*, at 730, "[t]he separated powers of our Government cannot be permitted to turn on judicial assessment of whether an officer exercising executive power is on good terms with Congress."

The Framers created a structure in which "[a] dependence on the people" would be the "primary control on the government." THE FEDERALIST No. 51, at 349 (J. Madison). That dependence is maintained, not just by "parchment barriers," *id.*, No. 48, at 333 (same), but by letting "[a]mbition . . . counteract ambition," giving each branch "the necessary constitutional means, and personal motives, to resist encroachments of the others," *id.*, No. 51, at 349. A key "constitutional means" vested in the President—perhaps *the* key means—was "the power of appointing, overseeing, and controlling those who execute the laws." 1 Annals of Cong., at 463. And while a government of "opposite and rival interests" may sometimes inhibit the smooth functioning of administration, THE FEDERALIST No. 51, at 349, "[t]he Framers recognized that, in the long term, structural protections against abuse of power were critical to preserving liberty." *Bowsher*, *supra*, at 730.

Calls to abandon those protections in light of "the era's perceived necessity," *New York*, 505 U.S., at 187, are not unusual. Nor is the argument from bureaucratic expertise limited only to the field of accounting. The failures of accounting regulation may be a "pressing national problem," but "a judiciary that licensed extraconstitutional government with each issue of comparable gravity would, in the long run, be far worse." Neither respondents nor the dissent explains why the Board's task, unlike so many others, requires *more* than one layer of insulation from the President—or, for that matter, why only two. The point is not to take issue with for-cause limitations in general; we do not do that. The question here is far more modest. We deal with the unusual situation, never before addressed by the Court, of two layers of for-cause tenure. And though it may be criticized as "elementary arithmetical logic," two layers are not the same as one.

The President has been given the power to oversee executive officers; he is not limited, as in Harry Truman's lament, to "persuad[ing]" his unelected subordinates "to do what they ought to do without persuasion." In its pursuit of a "workable government," Congress cannot reduce the Chief Magistrate to a cajoler-in-chief.

JUSTICE BREYER, with whom JUSTICE STEVENS, JUSTICE GINSBURG, and JUSTICE SOTO-MAYOR join, dissenting.

I agree that the Accounting Board members are inferior officers. But in my view the statute does not significantly interfere with the President's "executive Power." Art. II, § 1. It violates no separation-of-powers principle. And the Court's contrary holding threatens to disrupt severely the fair and efficient administration of the laws. I consequently dissent.

I

A

The legal question before us arises at the intersection of two general constitutional principles. On the one hand, Congress has broad power to enact statutes "necessary and proper" to the exercise of its specifically enumerated constitutional authority. Art. I, § 8, cl. 18. As Chief Justice Marshall wrote for the Court nearly 200 years ago, the Necessary and Proper Clause reflects the Framers' efforts to create a Constitution that would "endure for ages to come." *McCulloch v. Maryland*, 17 U.S. 316, 4 Wheat. 316, 415 (1819). On the other hand, the opening sections of Articles I, II, and III of the Constitution separately and respectively vest "all legislative Powers" in Congress, the "executive Power" in the President, and the "judicial Power" in the Supreme Court. In doing so, these provisions imply a structural separation-of-powers principle. See, *e.g.*, *Miller v. French*, 530 U.S. 327, 341–342 (2000). And that principle, along with the instruction in Article II, § 3 that the President "shall take Care that the Laws be faithfully executed," limits Congress' power to structure the Federal Government. See, *e.g.*, *INS v. Chadha*, 462 U.S. 919, 946 (1983); *Commodity Futures Trading Comm'n v. Schor*, 478 U.S. 833, 859–860 (1986).

But neither of these two principles is absolute in its application to removal cases. The Necessary and Proper Clause does not grant Congress power to free *all* Executive Branch officials from dismissal at the will of the President. Nor does the separation-of-powers principle grant the President an absolute authority to remove *any and all* Executive Branch officials at will. Rather, depending on, say, the nature of the office, its function, or its subject matter, Congress sometimes may, consistent with the Constitution, limit the President's authority to remove an officer from his post. See *Humphrey's Executor v. United States*, 295 U.S. 602 (1935), overruling in part *Myers, supra*; *Morrison v. Olson*, 487 U.S. 654 (1988). And we must here decide whether the circumstances surrounding the statute at issue justify such a limitation.

In answering the question presented, we cannot look to more specific constitutional text, such as the text of the Appointments Clause or the Presentment Clause, upon which the Court has relied in other separation-of-powers cases. See, *e.g.*, *Chadha, supra*, at 946; *Buckley, supra*, at 124–125. That is because, with the exception of the general "vesting" and "take care" language, the Constitution is completely "silent with respect to the power of removal from office."

Nor does history offer significant help. The President's power to remove Executive Branch officers "was not discussed in the Constitutional Convention." *Myers, supra,* at 109–110. The First Congress enacted federal statutes that limited the President's ability to *oversee* Executive Branch officials, including the Comptroller of the United States, federal district attorneys (precursors to today's United States Attorneys), and, to a lesser extent, the Secretary of the Treasury. But those statutes did not directly limit the President's authority to *remove* any of those officials—"a subject" that was "much disputed" during "the early history of this government," "and upon which a great diversity of opinion was entertained." Scholars, like Members of this Court, have continued to disagree, not only about the inferences that should be drawn from the inconclusive historical record, but also about the nature of the original disagreement. Compare *Myers, supra,* at 114 (majority opinion of Taft, C. J.), with, *e.g., Myers, supra,* at 194 (McReynolds, J., dissenting).

Nor does this Court's precedent fully answer the question presented. At least it does not clearly invalidate the provision in dispute. In *Myers, supra,* the Court invalidated—for the first and only time—a congressional statute on the ground that it unduly limited the President's authority to remove an Executive Branch official. But soon thereafter the Court expressly disapproved most of *Myers'* broad reasoning. See *Humphrey's Executor,* 295 U.S., at 626–627.

In short, the question presented lies at the intersection of two sets of conflicting, broadly framed constitutional principles. And no text, no history, perhaps no precedent provides any clear answer.

B

When previously deciding this kind of nontextual question, the Court has emphasized the importance of examining how a particular provision, taken in context, is likely to function. The Court has thereby written into law Justice Jackson's wise perception that "the Constitution . . . contemplates that practice will integrate the dispersed powers into *a workable government." Youngstown Sheet & Tube Co. v. Sawyer,* 343 U.S. 579, 635 (1952).

It is not surprising that the Court in these circumstances has looked to function and context, and not to bright-line rules. For one thing, that approach embodies the intent of the Framers. As Chief Justice Marshall long ago observed, our Constitution is fashioned so as to allow the three coordinate branches, including this Court, to exercise practical judgment in response to changing conditions and "exigencies," which at the time of the founding could be seen only "dimly," and perhaps not at all. *McCulloch,* 4 Wheat., at 415.

For another, a functional approach permits Congress and the President the flexibility needed to adapt statutory law to changing circumstances. That is why the "powers conferred upon the Federal Government by the Constitution were phrased in language broad enough to allow for the expansion of the Federal Government's role" over time. Indeed, the Federal Government at the time of the founding consisted of about 2,000 employees and served a population of about 4 million. Today, however, the Federal Government employs about *4.4 million workers* who serve a Nation of more than 310 million people living in a society characterized by rapid technological, economic, and social change.

The upshot is that today vast numbers of statutes governing vast numbers of subjects, concerned with vast numbers of different problems, provide for, or foresee, their execution or administration through the work of administrators organized within many different kinds of administrative structures, exercising different kinds of administrative authority, to achieve their legislatively mandated objectives. And, given the nature of the Government's work, it is not surprising that administrative units come in many different shapes and sizes.

The functional approach required by our precedents recognizes this administrative complexity and, more importantly, recognizes the various ways presidential power operates within this context—and the various ways in which a removal provision might affect that power. As human beings have known ever since Ulysses tied himself to the mast so as safely to hear the Sirens' song, sometimes it is necessary to disable oneself in order to achieve a broader objective. Thus, legally enforceable commitments—such as contracts, statutes that cannot instantly be changed, and, as in the case before us, the establishment of independent administrative institutions—hold the potential to empower precisely because of their ability to constrain. If the President seeks to regulate through impartial adjudication, then insulation of the adjudicator from removal at will can help him achieve that goal. And to free a technical decisionmaker from the fear of removal without cause can similarly help create legitimacy with respect to that official's regulatory actions by helping to insulate his technical decisions from nontechnical political pressure.

Neither is power always susceptible to the equations of elementary arithmetic. A rule that takes power from a President's friends and allies may weaken him. But a rule that takes power from the President's opponents may strengthen him. And what if the rule takes power from a functionally *neutral* independent authority? In that case, it is difficult to predict how the President's power is affected in the abstract.

These practical reasons not only support our precedents' determination that cases such as this should examine the specific functions and context at issue; they also indicate that judges should hesitate before second-guessing a "for cause" decision made by the other branches. Compared to Congress and the President, the Judiciary possesses an inferior understanding of the realities of administration, and the manner in which power, including and most especially political power, operates in context.

There is no indication that the two comparatively more expert branches were divided in their support for the "for cause" provision at issue here. In this case, the Act embodying the provision was passed by a vote of 423 to 3 in the House of Representatives and a by vote of 99 to 0 in the Senate. The creation of the Accounting Board was discussed at great length in both bodies without anyone finding in its structure any constitutional problem. The President signed the Act. And, when he did so, he issued a signing statement that critiqued multiple provisions of the Act but did not express any separation-of-powers concerns. See President's Statement on Signing the Sarbanes-Oxley Act of 2002.

Thus, here, as in similar cases, we should decide the constitutional question in light of the provision's practical functioning in context. And our decision should take account of the Judiciary's comparative lack of institutional expertise.

With respect I dissent.

EXERCISE 5:

1. What was the Court's holding?

2. What interpretive methods and sources did the Court and dissent draw upon to answer that question?

3. Which opinion was more faithful to the Decision of 1789 and the Framing and Ratification historical understanding?

4. Did the Court follow or deviate from its important precedents of *Myers*, *Humphrey's Executor*, and *Morrison*? Did the Court overrule any prior cases?

5. Who had the better of the argument regarding whether the double-for-cause removal provision violated Article II? Is this challenged provision more limiting of presidential power than prior removal provisions?

6. Were the majority and dissenting opinions formalist or functionalist? What were the best arguments for each respective perspective? In other words, what was the best argument for taking a formalist perspective? A functionalist perspective?

7. What kind of power do independent agencies exercise, according to *Free Enterprise Fund*? Is that consistent with *Humphrey's Executor*?

8. The *Free Enterprise Fund* double-insulation situation was memorably characterized by Judge Kavanaugh in his D.C. Circuit panel dissent as "*Humphrey's Executor* Squared." 537 F.3d 667, 685 (D.C. Cir. 2008). If *Humphrey's Executor* is good law, what is wrong with squaring it?

9. Do policy considerations support the majority or dissent?

10. A panel of the D.C. Circuit, speaking through Judge Kavanaugh, the same judge whose dissent was vindicated by the Court in *Free Enterprise Fund*, recently held that the Consumer Finance Protection Bureau was unconstitutionally insulated from presidential control because it had a single head, unlike multi-member independent agencies like the FCC or SEC. See *PHH, Inc. v. Consumer Finance Protection Bureau*, 839 F.3d 1 (D.C. Cir. 2016), *rehearing en banc granted* (Feb. 16, 2017). If *Humphrey's Executor* is questionable, should courts cabin it with fine distinctions like the no-double-insulation rule of *Free Enterprise Fund* and the no-single-headed agencies rule of *PHH*, or should the Court revisit *Humphrey's Executor* itself?

C. APPOINTMENTS

Part B of this Chapter concerned presidential removal power, an issue not addressed explicitly in the constitutional text. The President's appointment power, however, is set out explicitly in Art. II, sec. 2, cl. 2, which provides that the President "shall nominate, and by and with the Advice and Consent of the Senate, shall appoint Ambassadors, other public Ministers and Consuls, Judges of the supreme Court, and all other Officers of the United States, whose Appointments are not herein otherwise provided for, and which shall be established by Law: but the Congress may by Law vest the Appointment of such inferior Officers, as they think proper, in the President alone, in the Courts of Law, or in the Heads of Departments." This provision has several moving parts: Who counts as an "officer"? Which of these is an "inferior officer"? What is a "Head of Department" or "Court of Law"?

1. Congressional Appointment

A first point about the Appointments Clause is obvious, though: while Congress may establish "by law" who appoints inferior officers, it cannot appoint such officers directly.

BUCKLEY v. VALEO
424 U.S. 1 (1976)

Per Curiam.

These appeals present constitutional challenges to the key provisions of the Federal Elections Campaign Act of 1971 (Act), and related provisions of the Internal Revenue Code of 1954, all as amended in 1974.

The Court of Appeals, in sustaining the legislation in large part against constitutional challenges, viewed it as "by far the most comprehensive reform legislation [ever] passed by Congress concerning the election of the President, Vice-President, and members of Congress."

In this Court, appellants renew their attack on the Commission's composition and powers.

IV. THE FEDERAL ELECTION COMMISSION

The 1974 amendments to the Act create an eight-member Federal Election Commission (Commission) and vest in it primary and substantial responsibility for administering and enforcing the Act. The question that we address in this portion of the opinion is whether, in view of the manner in which a majority of its members are appointed, the Commission may under the Constitution exercise the powers conferred upon it.

[The Act] makes the Commission the principal repository of the numerous reports and statements which are required by [the Act] to be filed by those engaging in the regulated political activities. Its duties under §438(a) with respect to these reports and statements include filing and indexing, making them available for public inspection, preservation, and auditing and field investigations.

Beyond these recordkeeping, disclosure, and investigative functions, however, the Commission is given extensive rulemaking and adjudicative powers. Under §437d(a)(8) the Commission is empowered to make such rules "as are necessary to carry out the provisions of this Act." Section 437d(a)(9) authorizes it to "formulate general policy with respect to the administration of this Act" and enumerated sections of Title 18's Criminal Code, as to all of which provisions the Commission "has primary jurisdiction with respect to [their] civil enforcement." §437c(b). The Commission is authorized under §437f(a) to render advisory opinions with respect to activities possibly violating the Act, the Title 18 sections, or the campaign funding provisions of Title 26, the effect of which is that "[n]otwithstanding any other provision of law, any person with respect to whom an advisory opinion is rendered . . . who acts in good faith in accordance with the provisions and findings [thereof] shall be presumed to be in compliance with the [statutory provision] with respect to which such advisory opinion is rendered." §437f(b).

The Commission's enforcement power is both direct and wide ranging. It may institute a civil action for (i) injunctive or other relief against "any acts or practices which constitute or will constitute a violation of this Act." In no respect do the foregoing civil actions require the concurrence of or participation by the Attorney General; conversely, the decision not to seek judicial relief would appear to rest solely with the Commission. [I]f, after notice and opportunity for a hearing before it, the Commission finds an actual or threatened criminal violation, the Attorney General "upon request by the Commission . . . shall institute a civil action for relief." Finally, as "[a]dditional enforcement authority," §456(a) authorizes the Commission, after notice and opportunity for hearing, to make "a finding that a person . . . while a candidate for Federal office, failed to file" a required report of contributions or expenditures. If that finding is made within the applicable limitations period for prosecutions, the candidate is thereby "disqualified from becoming a candidate in any future election for Federal office for a period of time beginning on the date of such finding and ending one year after the expiration of the term of the Federal office for which such person was a candidate."

The body in which this authority is reposed consists of eight members. The Secretary of the Senate and the Clerk of the House of Representatives are *ex officio* members of the Commission without the right to vote. Two members are appointed by the President *pro tempore* of the Senate "upon the recommendations of the majority leader of the Senate and the minority leader of the Senate." Two more are to be appointed by the Speaker of the House of Representatives, likewise upon the recommendations of its respective majority and minority leaders. The remaining two members are appointed by the President. Each of the six voting members of the Commission must be confirmed by the majority of both Houses of Congress, and each of the three appointing authorities is forbidden to choose both of their appointees from the same political party.

B. The Merits

Appellants urge that since Congress has given the Commission wide-ranging rulemaking and enforcement powers with respect to the substantive provisions of the Act, Congress is precluded under the principle of separation of powers from vesting in itself the authority to appoint those who will exercise such authority. Their argument is based on the language of Art. II, §2, cl. 2, of the Constitution. Appellee Commission and *amici* in support of the Commission urge that the Framers of the Constitution, while mindful of the need for checks and balances among the three branches of the National Government, had no intention of denying to the Legislative Branch authority to appoint its own officers. Congress, either under the Appointments Clause or under its grants of substantive legislative authority and the Necessary and Proper Clause in Art. I, is in their view empowered to provide for the appointment to the Commission in the manner which it did because the Commission is performing "appropriate legislative functions."

1. Separation of Powers

We do not think appellants' arguments based upon Art. II, §2, cl. 2, of the Constitution may be so easily dismissed as did the majority of the Court of Appeals. Our inquiry of necessity touches upon the fundamental principles of the Government established by the Framers of the Constitution, and all litigants and all of the courts which have addressed themselves to the matter start on common ground in the recognition of the intent of the Framers that the powers of the three great branches of the National Government be largely separate from one another.

James Madison, writing in THE FEDERALIST No. 47, defended the work of the Framers against the charge that these three governmental powers were not *entirely* separate from one another in the proposed Constitution. He asserted that while there was some admixture, the Constitution was nonetheless true to Montesquieu's well-known maxim that the legislative, executive, and judicial departments ought to be separate and distinct:

> The reasons on which Montesquieu grounds his maxim are a further demonstration of his meaning. "When the legislative and executive powers are united in the same person or body," says he, "there can be no liberty, because apprehensions may arise lest *the same* monarch or senate should *enact* tyrannical laws to *execute* them in a tyrannical manner." Again: "Were the power of judging joined with the legislative, the life and liberty of the subject would be exposed to arbitrary control, for *the judge* would then be *the legislator.* Were it joined to the executive power, *the judge* might behave with all the violence of *an oppressor.*"

Yet it is also clear from the provisions of the Constitution itself, and from the Federalist Papers, that the Constitution by no means contemplates total separation of each of these three essential branches of Government. The President is a participant in the lawmaking process by virtue of his authority to veto bills enacted by Congress. The Senate is a participant in the appointive process by virtue of its authority to refuse to confirm persons nominated to office by the President. The men who met in Philadelphia in the summer of 1787 were practical statesmen, experienced in politics, who viewed the principle of separation of powers as a vital check against tyranny. But they likewise saw that a hermetic sealing off of the three branches of Government from one another would preclude the establishment of a Nation capable of governing itself effectively.

This Court has not hesitated to enforce the principle of separation of powers embodied in the Constitution when its application has proved necessary for the decisions of cases or controversies properly before it. The Court has held that executive or administrative duties of a nonjudicial nature may not be imposed on judges holding office under Art. III of the Constitution. *Hayburn's Case*, 2 U.S. 409 (1792). The Court has held that the President may not execute and exercise legislative authority belonging only to Congress. *Youngstown Sheet & Tube Co. v. Sawyer.*

2. The Appointments Clause

The principle of separation of powers was not simply an abstract generalization in the minds of the Framers: it was woven into the document that they drafted in Philadelphia in the summer of 1787. Article I, § 1, declares: "All legislative Powers herein granted shall be vested in a Congress of the United States." Article II, § 1, vests the executive power "in a President of the United States of America," and Art. III, § 1, declares that "The judicial Power of the United States, shall be vested in one supreme Court, and in such inferior Courts as the Congress may from time to time ordain and establish."

It is in the context of these cognate provisions of the document that we must examine the language of Art. II, § 2, cl. 2, which appellants contend provides the only authorization for appointment of those to whom substantial executive or administrative authority is given by statute. The Appointments Clause could, of course, be read as merely dealing with etiquette or protocol in describing "Officers of the United States," but the drafters had a less frivolous purpose in mind. This conclusion is supported by language from *United States v. Germaine*, 99 U.S. 508, 509–10 (1879):

> The Constitution for purposes of appointment very clearly divides all its officers into two classes. The primary class requires a nomination by the President and confirmation by the Senate. But foreseeing that when offices became numerous, and sudden removals necessary, this mode might be inconvenient, it was provided that, in regard to officers inferior to those specially mentioned, Congress might by law vest their appointment in the President alone, in the courts of law, or in the heads of departments. *That all persons who can be said to hold an office under the government about to be established under the Constitution were intended to be included within one or the other of these modes of appointment there can be but little doubt.*

We think that the term "Officers of the United States" as used in Art. II, defined to include "all persons who can be said to hold an office under the government" in *United States v. Germaine* is a term intended to have substantive meaning. We think its fair import is that any appointee exercising significant authority pursuant to the laws of the United States is an "Officer of the United States," and must, therefore, be appointed in the manner prescribed by § 2, cl. 2, of that Article.

If "all persons who can be said to hold an office under the government about to be established under the Constitution were intended to be included within one or the other of these modes of appointment," *United States v. Germaine*, it is difficult to see how the members of the Commission may escape inclusion. If a postmaster first class, *Myers v. United States*, 272 U.S. 52 (1926), and the clerk of a district court, *Ex parte Hennen*, 38 U.S. 225 (1839), are inferior officers of the United States within the meaning of the Appointments Clause, as they are, surely the Commissioners before us are at the very least such "inferior Officers" within the meaning of that Clause.

Although two members of the Commission are initially selected by the President, his nominations are subject to confirmation not merely by the Senate, but by the House of Representatives as well. The remaining four voting members of the Commission are appointed by the President *pro tempore* of the Senate and by the Speaker of the House. While the second part of the Clause authorizes Congress to vest the appointment of the officers described in that part in "the Courts of Law, or in the Heads of Departments," neither the Speaker of the House nor the President *pro tempore* of the Senate comes within this language.

The phrase "Heads of Departments," used as it is in conjunction with the phrase "Courts of Law," suggests that the Departments referred to are themselves in the Executive Branch or at least have some connection with that branch. While the Clause expressly authorizes Congress to vest the appointment of certain officers in the "Courts of Law," the absence of similar language to include Congress must mean that neither Congress nor its officers were included within the language "Heads of Departments" in this part of cl. 2.

Thus with respect to four of the six voting members of the Commission, neither the President, the head of any department, nor the Judiciary has any voice in their selection.

The Appointments Clause specifies the method of appointment only for "Officers of the United States" whose appointment is not "otherwise provided for" in the Constitution. But there is no provision of the Constitution remotely providing any alternative means for the selection of the members of the Commission or for anybody like them. Appellee Commission has argued, and the Court of Appeals agreed, that the Appointments Clause of Art. II should not be read to exclude the "inherent power of Congress" to appoint its own officers to perform functions necessary to that body as an institution. But there is no need to read the Appointments Clause contrary to its plain language in order to reach the result sought by the Court of Appeals. Article I, § 3, cl. 5, expressly authorizes the selection of the President *pro tempore* of the Senate, and § 2, cl. 5, of that Article provides for the selection of the Speaker of the House. Ranking nonmembers, such as the Clerk of the House of Representatives, are elected under the internal rules of each House and are designated by statute as "officers of the Congress."

Appellee Commission and *amici* contend somewhat obliquely that because the Framers had no intention of relegating Congress to a position below that of the coequal Judicial and Executive Branches of the National Government, the Appointments Clause must somehow be read to include Congress or its officers as among those in whom the appointment power may be vested. But the debates of the Constitutional Convention, and the Federalist Papers, are replete with expressions of fear that the Legislative Branch of the National Government will aggrandize itself at the expense of the other two branches. The debates during the Convention, and the evolution of the draft version of the Constitution, seem to us to lend considerable support to our reading of the language of the Appointments Clause itself.

In the final version, the Senate is shorn of its power to appoint Ambassadors and Judges of the Supreme Court. The President is given, not the power to *appoint* public officers of the United States, but only the right to *nominate* them, and a provision is inserted by virtue of which Congress may require Senate confirmation of his nominees. It would seem a fair surmise that a compromise had been made. But no change was made in the concept of the term "Officers of the United States," which since it had first appeared had been taken by all concerned to embrace all appointed officials exercising responsibility under the public laws of the Nation.

The position that because Congress has been given explicit and plenary authority to regulate a field of activity, it must therefore have the power to appoint those who are to administer the regulatory statute is both novel and contrary to the language of the Appointments Clause. Unless their selection is elsewhere provided for, *all* Officers of the United States are to be appointed in accordance with the Clause. Principal officers are selected by the President with the advice and consent of the Senate. Inferior officers Congress may allow to be appointed by the President alone, by the heads of departments, or by the Judiciary. No class or type of officer is excluded because of its special functions. The President appoints judicial as well as executive officers. Neither has it been disputed—and apparently it is not now disputed—that the Clause controls the appointment of the members of a typical administrative agency even though its functions, as this Court recognized in *Humphrey's Executor v. United States*, 295 U.S. 602, 624 (1935), may be "predominantly quasi-judicial and quasi-legislative" rather than executive. The Court in that case carefully emphasized that although the members of such agencies were to be independent of the Executive in their day-to-day operations, the Executive was not excluded from selecting them. *Id.* at 625–26.

We are also told by appellees and *amici* that Congress had good reason for not vesting in a Commission composed wholly of Presidential appointees the authority to administer the Act, since the administration of the Act would undoubtedly have a bearing on any incumbent President's campaign for re-election. While one cannot dispute the basis for this sentiment as a practical matter, it would seem that those who sought to challenge incumbent Congressmen might have equally good reason to fear a Commission which was unduly responsive to members of Congress whom they were seeking to unseat. But such fears, however rational, do not by themselves warrant a distortion of the Framers' work.

Appellee Commission and *amici* finally contend, and the majority of the Court of Appeals agreed with them, that whatever shortcomings the provisions for the appointment of members of the Commission might have under Art. II, Congress had ample authority under the Necessary and Proper Clause of Art. I to effectuate this result. We do not agree. So framed, the claim that Congress may provide for this manner of appointment under the Necessary and Proper Clause of Art. I stands on no better footing than the claim that it may provide for such manner of appointment because of its substantive authority to regulate federal elections. Congress could not, merely because it concluded that such a measure was "necessary and proper" to the discharge of its substantive legislative authority, pass a bill of attainder or *ex post facto* law contrary to the prohibitions contained in § 9 of Art. I. No more may it vest in itself, or in its officers, the authority to appoint officers of the United States when the Appointments Clause by clear implication prohibits it from doing so.

3. The Commission's Powers

Thus, on the assumption that all of the powers granted in the statute may be exercised by an agency whose members *have been* appointed in accordance with the Appointments Clause, the ultimate question is which, if any, of those powers may be exercised by the present voting Commissioners, none of whom *was* appointed as provided by that Clause.

Insofar as the powers confided in the Commission are essentially of an investigative and informative nature, falling in the same general category as those powers which Congress might delegate to one of its own committees, there can be no question that the Commission as presently constituted may exercise them. *McGrain v. Daugherty*, 273 U.S. 135 (1927).

But when we go beyond this type of authority to the more substantial powers exercised by the Commission, we reach a different result. The Commission's enforcement power, exemplified by its discretionary power to seek judicial relief, is authority that cannot possibly be regarded as merely in aid of the legislative function of Congress. A lawsuit is the ultimate remedy for a breach of the law, and it is to the President, and not to the Congress, that the Constitution entrusts the responsibility to "take Care that the Laws be faithfully executed." Art. II, § 3.

We hold that these provisions of the Act, vesting in the Commission primary responsibility for conducting civil litigation in the courts of the United States for vindicating public rights, violate Art. II, § 2, cl. 2, of the Constitution. Such functions may be discharged only by persons who are "Officers of the United States" within the language of that section.

[T]he judgment of the Court of Appeals is affirmed in part and reversed in part.

JUSTICE STEVENS took no part in the consideration or decision of these cases.

CHIEF JUSTICE BURGER, concurring in part and dissenting in part. [Opinion omitted.]

JUSTICE WHITE, concurring in part and dissenting in part. [Opinion omitted.]

[The separate opinions of Justices Marshall, Blackmun, and Rehnquist, each of whom concurred in Part IV of the Court's opinion and dissented on other matters, have been omitted.]

EXERCISE 6:

Consider the following questions in regard to *Buckley v. Valeo*:

1. What is the test for distinguishing an "Officer of the United States" from an "employee" of the central government or an "Officer of Congress"? What basis does the Court give for this distinction?

In *Freytag v. Commissioner*, 501 U.S. 868, 881–82 (1991), the Court applied the *Buckley* officer/employee test and found that special trial judges serving the Tax Court were officers, not employees:

> The Commissioner reasons that special trial judges may be deemed employees . . . because they lack authority to enter a final decision. But this argument ignores the significance of the duties and discretion that special trial judges possess. The office of special trial judge is "established by Law," Art. II, § 2, cl. 2, and the duties, salary, and means of appointment for that office are specified by statute. . . . These characteristics distinguish special trial judges from special masters, who are hired by Article III courts on a temporary, episodic basis, whose positions are not established by law, and whose duties and functions are not delineated in a statute. Furthermore, special trial judges perform more than ministerial tasks. They take testimony, conduct trials, rule on the admissibility of evidence, and have the power to enforce compliance with discovery orders. In the course of carrying out these important functions, the special trial judges exercise significant discretion.
>
> Even if the duties of special trial judges . . . were not as significant as we and the two courts have found them to be, our conclusion would be unchanged. . . . Special trial judges are not inferior officers for purposes of some of their duties . . . but mere employees with respect to other responsibilities. The fact that an inferior officer on occasion performs duties that may be performed by an employee not subject to the Appointments Clause does not transform his status under the Constitution.

Whether Administrative Law Judges at the Securities and Exchange Commission are "employees" has split the circuits. *Compare Raymond J. Lucia Companies, Inc. v. SEC,*

832 F.3d 277 (D.C. Cir. 2016) (holding that they are); with *Bandimere v. SEC*, 844 F.3d 1168 (10th Cir. 2016) (holding, over a dissent, that they are not, and hence violate the Appointments Clause). The D.C. Circuit granted rehearing en banc in the *Raymond J. Lucia* case, but split 5–5. With the circuit split thus intact, the issue thus seems likely to reach the Supreme Court in 2018.

For recent academic criticism of this aspect of *Buckley* on the basis of the original meaning, see Jennifer Mascott, *Who Are "Officers of the United States"?*, 70 Stan. L. Rev. __ (forthcoming 2018), available at https://papers.ssrn.com/paper=2918952. Mascott uses "corpus linguistics"—computer-aided analysis of a large corpus of naturally-occurring language—and a detailed analysis of the acts of the First Congress to argue that "anyone with continuing responsibility for a federal statutory duty" is subject to the Appointments Clause.

2. Which functions, if any, vested in the FEC could be exercised without significant constitutional problems? Why are they not subject to the Appointments Clause of Article II?

3. Which functions, if any, vested in the FEC were "executive" functions that could be exercised only by one or more "Officers of the United States"?

4. What constitutional issues, if any, were presented by the inclusion of the *ex officio* members of the FEC?

5. What constitutional issues, if any, were presented with respect to the presidential appointees to the FEC?

6. What constitutional issues, if any, were presented with respect to the congressional appointees to the FEC?

7. May Congress appoint officers that exercise executive power? Describe the forms of arguments utilized by the majority to support its conclusion that the method of appointing FEC commissioners violated the Constitution.

8. Is the Court's opinion formalist or functionalist? Explain your answer.

9. With respect to the issues addressed by the Court, what interpretation of the Constitution is suggested by practical policy and political considerations? What weight does the Court give to such matters?

10. Throughout *Buckley v. Valeo*, did the Court fairly characterize *Myers* and *Humphrey's Executor*, two of its important precedents on *removal* of officers?

11. Despite *Buckley*, Congress continued to use direct congressional appointment of officials, and had them struck down in later cases. *Metropolitan Washington Airports Authority v. Citizens for Abatement of Aircraft Noise, Inc.*, 501 U.S. 252 (1991), involved a federal statute transferring control of D.C. airports from the federal government to a new entity itself governed by a board consisting of nine members of Congress. The dissent claimed that the airports authority was merely the creature of state law, but the Court disagreed, holding that it exercised federal power. What kind of federal power—executive or legislative—did not matter. "If the power is executive, the Constitution does not permit an agent of Congress to exercise it. If

the power is legislative, Congress must exercise it in conformity with the bicameralism and presentment requirements of Art. I, § 7." *Id.* at 276.

12. Like almost all of the executive-power issues in this volume, legislative appointment is a fascinatingly complicated issue under state constitutional law, as well as federal constitutional law. Most states actually allow legislative appointments. *Marine Forests Society v. California Coastal Commission*, 113 P.3d 1062, 1085–86 (Cal. 2005) (reversing an intermediate-state-court decision invalidating legislative appointments, and listing states on either side of the issue). State executive power is generally divided among several elected executive officials, both at the state level (among a governor, attorney general, and secretary of state, for instance) and between the state and local levels (between these officials and local governments). Very little scholarly attention tends to be paid to these issues of state-constitutional law; the field is ripe for well-done fifty-state surveys of the ground. The annual Book of the States, published by the Council of State Governments, has extremely useful surveys of both developments and the state-constitutional rules in each state, and political-science scholars have long paid the field significant attention. Law schools and lawyers have, however, tended to neglect it. Each state's constitutional law tends to develop in relative isolation simply for lack of an adequate fifty-state map of separation-of-powers law. The prominence of federal separation-of-powers law makes it relatively easy to construct such a survey with electronic databases: simply reviewing the citations to a federal separation-of-powers case with a filter on state cases will generally turn up a wealth of material not previously canvassed by scholars.

2. "Inferior Officers," "Courts of Law," and "Heads of Departments"

In Section B, we covered the removal issues in the independent counsel statute. Here, we consider the case's two Appointments-Clause issues: (1) whether the independent counsel is an "inferior officer" who need not be presidentially-appointed and Senate-confirmed, and (2) whether "courts of law" may appoint such an executive officer.

MORRISON v. OLSON
487 U.S. 654 (1988)

Chief Justice Rehnquist delivered the opinion of the Court.

This case presents us with a challenge to the independent counsel provisions of the Ethics in Government Act of 1978. We hold today that these provisions of the Act do not violate the Appointments Clause of the Constitution, Art. II, § 2, cl. 2 . . . [The background to the Independent Counsel Act we summarized above in Section B.]

III

The parties do not dispute that "[t]he Constitution for purposes of appointment . . . divides all its officers into two classes." *United States v. Germaine*, 99 U.S. 508, 509 (1879). As we stated in *Buckley v. Valeo*, 424 U.S. 1, 132 (1976): "[P]rincipal officers are selected by the President with the advice and consent of the Senate. Inferior officers Congress may allow to be appointed by the President alone, by the heads of departments, or by the Judiciary." The initial question is, accordingly, whether appellant is an "inferior" or a "principal" officer. If she is the latter then the Act is in violation of the Appointments Clause.

The line between "inferior" and "principal" officers is one that is far from clear, and the Framers provided little guidance into where it should be drawn. *See, e.g.,* 2 JOSEPH STORY, COMMENTARIES ON THE CONSTITUTION § 1536, pp. 397–98 (3d ed. 1858) ("In the practical course of the government there does not seem to have been any exact line drawn, who are and who are not to be deemed *inferior* officers, in the sense of the constitution, whose appointment does not necessarily require the concurrence of the senate"). We need not attempt here to decide exactly where the line falls between the two types of officers, because in our view appellant clearly falls on the "inferior officer" side of that line. Several factors lead to this conclusion.

First, appellant is subject to removal by a higher Executive Branch official. Although appellant may not be "subordinate" to the Attorney General (and the President) insofar as she possesses a degree of independent discretion to exercise the powers delegated to her under the Act, the fact that she can be removed by the Attorney General indicates that she is to some degree "inferior" in rank and authority. Second, appellant is empowered by the Act to perform only certain, limited duties. An independent counsel's role is restricted primarily to investigation and, if appropriate, prosecution for certain federal crimes. Admittedly, the Act delegates to appellant "full power and independent authority to exercise all investigative and prosecutorial functions and powers of the Department of Justice," § 594(a), but this grant of authority does not include any authority to formulate policy for the Government or the Executive Branch, nor does it give appellant any administrative duties outside of those necessary to operate her office. The Act specifically provides that in policy matters appellant is to comply to the extent possible with the policies of the Department. § 594(f).

Third, appellant's office is limited in jurisdiction. Not only is the Act itself restricted in applicability to certain federal officials suspected of certain serious federal crimes, but an independent counsel can only act within the scope of the jurisdiction that has been granted by the Special Division pursuant to a request by the Attorney General. Finally, appellant's office is limited in tenure. There is concededly no time limit on the appointment of a particular counsel. Nonetheless, the office of independent counsel is "temporary" in the sense that an independent counsel is appointed essentially to accomplish a single task, and when that task is over the office is terminated, either by the counsel herself or by action of the Special Division. In our view, these factors relating to the "ideas of tenure, duration . . . and duties" of the independent counsel, *Germaine*, 99 U.S. at 511, are sufficient to establish that appellant is an "inferior" officer in the constitutional sense.

This does not, however, end our inquiry under the Appointments Clause. Appellees argue that even if appellant is an "inferior" officer, the Clause does not empower Congress to place the power to appoint such an officer outside the Executive Branch. On its face, the language of [the] "excepting clause" [of the Appointments Clause] admits of no limitation on interbranch appointments. Indeed, the inclusion of "as they think proper" seems clearly to give Congress significant discretion to determine whether it is "proper" to vest the appointment of, for example, executive officials in the "courts of Law." We recognized as much in one of our few decisions in this area, *Ex parte Siebold*, where we stated:

> It is no doubt usual and proper to vest the appointment of inferior officers in that department of the government, executive or judicial, or in that particular executive department to which the duties of such officers appertain. But there is no absolute requirement to this effect in the Constitution; and, if there were, it would be difficult in many cases to determine to which department an office properly belonged.

> But as the Constitution stands, the selection of the appointing power, as between the functionaries named, is a matter resting in the discretion of Congress.

100 U.S. 371, 397–98.

We also note that the history of the Clause provides no support for appellees' position. Throughout most of the process of drafting the Constitution, the Convention concentrated on the problem of who should have the authority to appoint judges. At the suggestion of James Madison, the Convention adopted a proposal that the Senate should have this authority, 1 MAX FARRAND, RECORDS OF THE FEDERAL CONVENTION OF 1787, pp. 232–233 (1966), and several attempts to transfer the appointment power to the President were rejected. *See* 2 *id.* at 42–44. The August 6, 1787, draft of the Constitution reported by the Committee of Detail retained Senate appointment of Supreme Court Judges, provided also for Senate appointment of ambassadors, and vested in the President the authority to "appoint officers in all cases not otherwise provided for by this Constitution." *Id.* at 183, 185. This scheme was maintained until September 4, when the Committee of Eleven reported its suggestions to the Convention. This Committee suggested that the Constitution be amended to state that the President "shall nominate and by and with the advice and consent of the Senate shall appoint ambassadors, and other public Ministers, Judges of the Supreme Court, and all other Officers of the [United States], whose appointments are not otherwise herein provided for." *Id.* at 498–99. After the addition of "Consuls" to the list, the Committee's proposal was adopted, *id.* at 539, and was subsequently reported to the Convention by the Committee of Style. *See id.* at 599. It was at this point, on September 15, that Gouverneur Morris moved to add the Excepting Clause to Art. II, § 2. *Id.* at 627. The one comment made on this motion was by Madison, who felt that the Clause did not go far enough in that it did not allow Congress to vest appointment powers in "Superior Officers below Heads of Departments." The first vote on Morris' motion ended in a tie. It was then put forward a second time, with the urging that "some such provision [was] too necessary, to be omitted." This time the proposal was adopted. *Id.* at 627–28. As this discussion shows, there was little or no debate on the question whether the Clause empowers Congress to provide for interbranch appointments, and there is nothing to suggest that the Framers intended to prevent Congress from having that power.

We have recognized that courts may appoint private attorneys to act as prosecutor for judicial contempt judgments. [W]e approved court appointment of United States commissioners, who exercised certain limited prosecutorial powers. In *Siebold*, as well, we indicated that judicial appointment of federal marshals, who are "executive officer[s]," would not be inappropriate. Lower courts have also upheld interim judicial appointments of United States Attorneys and Congress itself has vested the power to make these interim appointments in the district courts. Congress, of course, was concerned when it created the office of independent counsel with the conflicts of interest that could arise in situations when the Executive Branch is called upon to investigate its own high-ranking officers. If it were to remove the appointing authority from the Executive Branch, the most logical place to put it was in the Judicial Branch. In the light of the Act's provision making the judges of the Special Division ineligible to participate in any matters relating to an independent counsel they have appointed, we do not think that appointment of the independent counsel by the court runs afoul of the constitutional limitation on "incongruous" interbranch appointments.

JUSTICE SCALIA, dissenting.

[T]his suit is about [p]ower. The allocation of power among Congress, the President, and the courts in such fashion as to preserve the equilibrium the Constitution sought to establish—so that "a gradual concentration of the several powers in the same department," FEDERALIST No. 51 (J. Madison), can effectively be resisted. Frequently an issue of this sort will come before the Court clad, so to speak, in sheep's clothing: the potential of the asserted principle to effect important change in the equilibrium of power is not immediately evident, and must be discerned by a careful and perceptive analysis. But this wolf comes as a wolf.

I

As a practical matter, it would be surprising if the Attorney General had any choice (assuming this statute is constitutional) but to seek appointment of an independent counsel to pursue the charges against the principal object of the congressional request, Mr. Olson. Merely the political consequences (to him and the President) of seeming to break the law by refusing to do so would have been substantial. How could it not be, the public would ask, that a 3,000-page indictment drawn by our representatives over 2 1/2 years does not even establish "reasonable grounds to believe" that further investigation or prosecution is warranted with respect to at least the principal alleged culprit? But the Act establishes more than just practical compulsion. Although the Court's opinion asserts that the Attorney General had "no duty to comply with the [congressional] request," that is not entirely accurate. He had a duty to comply unless he could conclude that there were "no reasonable grounds to believe," not that prosecution was warranted, but merely that "further investigation" was warranted, 28 U.S.C. § 592(b)(1), after a 90-day investigation in which he was prohibited from using such routine investigative techniques as grand juries, plea bargaining, grants of immunity, or even subpoenas, *see* § 592(a)(2). The Court also makes much of the fact that "the courts are specifically prevented from reviewing the Attorney General's decision not to seek appointment." Yes, but Congress is not prevented from reviewing it. The context of this statute is acrid with the smell of threatened impeachment. Where, as here, a request for appointment of an independent counsel has come from the Judiciary Committee of either House of Congress, the Attorney General must, if he decides not to seek appointment, explain to that Committee why. *See also* 28 U.S.C. § 595(c) (independent counsel must report to the House of Representatives information "that may constitute grounds for an impeachment").

Thus, by the application of this statute in the present case, Congress has effectively compelled a criminal investigation of a high-level appointee of the President in connection with his actions arising out of a bitter power dispute between the President and the Legislative Branch. Mr. Olson may or may not be guilty of a crime; we do not know. But we do know that the investigation of him has been commenced, not necessarily because the President or his authorized subordinates believe it is in the interest of the United States, in the sense that it warrants the diversion of resources from other efforts, and is worth the cost in money and in possible damage to other governmental interests; and not even, leaving aside those normally considered factors, because the President or his authorized subordinates necessarily believe that an investigation is likely to unearth a violation worth prosecuting; but only because the Attorney General cannot affirm, as Congress demands, that there are no reasonable grounds to believe that further investigation is warranted. The decisions regarding the scope of that further investigation, its duration, and, finally, whether or not prosecution should ensue, are likewise beyond the control of the President and his subordinates.

III

As I indicated earlier, the basic separation-of-powers principles I have discussed are what give life and content to our jurisprudence concerning the President's power to appoint and remove officers. The same result of unconstitutionality is therefore plainly indicated by our case law in these areas.

Because appellant (who all parties and the Court agree is an officer of the United States) was not appointed by the President with the advice and consent of the Senate, but rather by the Special Division of the United States Court of Appeals, her appointment is constitutional only if (1) she is an "inferior" officer within the meaning of the above Clause, and (2) Congress may vest her appointment in a court of law.

As to the first of these inquiries, the Court does not attempt to "decide exactly" what establishes the line between principal and "inferior" officers, but is confident that, whatever the line may be, appellant "clearly falls on the 'inferior officer' side" of it. The Court gives three reasons. The first of these lends no support to the view that appellant is an inferior officer. Appellant is removable only for "good cause" or physical or mental incapacity. 28 U.S.C. § 596(a)(1). By contrast, most (if not all) *principal* officers in the Executive Branch may be removed by the President *at will*. I fail to see how the fact that appellant is more difficult to remove than most principal officers helps to establish that she is an inferior officer. If it were common usage to refer to someone as "inferior" who is subject to removal for cause by another, then one would say that the President is "inferior" to Congress.

The second reason offered by the Court — that appellant performs only certain, limited duties — may be relevant to whether she is an inferior officer, but it mischaracterizes the extent of her powers. As the Court states: "Admittedly, the Act delegates to appellant [the] 'full power and independent authority to exercise all investigative and prosecutorial functions and powers of the Department of Justice.'" Moreover, in addition to this general grant of power she is given a broad range of specifically enumerated powers, including a power not even the Attorney General possesses: to "contes[t] in court . . . any claim of privilege or attempt to withhold evidence on grounds of national security." § 594(a)(6).

The final set of reasons given by the Court for why the independent counsel clearly is an inferior officer emphasizes the limited nature of her jurisdiction and tenure. Taking the latter first, I find nothing unusually limited about the independent counsel's tenure. To the contrary, unlike most high-ranking Executive Branch officials, she continues to serve until she (or the Special Division) decides that her work is substantially completed. *See* §§ 596(b)(1), (b)(2). This particular independent prosecutor has already served more than two years, which is at least as long as many Cabinet officials. As to the scope of her jurisdiction, there can be no doubt that is small (though far from unimportant). But within it she exercises more than the full power of the Attorney General . . . .

More fundamentally, however, it is not clear from the Court's opinion why the factors it discusses — even if applied correctly to the facts of this case — are determinative of the question of inferior officer status. The apparent source of these factors is a statement in *United States v. Germaine*, 99 U.S. 508 (1879) (discussing *United States v. Hartwell*, 73 U.S. 385, 393 (1868)), that "the term [officer] embraces the ideas of tenure, duration, emolument, and duties." Besides the fact that this was dictum, it was dictum in a case where the distinguishing characteristics of inferior officers versus superior officers were in no way relevant, but rather only the distinguishing characteristics of an "officer of the United States" (to which the criminal statute at issue applied) as opposed to a mere employee. Rather than erect a theory of who is an inferior officer on the foundation of such an irrelevancy, I think it preferable to look to the text of the Constitution and the division of power that it establishes. These demonstrate, I think, that the independent counsel is not an inferior officer because she is not *subordinate* to any officer in the Executive Branch (indeed, not even to the President). Dictionaries in use at the time of the Constitutional Convention gave the word "inferiour" two meanings which it still bears today: (1) "[l]ower in place, . . . station, . . . rank of life, . . . value or excellency," and (2) "[s]ubordinate." SAMUEL JOHNSON, DICTIONARY OF THE ENGLISH LANGUAGE (6th ed. 1785). In a document dealing with the structure (the constitution) of a government, one would naturally expect the word to bear the latter meaning—indeed, in such a context it would be unpardonably careless to use the word unless a relationship of subordination was intended.

That "inferior" means "subordinate" is also consistent with what little we know about the evolution of the Appointments Clause. As originally reported to the Committee on Style, the Appointments Clause provided no "exception" from the standard manner of appointment (President with the advice and consent of the Senate) for inferior officers. 2 MAX FARRAND, RECORDS OF THE FEDERAL CONVENTION OF 1787, pp. 498–499, 599 (rev. ed. 1966). To be sure, it is not a *sufficient* condition for "inferior" officer status that one be subordinate to a principal officer. Even an officer who is subordinate to a department head can be a principal officer. That is clear from the brief exchange following Gouverneur Morris' suggestion of the addition of the exceptions clause for inferior officers. Madison responded: "It does not go far enough if it be necessary at all—Superior Officers below Heads of Departments ought in some cases to have the appointment of the lesser offices." 2 MAX FARRAND, RECORDS OF THE FEDERAL CONVENTION of 1787, p. 627 (rev. ed. 1966). But it is surely a *necessary* condition for inferior officer status that the officer be subordinate to another officer.

The independent counsel is not even subordinate to the President. The Court essentially admits as much, noting that "appellant may not be 'subordinate' to the Attorney General (and the President) insofar as she possesses a degree of independent discretion to exercise the powers delegated to her under the Act." In fact, there is no doubt about it. As noted earlier, the Act specifically grants her the "full power and independent authority to exercise all investigative and prosecutorial functions of the Department of Justice," 28 U.S.C. § 594(a), and makes her removable only for "good cause," a limitation specifically intended to ensure that she be *independent* of, not *subordinate* to, the President and the Attorney General. *See* H.R. Conf. Rep. No. 100-452, p. 37 (1987).

Because appellant is not subordinate to another officer, she is not an "inferior" officer and her appointment other than by the President with the advice and consent of the Senate is unconstitutional.

EXERCISE 7:

Consider the following questions in connection with *Morrison v. Olson*:

1. With respect to the majority's analysis under the Appointments Clause, what four factors did the Court find indicated that the independent counsel was only an inferior officer? Assuming those four factors specify the appropriate test, when you apply them to the independent counsel, do you reach the same result as the Court?

2. With respect to the majority's analysis under the Appointments Clause, do you agree with the permissibility of "interbranch appointments"? Why or why not? If such appointments were prohibited, would any text of the Appointments Clause be rendered superfluous? Could Congress authorize the Attorney General to appoint clerks for all the Article III courts? Could Congress authorize the U.S. Supreme Court to appoint the Solicitor General?

3. In dissent, Justice Scalia reviewed the four criteria considered by the majority in determining whether the IC was a principal or inferior officer. Did he succeed in demonstrating that the majority misapplied their own criteria? What alternative test did Justice Scalia advance?

4. What manner of argument did Justice Scalia assert to support his alternative test for distinguishing principal from inferior officers?

———————

While *Morrison* held that "Courts of Law" from Article III could make interbranch appointments, the Court held three years later that "Courts of Law"—in particular, the Tax Court—might themselves be located in the executive branch. *Freytag v. Commissioner*, 501 U.S. 868 (1991). While it was unanimous on the result, the Court split 5–4 on the rationale; Justice Scalia for 4 justices held that a "Court of Law" must be composed of Article III judges. The majority held that the Tax Court could not be a "Head of Department," as Justice Scalia's concurrence-in-judgment would have held that it was, because those were only "executive divisions like the Cabinet-level departments."

FREE ENTERPRISE FUND v. PUBLIC COMPANY ACCOUNTING OVERSIGHT BOARD
561 U.S. 477 (2010)

[P]etitioners argue, the Commission is not a "Departmen[t]" like the "Executive departments" (e.g., State, Treasury, Defense) listed in 5 U.S.C. § 101. In *Freytag*, 501 U.S., at 887, n. 4, 111 S.Ct. 2631, we specifically reserved the question whether a "principal agenc[y], such as . . . the Securities and Exchange Commission," is a "Departmen[t]" under the Appointments Clause. Four Justices, however, would have concluded that the Commission is indeed such a "Departmen[t]," see *id.*, at 918 (Scalia, J., concurring in part and concurring in judgment), because it is a "free-standing, self-contained entity in the Executive Branch."

Respondents urge us to adopt this reasoning as to those entities not addressed by our opinion in Freytag, and we do. Respondents' reading of the Appointments Clause is consistent with the common, near-contemporary definition of a "department" as a "separate allotment or part of business; a distinct province, in which a class of duties are allotted to a particular person." 1 N. Webster, American Dictionary of the English Language (1828) (def. 2) (1995 facsimile ed.). It is also consistent with the early practice of Congress, which in 1792 authorized the Postmaster General to appoint "an assistant, and deputy postmasters, at all places where such shall be found necessary," § 3, 1 Stat. 234 — thus treating him as the "Hea[d] of [a] Departmen[t]" without the title of Secretary or any role in the President's Cabinet. And it is consistent with our prior cases, which have never invalidated an appointment made by the head of such an establishment. Because the Commission is a freestanding component of the Executive Branch, not subordinate to or contained within any other such component, it constitutes a "Departmen[t]" for the purposes of the Appointments Clause.

But petitioners are not done yet. They argue that the full Commission cannot constitutionally appoint Board members, because only the Chairman of the Commission is the Commission's "Hea[d]." The Commission's powers, however, are generally vested in the Commissioners jointly, not the Chairman alone. The Commissioners do not report to the Chairman, who exercises administrative and executive functions subject to the full Commission's policies. The Chairman is also appointed from among the Commissioners by the President alone, which means that he cannot be regarded as "the head of an agency" for purposes of the Reorganization Act. (The Commission as a whole, on the other hand, does meet the requirements of the Act, including its provision that "the head of an agency [may] be an individual or a commission or board with more than one member.")

As a constitutional matter, we see no reason why a multimember body may not be the "Hea[d]" of a "Departmen[t]" that it governs. The Appointments Clause necessarily contemplates collective appointments by the " Courts of Law," Art. II, § 2, cl. 2, and each House of Congress, too, appoints its officers collectively, see Art. I, § 2, cl. 5; id., § 3, cl. 5. Petitioners argue that the Framers vested the nomination of principal officers in the President to avoid the perceived evils of collective appointments, but they reveal no similar concern with respect to inferior officers, whose appointments may be vested elsewhere, including in multimember bodies. Practice has also sanctioned the appointment of inferior officers by multimember agencies. See Freytag, supra, at 918 (Scalia, J., concurring in part and concurring in judgment); see also Classification Act of 1923, ch. 265, § 2, 42 Stat. 1488 (defining "the head of the department" to mean "the officer or group of officers . . . who are not subordinate or responsible to any other officer of the department" (emphasis added)); 37 Op. Atty. Gen. 227, 231 (1933) (endorsing collective appointment by the Civil Service Commission). We conclude that the Board members have been validly appointed by the full Commission.

EXERCISE 8:

1. Does *Free Enterprise Fund* suggest that the Court might follow Justice Scalia's concurrence-in-judgment on the "Courts of Law" issue?

2. Does the victory of Scalia's view on one Appointments-Clause issue presage his victory on others as well?

3. What should lower courts do if they think the Supreme Court will overrule a case? The Seventh Circuit once predicted accurately that the Supreme Court would overrule an earlier case, but was rebuked in the course of being affirmed. *Rodriguez de Quijas v. Shearson/American Express*, 490 U.S. 477, 484 (1989). By contrast, the Second Circuit was later reversed but commended for following soon-to-be-obsolete precedent in *Agostini v. Felton*, 521 U.S. 203, 214, 237 (1997).

Nine years after *Morrison*, the Court returned to the "inferior officer" question, but this time, Justice Scalia wrote for the Court rather than dissenting alone.

EDMOND v. UNITED STATES

520 U.S. 651 (1997)

JUSTICE SCALIA delivered the opinion of the Court.

We must determine in this case whether Congress has authorized the Secretary of Transportation to appoint civilian members of the Coast Guard Court of Criminal Appeals, and if so, whether this authorization is constitutional under the Appointments Clause of Article II.

I.

The Coast Guard Court of Criminal Appeals (formerly known as the Coast Guard Court of Military Review) is an intermediate court within the military justice system. [It] hears appeals from decisions of courts-martial, and its decisions are subject to review by the United States Court of Appeals for the Armed Forces. Appellate military judges who are assigned to a Court of Criminal Appeals must be members of the bar, but may be commissioned officers or civilians.

II.

Petitioners argue that the Secretary's civilian appointments to the Coast Guard Court of Criminal Appeals are invalid for two reasons: first, the Secretary lacks authority under 49 U.S.C. § 323(a) to appoint members of the court; second, judges of military Courts of Criminal Appeals are principal, not inferior, officers within the meaning of the Appointments Clause, and must therefore be appointed by the President with the advice and consent of the Senate. We consider these contentions in turn.

[The Court construed 49 U.S.C. § 323(a) as statutory authorization for the Secretary to make the challenged appointments.]

III.

As we recognized in *Buckley v. Valeo*, 424 U.S. 1 (1976), the Appointments Clause of Article II is more than a matter of "etiquette or protocol"; it is among the significant structural safeguards of the constitutional scheme. By vesting the President with the exclusive power to select the principal (noninferior) officers of the United States, the Appointments Clause prevents congressional encroachment upon the Executive and Judicial Branches. This disposition was also designed to assure a higher quality of appointments: The Framers anticipated that the President would be less vulnerable to interest-group pressure and personal favoritism than would a collective body. "The sole and undivided responsibility of one man will naturally beget a livelier sense of duty, and a more exact regard to reputation." THE FEDERALIST No. 76 (A. Hamilton). The President's power to select principal officers of the United States was not left unguarded, however, as Article II further requires the "Advice and Consent of the Senate." This serves both to curb Executive abuses of the appointment power and "to promote a judicious choice of [persons] for filling the offices of the union," THE FEDERALIST No. 76. By requiring the joint participation of the President and the Senate, the Appointments Clause was designed to ensure public accountability for both the making of a bad appointment and the rejection of a good one. [Alexander] Hamilton observed:

> The blame of a bad nomination would fall upon the president singly and absolutely. The censure of rejecting a good one would lie entirely at the door of the senate; aggravated by the consideration of their having counteracted the good intentions of the executive. If an ill appointment should be made, the executive for nominating, and the senate for approving, would participate, though in different degrees, in the opprobrium and disgrace.

THE FEDERALIST No. 77 (A. Hamilton).

The prescribed manner of appointment for principal officers is also the default manner of appointment for inferior officers. "[B]ut," the Appointments Clause continues, "the Congress may by Law vest the Appointment of such inferior Officers, as they think proper, in the President alone, in the Courts of Law, or in the Heads of Departments." This provision, sometimes referred to as the "Excepting Clause," was added to the proposed Constitution on the last day of the Grand Convention, with little discussion. *See* 2 MAX FARRAND, RECORDS OF THE FEDERAL CONVENTION OF 1787, pp. 627–28 (1911). As one of our early opinions suggests, its obvious purpose is administrative convenience — but that convenience was deemed to outweigh the benefit of the more cumbersome procedure only with respect to the appointment of "inferior Officers."

Our cases have not set forth an exclusive criterion for distinguishing between principal and inferior officers for Appointments Clause purposes. Among the offices that we have found to be inferior are that of a district court clerk, an election supervisor, a vice consul charged temporarily with the duties of the consul, and a "United States commissioner" in district court proceedings. Most recently, in

Morrison v. Olson, 487 U.S. 654 (1988), we held that the independent counsel created by provisions of the Ethics in Government Act of 1978 was an inferior officer. In reaching that conclusion, we relied on several factors: that the independent counsel was subject to removal by a higher officer (the Attorney General), that she performed only limited duties, that her jurisdiction was narrow, and that her tenure was limited.

Petitioners are quite correct that the last two of these conclusions do not hold with regard to the office of military judge at issue here. It is not "limited in tenure," as that phrase was used in *Morrison*. Nor are military judges "limited in jurisdiction," as used in *Morrison*. However, *Morrison* did not purport to set forth a definitive test for whether an office is "inferior" under the Appointments Clause. To the contrary, it explicitly stated: "We need not attempt here to decide exactly where the line falls between the two types of officers, because in our view [the independent counsel] clearly falls on the 'inferior officer' side of that line."

To support principal-officer status, petitioners emphasize the importance of the responsibilities that the Court of Criminal Appeals judges bear. They review those court-martial proceedings that result in the most serious sentences, including those "in which the sentence, as approved, extends to death, dismissal . . . dishonorable or bad-conduct discharge, or confinement for one year or more." They must ensure that the court-martial's finding of guilt and its sentence are "correct in law and fact" which includes resolution of constitutional challenges. And finally, unlike most appellate judges, Court of Criminal Appeals judges are not required to defer to the trial court's factual findings. We do not dispute that military appellate judges are charged with exercising significant authority on behalf of the United States. This, however, is also true of offices that we have held were "inferior" within the meaning of the Appointments Clause. The exercise of "significant authority pursuant to the laws of the United States" marks, not the line between principal and inferior officer for Appointments Clause purposes, but rather, as we said in *Buckley*, the line between officer and nonofficer.

Generally speaking, the term "inferior officer" connotes a relationship with some higher ranking officer or officers below the President: Whether one is an "inferior" officer depends on whether he has a superior. It is not enough that other officers may be identified who formally maintain a higher rank, or possess responsibilities of greater magnitude. Rather, in the context of a Clause designed to preserve political accountability relative to important Government assignments, we think it evident that "inferior officers" are officers whose work is directed and supervised at some level by others who were appointed by Presidential nomination with the advice and consent of the Senate.

This understanding of the Appointments Clause conforms with the views of the first Congress. On July 27, 1789, Congress established the first Executive department, the Department of Foreign Affairs. In doing so, it expressly designated the Secretary of the Department as a "principal officer," and his subordinate, the Chief Clerk of the

Department, as an "inferior officer." Congress used similar language in establishing the Department of War, repeatedly referring to the Secretary of that department as a "principal officer," and the Chief Clerk, who would be "employed" within the Department as the Secretary "shall deem proper," as an "inferior officer."

Supervision of the work of Court of Criminal Appeals judges is divided between the Judge Advocate General ["JAG"] (who in the Coast Guard is subordinate to the Secretary of Transportation) and the Court of Appeals for the Armed Forces. The [JAG] exercises administrative oversight over the Court of Criminal Appeals. It is conceded by the parties that the [JAG] may also remove a Court of Criminal Appeals judge from his judicial assignment without cause. The power to remove officers, we have recognized, is a powerful tool for control.

The [JAG]'s control over Court of Criminal Appeals judges is, to be sure, not complete. He may not attempt to influence (by threat of removal or otherwise) the outcome of individual proceedings and has no power to reverse decisions of the court. This latter power does reside, however, in another Executive Branch entity, the Court of Appeals for the Armed Forces.[1] The scope of review is narrower than that exercised by the Court of Criminal Appeals. This limitation upon review does not in our opinion render the judges of the Court of Criminal Appeals principal officers. What is significant is that the judges of the Court of Criminal Appeals have no power to render a final decision on behalf of the United States unless permitted to do so by other Executive officers.

Accordingly, we affirm the judgment of the Court of Appeals for the Armed Forces with respect to each petitioner.

JUSTICE SOUTER, concurring in part and concurring in the judgment.

I join in Parts I and II of the Court's opinion and agree with the reasoning in Part III insofar as it describes an important, and even necessary, reason for holding judges of the Coast Guard Court of Criminal Appeals to be inferior officers within the meaning of the Appointments Clause.

Because the term "inferior officer" implies an official superior, one who has no superior is not an inferior officer. It does not follow, however, that if one is subject to some supervision and control, one is an inferior officer. Having a superior officer is necessary for inferior officer status, but not sufficient to establish it. Accordingly, in *Morrison*, the Court's determination that the independent counsel was "to some degree 'inferior'" to the Attorney General did not end the enquiry. The Court went on to weigh the duties, jurisdiction, and tenure associated with the office before concluding that the independent counsel was an inferior officer. Thus, under *Morrison*, the Solicitor General of the United States, for example, may well be a principal officer, despite his statutory "inferiority" to the Attorney General. The mere existence of a "superior" is not dispositive.

---

1. [T]he Court of Appeals for the Armed Forces "is established under Article I of the Constitution," and "is located for administrative purposes only in the Department of Defense."

EXERCISE 9:

Consider the following questions in connection with *Edmond v. United States*:

1. What distinguishes "officers" of the United States from mere "employees"? Is *Edmond* consistent with prior precedent on that point?

2. According to *Edmond*, what distinguishes "principal officers" from "inferior officers"? Is *Edmond* consistent with prior precedent on that point?

3. What interpretative methods and sources did the Court draw upon to answer those questions?

4. What are the constitutionally permissible means of appointment of judges to the U.S. District Courts and U.S. Courts of Appeals?

5. If your instructor assigned Volume 1, consider whether sitting Justices of the U.S. Supreme Court needed a second commission to resume holding Circuit Courts upon passage of the federal Judiciary Act of 1802. These officers had been nominated by the President, confirmed by the Senate, and commissioned to serve on the Supreme Court. Could Congress expand their duties to include serving on separate courts? Or, was Circuit Judge a distinct office requiring a separate appointment and commission?

3. Recess Appointments

Art. II, § 2, cl. 2 is not the only clause governing appointments; the next clause covers "vacancies that may happen during the Recess of the Senate." While the Clause has an extremely detailed history — largely left out of the excerpt here — the Supreme Court considered it for the first time only in 2014. The case is important chiefly for the light it sheds on interpretive methodology: what is the proper relationship between text and history when there are no judicial precedents in the way?

NLRB v. NOEL CANNING
134 S.Ct. 2550 (2014)

Justice Breyer delivered the opinion of the Court.

Ordinarily the President must obtain "the Advice and Consent of the Senate" before appointing an "Office[r] of the United States." U. S. Const., Art. II, § 2, cl. 2. But the Recess Appointments Clause creates an exception. It gives the President alone the power "to fill up all Vacancies that may happen during the Recess of the Senate, by granting Commissions which shall expire at the End of their next Session." Art. II, § 2, cl. 3. We here consider three questions about the application of this Clause.

The first concerns the scope of the words "recess of the Senate." Does that phrase refer only to an inter-session recess (i.e., a break between formal sessions of Congress), or does it also include an intra-session recess, such as a summer recess in the midst of a session? We conclude that the Clause applies to both kinds of recess.

The second question concerns the scope of the words "vacancies that may happen." Does that phrase refer only to vacancies that first come into existence during a recess, or does it also include vacancies that arise prior to a recess but continue to exist during the recess? We conclude that the Clause applies to both kinds of vacancy.

The third question concerns calculation of the length of a "recess." . . . In calculating the length of a recess are we to ignore the pro forma sessions, thereby treating the series of brief recesses as a single, month-long recess? We conclude that we cannot ignore these pro forma sessions.

Our answer to the third question means that, when the appointments before us took place, the Senate was in the midst of a 3-day recess. Three days is too short a time to bring a recess within the scope of the Clause.

II

[I]n interpreting the Clause, we put significant weight upon historical practice. For one thing, the interpretive questions before us concern the allocation of power between two elected branches of Government. Long ago Chief Justice Marshall wrote that "a doubtful question, one on which human reason may pause, and the human judgment be suspended, in the decision of which the great principles of liberty are not concerned, but the respective powers of those who are equally the representatives of the people, are to be adjusted; if not put at rest by the practice of the government, ought to receive a considerable impression from that practice." *McCulloch v. Maryland*, 4 Wheat. [17 U.S.] 316, 401 (1819). And we later confirmed that "[l]ong settled and established practice is a consideration of great weight in a proper interpretation of constitutional provisions" regulating the relationship between Congress and the President. *The Pocket Veto Case*, 279 U. S. 655, 689 (1929); see also id., at 690 ("[A] practice of at least twenty years duration 'on the part of the executive department, acquiesced in by the legislative department, . . . is entitled to great regard in determining the true construction of a constitutional provision the phraseology of which is in any respect of doubtful meaning'" (quoting *State v. South Norwalk*, 77 Conn. 257, 264, 58 A. 759, 761 (1904))).

These precedents show that this Court has treated practice as an important interpretive factor even when the nature or longevity of that practice is subject to dispute, and even when that practice began after the founding era.

III

The first question concerns the scope of the phrase "*the recess* of the Senate." Art. II, § 2, cl. 3 (emphasis added). The Constitution provides for congressional elections every two years. And the 2-year life of each elected Congress typically consists of two formal 1-year sessions, each separated from the next by an "inter-session recess."

The Senate and the House also take breaks in the midst of a session. The Senate or the House announces any such "intra-session recess" by adopting a resolution stating that it will "adjourn" to a fixed date, a few days or weeks or even months later.

All agree that the phrase "the recess of the Senate" covers inter-session recesses. The question is whether it includes intra-session recesses as well.

In our view, the phrase "the recess" includes an intra-session recess of substantial length. Its words taken literally can refer to both types of recess. Founding-era dictionaries define the word "recess," much as we do today, simply as "a period of cessation from usual work."

We recognize that the word "the" in "*the* recess" might suggest that the phrase refers to the single break separating formal sessions of Congress. That is because the word "the" frequently (but not always) indicates "a particular thing." [The Court cites Samuel Johnson's Dictionary.] But the word can also refer "to a term used generically or universally." 17 OED 879. . . . Reading "the" generically in this way, there is no linguistic problem applying the Clause's phrase to both kinds of recess.

The constitutional text is thus ambiguous. And we believe the Clause's purpose demands the broader interpretation. The Clause gives the President authority to make appointments during "the recess of the Senate" so that the President can ensure the continued functioning of the Federal Government when the Senate is away.

History also offers strong support for the broad interpretation. We concede that pre-Civil War history is not helpful. But it shows only that Congress generally took long breaks between sessions, while taking no significant intra-session breaks at all (five times it took a break of a week or so at Christmas).

We are aware of, but we are not persuaded by, three important arguments to the contrary. First, some argue that the Founders would likely have intended the Clause to apply only to inter-session recesses, for they hardly knew any other. See, e.g., Brief for Originalist Scholars as Amici Curiae 27–29. Indeed, from the founding until the Civil War inter-session recesses were the only kind of significant recesses that Congress took. The problem with this argument, however, is that it does not fully describe the relevant founding intent. The question is not: Did the Founders at the time think about intra-session recesses? Perhaps they did not. The question is: Did the Founders intend to restrict the scope of the Clause to the form of congressional recess then prevalent, or did they intend a broader scope permitting the Clause to apply, where appropriate, to somewhat changed circumstances? The Founders knew they were writing a document designed to apply to ever-changing circumstances over centuries.

Second, some argue that the intra-session interpretation permits the President to make "illogic[ally]" long recess appointments. We agree that the intra-session interpretation permits somewhat longer recess appointments, but we do not agree that this consequence is "illogical." . . . [T]he Clause ensures that the President and Senate always have at least a full session to go through the nomination and confirmation process.

Third, the Court of Appeals believed that application of the Clause to intra-session recesses would introduce "vagueness" into a Clause that was otherwise clear. One can find problems of uncertainty, however, either way. In 1867, for example,

President Andrew Johnson called a special session of Congress, which took place during a lengthy intra-session recess. Consider the period of time that fell just after the conclusion of that special session. Did that period remain an intra-session recess, or did it become an inter-session recess?

The greater interpretive problem is determining how long a recess must be in order to fall within the Clause. Is a break of a week, or a day, or an hour too short to count as a "recess"? The Clause itself does not say. Even the Solicitor General, arguing for a broader interpretation, acknowledges that there is a lower limit applicable to both kinds of recess. He argues that the lower limit should be three days by analogy to the Adjournments Clause of the Constitution.

We agree with the Solicitor General that a 3-day recess would be too short. . . . The Adjournments Clause reflects the fact that a 3-day break is not a significant interruption of legislative business. As the Solicitor General says, it is constitutionally de minimis. A Senate recess that is so short that it does not require the consent of the House is not long enough to trigger the President's recess-appointment power.

[T]hough Congress has taken short breaks for almost 200 years, and there have been many thousands of recess appointments in that time, we have not found a single example of a recess appointment made during an intra-session recess that was shorter than 10 days. Nor has the Solicitor General.

We therefore conclude, in light of historical practice, that a recess of more than 3 days but less than 10 days is presumptively too short to fall within the Clause. We add the word "presumptively" to leave open the possibility that some very unusual circumstance—a national catastrophe, for instance, that renders the Senate unavailable but calls for an urgent response—could demand the exercise of the recess-appointment power during a shorter break. (It should go without saying—except that Justice Scalia compels us to say it—that political opposition in the Senate would not qualify as an unusual circumstance.)

In sum, we conclude that the phrase "the recess" applies to both intra-session and inter-session recesses. If a Senate recess is so short that it does not require the consent of the House, it is too short to trigger the Recess Appointments Clause. See Art. I, § 5, cl. 4. And a recess lasting less than 10 days is presumptively too short as well.

IV

The second question concerns the scope of the phrase "vacancies *that may happen* during the recess of the Senate." Art. II, § 2, cl. 3 (emphasis added). All agree that the phrase applies to vacancies that initially occur during a recess. But does it also apply to vacancies that initially occur before a recess and continue to exist during the recess? In our view the phrase applies to both kinds of vacancy.

We believe that the Clause's language, read literally, permits, though it does not naturally favor, our broader interpretation. We concede that the most natural meaning of "happens" as applied to a "vacancy" (at least to a modern ear) is that the vacancy "happens" when it initially occurs. See [Johnson's Dictionary] (defining "happen" in relevant part as meaning "[t]o fall out; to chance; to come to pass"). But that is not the only possible way to use the word.

We can still understand this earlier use of "happen" if we think of it used together with another word that, like "vacancy," can refer to a continuing state, say, a financial crisis. A statute that gives the President authority to act in respect to "any financial crisis that may happen during his term" can easily be interpreted to include crises that arise before, and continue during, that term. Perhaps that is why the Oxford English Dictionary defines "happen" in part as "chance to be," rather than "chance to occur." 6 OED 1096 (emphasis added); *see also* 19 OED 383 (defining "vacancy" as the "condition of an office or post being . . . vacant").

In any event, the linguistic question here is not whether the phrase can be, but whether it must be, read more narrowly. The question is whether the Clause is ambiguous. And the broader reading, we believe, is at least a permissible reading of a "doubtful" phrase. We consequently go on to consider the Clause's purpose and historical practice.

The Clause's purpose strongly supports the broader interpretation. That purpose is to permit the President to obtain the assistance of subordinate officers when the Senate, due to its recess, cannot confirm them.

We do not agree with Justice Scalia's suggestion that the Framers would have accepted the catastrophe envisioned by [Attorney General] Wirt [in 1823] because Congress can always provide for acting officers, see 5 U. S. C. §3345, and the President can always convene a special session of Congress, see U. S. Const., Art. II, §3. Acting officers may have less authority than Presidential appointments. 6 Op. OLC 119, 121 (1982). Moreover, to rely on acting officers would lessen the President's ability to staff the Executive Branch with people of his own choosing, and thereby limit the President's control and political accountability. *Cf. Free Enterprise Fund v. Public Company Accounting Oversight Bd.*, 561 U. S. 477–498 (2010). Special sessions are burdensome (and would have been especially so at the time of the founding). The point of the Recess Appointments Clause was to avoid reliance on these inadequate expedients.

At the same time, we recognize one important purpose-related consideration that argues in the opposite direction. A broad interpretation might permit a President to avoid Senate confirmations as a matter of course. If the Clause gives the President the power to "fill up all vacancies" that occur before, and continue to exist during, the Senate's recess, a President might not submit any nominations to the Senate. He might simply wait for a recess and then provide all potential nominees with recess appointments. He might thereby routinely avoid the constitutional need to obtain the Senate's "advice and consent."

Wirt thought considerations of character and politics would prevent Presidents from abusing the Clause in this way. . . . It is often less desirable for a President to make a recess appointment. A recess appointee only serves a limited term. That, combined with the lack of Senate approval, may diminish the recess appointee's ability, as a practical matter, to get a controversial job done. And even where the President and Senate are at odds over politically sensitive appointments, compromise is normally possible.

While we concede that both interpretations carry with them some risk of undesirable consequences, we believe the narrower interpretation risks undermining constitutionally conferred powers more seriously and more often. It would prevent the President from making any recess appointment that arose before a recess, no matter who the official, no matter how dire the need, no matter how uncontroversial the appointment, and no matter how late in the session the office fell vacant.

Historical practice over the past 200 years strongly favors the broader interpretation. The tradition of applying the Clause to pre-recess vacancies dates at least to President James Madison.

In light of some linguistic ambiguity, the basic purpose of the Clause, and the historical practice we have described, we conclude that the phrase "all vacancies" includes vacancies that come into existence while the Senate is in session.

V

The third question concerns the calculation of the length of the Senate's "recess."

The Solicitor General argues that we must treat the pro forma sessions as periods of recess. He says that these "sessions" were sessions in name only because the Senate was in recess as a functional matter.

In our view, however, the pro forma sessions count as sessions, not as periods of recess. We hold that, for purposes of the Recess Appointments Clause, the Senate is in session when it says it is, provided that, under its own rules, it retains the capacity to transact Senate business.

Applying this standard, we find that the pro forma sessions were sessions for purposes of the Clause. First, the Senate said it was in session. Second, the Senate's rules make clear that during its pro forma sessions, despite its resolution that it would conduct no business, the Senate retained the power to conduct business. During any pro forma session, the Senate could have conducted business simply by passing a unanimous consent agreement. By way of contrast, we do not see how the Senate could conduct business during a recess. It could terminate the recess and then, when in session, pass a bill. But in that case, of course, the Senate would no longer be in recess. It would be in session. And that is the crucial point. Senate rules make clear that, once in session, the Senate can act even if it has earlier said that it would not.

We do not believe . . . that engaging in the kind of factual appraisal that the Solicitor General suggests is either legally or practically appropriate.

Justice Scalia, with whom The Chief Justice, Justice Thomas, and Justice Alito join, concurring in the judgment.

To prevent the President's recess-appointment power from nullifying the Senate's role in the appointment process, the Constitution cabins that power in two significant ways. First, it may be exercised only in "the Recess of the Senate," that is, the intermission between two formal legislative sessions. Second, it may be used to fill only those vacancies that "happen during the Recess," that is, offices that become vacant during that intermission. Both conditions are clear from the Constitution's text and structure, and both were well understood at the founding.

I. Our Responsibility

Of course, where a governmental practice has been open, widespread, and unchallenged since the early days of the Republic, the practice should guide our interpretation of an ambiguous constitutional provision. *See, e.g., . . . Youngstown Sheet & Tube Co. v. Sawyer*, 343 U. S. 579, 610 (1952) (Frankfurter, J., concurring) (arguing that "a systematic, unbroken, executive practice, long pursued to the knowledge of the Congress and never before questioned" should inform interpretation of the "Executive Power" vested in the President) . . . . Plainly, then, a self-aggrandizing practice adopted by one branch well after the founding, often challenged, and never before blessed by this Court—in other words, the sort of practice on which the majority relies in this case—does not relieve us of our duty to interpret the Constitution in light of its text, structure, and original understanding.

Ignoring our more recent precedent in this area, which is extensive, the majority relies on *The Pocket Veto Case*, 279 U. S. 655, 689 (1929), for the proposition that when interpreting a constitutional provision "regulating the relationship between Congress and the President," we must defer to the settled practice of the political branches if the provision is "in any respect of doubtful meaning." The language the majority quotes from that case was pure dictum. The Pocket Veto Court had to decide whether a bill passed by the House and Senate and presented to the President less than 10 days before the adjournment of the first session of a particular Congress, but neither signed nor vetoed by the President, became a law. Most of the opinion analyzed that issue like any other legal question and concluded that treating the bill as a law would have been inconsistent with the text and structure of the Constitution. Only near the end of the opinion did the Court add that its conclusion was "confirmed" by longstanding Presidential practice in which Congress appeared to have acquiesced. 279 U. S., at 688–689. We did not suggest that the case would have come out differently had the longstanding practice been otherwise.[1]

II. Intra-Session Breaks

The first question presented is whether "the Recess of the Senate," during which the President's recess-appointment power is active, is (a) the period between two

---

1. The other cases cited by the majority in which we have afforded significant weight to historical practice, at 8, are consistent with the principles described above. Nearly all involved venerable and unchallenged practices, and constitutional provisions that were either deeply ambiguous or plainly supportive of the practice.

of the Senate's formal sessions, or (b) any break in the Senate's proceedings. I would hold that "the Recess" is the gap between sessions and that the appointments at issue here are invalid because they undisputedly were made during the Senate's session.

A. Plain Meaning

A sensible interpretation of the Recess Appointments Clause should start by recognizing that the Clause uses the term "Recess" in contradistinction to the term "Session." As Alexander Hamilton wrote: "The time within which the power is to operate 'during the recess of the Senate' and the duration of the appointments 'to the end of the next session' of that body, conspire to elucidate the sense of the provision." The Federalist No. 67, p. 455 (J. Cooke ed. 1961).

In the founding era, the terms "recess" and "session" had well-understood meanings in the marking-out of legislative time. . . . The period between two sessions was known as "the recess." . . . By contrast, other provisions of the Constitution use the verb "adjourn" rather than "recess" to refer to the commencement of breaks during a formal legislative session. See, e.g., Art. I, § 5, cl. 1; id., § 5, cl. 4.

More importantly, neither the Solicitor General nor the majority argues that the Clause uses "session" in its loose, colloquial sense. And if "the next Session" denotes a formal session, then "the Recess" must mean the break between formal sessions. As every commentator on the Clause until the 20th century seems to have understood, the "Recess" and the "Session" to which the Clause refers are mutually exclusive, alternating states.

Besides being linguistically unsound, the majority's reading yields the strange result that an appointment made during a short break near the beginning of one official session will not terminate until the end of the following official session, enabling the appointment to last for up to two years. . . . The Clause's self-evident design is to have the President's unilateral appointment last only until the Senate has "had an opportunity to act on the subject." 3 J. Story, Commentaries on the Constitution of the United States § 1551, p. 410 (1833) (emphasis added).

One way to avoid the linguistic incongruity of the majority's reading would be to read both "the Recess" and "the next Session" colloquially, so that the recess-appointment power would be activated during any temporary suspension of Senate proceedings, but appointments made pursuant to that power would last only until the beginning of the next suspension (which would end the next colloquial session). That approach would be more linguistically defensible than the majority's. But it would not cure the most fundamental problem with giving "Recess" its colloquial, rather than its formal, meaning: Doing so leaves the recess-appointment power without a textually grounded principle limiting the time of its exercise.

The dictionary definitions of "recess" on which the majority relies provide no such principle. On the contrary, they make clear that in colloquial usage, a recess could include any suspension of legislative business, no matter how short. See 2 S. Johnson, A Dictionary of the English Language 1602 (4th ed. 1773). Webster even provides a stark illustration: "[T]he house of representatives had a recess of half an hour." 2 Webster, supra. The notion that the Constitution empowers the President to make unilateral appointments every time the Senate takes a half-hour lunch break is so absurd as to be self-refuting. But that, in the majority's view, is what the text authorizes.

The boundlessness of the colloquial reading of "the Recess" thus refutes the majority's assertion that the Clause's "purpose" of "ensur[ing] the continued functioning of the Federal Government" demands that it apply to intra-session breaks as well as inter-session recesses. The majority disregards another self-evident purpose of the Clause: to preserve the Senate's role in the appointment process — which the founding generation regarded as a critical protection against "'despotism,'" Freytag, 501 U. S., at 883 — by clearly delineating the times when the President can appoint officers without the Senate's consent. Today's decision seriously undercuts that purpose. In doing so, it demonstrates the folly of interpreting constitutional provisions designed to establish "a structure of government that would protect liberty," Bowsher, 478 U. S., at 722, on the narrow-minded assumption that their only purpose is to make the government run as efficiently as possible. "Convenience and efficiency," we have repeatedly recognized, "are not the primary objectives" of our constitutional framework. Free Enterprise Fund, 561 U. S., at 499 (internal quotation marks omitted).

Relatedly, the majority contends that the Clause's supposed purpose of keeping the wheels of government turning demands that we interpret the Clause to maintain its relevance in light of the "new circumstance" of the Senate's taking an increasing number of intra-session breaks that exceed three days.

Even if I accepted the canard that courts can alter the Constitution's meaning to accommodate changed circumstances, I would be hard pressed to see the relevance of that notion here. The rise of intra-session adjournments has occurred in tandem with the development of modern forms of communication and transportation that mean the Senate "is always available" to consider nominations, even when its Members are temporarily dispersed for an intra-session break.

To avoid the absurd results that follow from its colloquial reading of "the Recess," the majority is forced to declare that some intra-session breaks — though undisputedly within the phrase's colloquial meaning — are simply "too short to trigger the Recess Appointments Clause." But it identifies no textual basis whatsoever for limiting the length of "the Recess," nor does it point to any clear standard for determining how short is too short.

Even if the many questions raised by the majority's failure to articulate a standard could be answered, a larger question would remain: If the Constitution's text empowers the President to make appointments during any break in the Senate's proceedings, by what right does the majority subject the President's exercise of that power to vague, court-crafted limitations with no textual basis?

An interpretation that calls for this kind of judicial adventurism cannot be correct.

B. Historical Practice

The historical practice of the political branches is, of course, irrelevant when the Constitution is clear. But even if the Constitution were thought ambiguous on this point, history does not support the majority's interpretation. . . .

What does all this amount to? In short: Intra-session recess appointments were virtually unheard of for the first 130 years of the Republic, were deemed unconstitutional by the first Attorney General to address them, were not openly defended by the Executive until 1921, were not made in significant numbers until after World War II, and have been repeatedly criticized as unconstitutional by Senators of both parties. It is astonishing for the majority to assert that this history lends "strong support," ante, at 11, to its interpretation of the Recess Appointments Clause.

III. Pre-Recess Vacancies

I would hold that the recess-appointment power is limited to vacancies that arise during the recess in which they are filled.

A. Plain Meaning

As the majority concedes, "the most natural meaning of 'happens' as applied to a 'vacancy' . . . is that the vacancy 'happens' when it initially occurs." The majority adds that this meaning is most natural "to a modern ear," but it fails to show that founding-era ears heard it differently. "Happen" meant then, as it does now, "[t]o fall out; to chance; to come to pass." 1 Johnson, Dictionary of the English Language 913. Thus, a vacancy that happened during the Recess was most reasonably understood as one that arose during the recess. It was, of course, possible in certain contexts for the word "happen" to mean "happen to be" rather than "happen to occur," as in the idiom "it so happens." But that meaning is not at all natural when the subject is a vacancy, a state of affairs that comes into existence at a particular moment in time.

In any event, no reasonable reader would have understood the Recess Appointments Clause to use the word "happen" in the majority's "happen to be" sense, and thus to empower the President to fill all vacancies that might exist during a recess, regardless of when they arose. For one thing, the Clause's language would have been a surpassingly odd way of giving the President that power. The Clause easily could have been written to convey that meaning clearly: It could have referred to "all Vacancies that may exist during the Recess," or it could have omitted the qualifying phrase entirely and simply authorized the President to "fill up all Vacancies during the Recess." Given those readily available alternative phrasings, the reasonable reader might have wondered, why would any intelligent drafter intending the majority's reading have inserted the words "that may happen" — words that, as the majority admits, make the majority's desired reading awkward and unnatural, and that must be effectively read out of the Clause to achieve that reading?

The original understanding of the Clause was consistent with what the majority concedes is the text's "most natural meaning." In 1792, Attorney General Edmund Randolph, who had been a leading member of the Constitutional Convention, provided the Executive Branch's first formal interpretation of the Clause. He advised President Washington that the Constitution did not authorize a recess appointment to fill the office of Chief Coiner of the United States Mint, which had been created by Congress on April 2, 1792, during the Senate's session.

The majority, however, relies heavily on a contrary account of the Clause given by Attorney General William Wirt in 1823. Wirt notably began—as does the majority—by acknowledging that his predecessors' reading was "most accordant with the letter of the constitution." But he thought the "most natural" reading had to be rejected because it would interfere with the "substantial purpose of the constitution," namely, "keep[ing] . . . offices filled." He was chiefly concerned that giving the Clause its plain meaning would produce "embarrassing inconveniences" if a distant office were to become vacant during the Senate's session, but news of the vacancy were not to reach the President until the recess.

[T]he Constitution provides ample means, short of rewriting its text, for dealing with the hypothetical dilemma Wirt posed. Congress can authorize "acting" officers to perform the duties associated with a temporarily vacant office—and has done that, in one form or another, since 1792. And on "extraordinary Occasions" the President can call the Senate back into session to consider a nomination. Art. II, § 3. If the Framers had thought those options insufficient and preferred to authorize the President to make recess appointments to fill vacancies arising late in the session, they would have known how to do so.

More fundamentally, Wirt and the majority are mistaken to say that the Constitution's "'substantial purpose'" is to "'keep . . . offices filled.'" The Constitution is not a road map for maximally efficient government, but a system of "carefully crafted restraints" designed to "protect the people from the improvident exercise of power."

B. Historical Practice

For the reasons just given, it is clear that the Constitution authorizes the President to fill unilaterally only those vacancies that arise during a recess, not every vacancy that happens to exist during a recess. Again, however, the majority says "[h]istorical practice" requires the broader interpretation. And again the majority is mistaken. Even if the Constitution were wrongly thought to be ambiguous on this point, a fair recounting of the relevant history does not support the majority's interpretation.

In sum: Washington's and Adams' Attorneys General read the Constitution to restrict recess appointments to vacancies arising during the recess, and there is no evidence that any of the first four Presidents consciously departed from that reading. The contrary reading was first defended by an executive official in 1823, was vehemently rejected by the Senate in 1863, was vigorously resisted by legislation in place from 1863 until 1940, and is arguably inconsistent with legislation in place from 1940 to the present. The Solicitor General has identified only about 100 appointments that have ever been made under the broader reading, and while it seems likely that a good deal more have been made in the last few decades, there is good reason to doubt that many were made before 1940 (since the appointees could not have been compensated). I can conceive of no sane constitutional theory under which this evidence of "historical practice"—which is actually evidence of a long-simmering inter-branch conflict—would require us to defer to the views of the Executive Branch.

IV. Conclusion

What the majority needs to sustain its judgment is an ambiguous text and a clear historical practice. What it has is a clear text and an at-best-ambiguous historical practice. Even if the Executive could accumulate power through adverse possession by engaging in a consistent and unchallenged practice over a long period of time, the oft-disputed practices at issue here would not meet that standard.

EXERCISE 10:

Consider the following questions in connection with *NLRB v. Noel Canning*:

1. How did the majority read the text of the Recess Appointments Clause? How did the concurrence-in-judgment?

2. What meaning does "that may happen" add to the meaning of the Recess Appointments Clause, according to the Court? Is that reading plausible?

3. What meaning does "that may happen" add to the meaning of the Recess Appointments Clause, according to the concurrence-in-judgment? Is that reading plausible?

4. What is the function of the "end of the next session" time limit on recess appointments, according to the Court? Is that assessment of function plausible?

5. What is the function of the "end of the next session" time limit on recess appointments, according to the concurrence-in-judgment? Is that assessment of function plausible?

6. Why according to the majority must an intra-session break be "substantial" in order to count as a Recess-Appointments-Clause recess? What does that mean?

7. Why does the Court use Founding-era dictionaries to interpret the Recess Appointments Clause, as opposed to dictionaries from today? Is the Court implicitly originalist?

8. Would it be possible for the President to reappoint a recess-appointee again under the Court's approach? Does it depend on the Senate's practices? What about the dissent's approach?

9. What is the role of subsequent practice history in constitutional interpretation, according to the majority? According to the concurrence-in-judgment?

One distinction that might be drawn—but which neither opinion did clearly—would be between *constitutive* and *epistemic* views of the relation of practice to constitutional interpretation. A common-law constitutionalist would say that the *object of interpretation*—the constitutional reality in virtue of which claims that "the Constitution prohibits X" or "the Constitution allows X" are true or false—consists in part of subsequent practice. To be contrary to subsequent practice, or to be consistent with subsequent practice, is part of *what it means to be* constitutionally required or allowed: our "constitutional ontology," on this reading, is spread out over time, with some bits located at the founding and some bits located later in history.

On the other hand, subsequent practice might be interpretively relevant *epistemically*—that is, as one of the considerations that tells us whether we *know* what the Constitution requires, even though the underlying reality in virtue of which those requirements exist is located only at the Founding itself, not in subsequent history. There are at least two ways that subsequent practice could be relevant to constitutional epistemology, but not constitutional ontology. First, early interpreters could be reliable guides to the original meaning. Second, the existence of historical practice might be epistemically relevant because it *raises the stakes*: the existence of reliance interests and other investments rooted in settled practice means that we should only enforce the original meaning in preference to these practices if we are very sure that we are right.

Note that these same three ways to understand subsequent practice—as constitutive, as reliable, or as raising the stakes—are also ways to understand subsequent judicial precedent. That is, judicial precedent might be seen as *part of the reality that makes constitutional requirements into constitutional requirements*—the constitutive/ontological option. Or, judicial precedent might be, epistemically, a reliable guide to original meaning. Finally, judicial precedent might be an important apple cart that we would not want to overturn unless we are very sure we need to do so in order to be faithful to the Constitution itself.

What evidence from the Court's opinion or the concurrence-in-judgment suggests one of these three approaches to subsequent practice? Which approach to subsequent practice seems best?

10. How did the majority and concurrence-in-judgment treat Justice Frankfurter's concurring opinion in *Youngstown*? We will cover *Youngstown* itself in Chapter 2, but Frankfurter's approach to interpretation—particularly the interaction of text and history—attracted the attention of all of the Justices in *Noel Canning*.

11. Is the majority's approach to the third issue—holding that pro-forma sessions interrupt a recess for the purpose of applying its rule limiting recess appointments to extended recesses—faithful to the quorum requirement of Art. I sec. 5 c. 1 ("a Majority of each shall constitute a Quorum to do Business; but a smaller Number may adjourn from day to day")? If only a few Senators are present such that the Senate may not constitutionally "do Business," what good is that to a President who needs a nominee confirmed quickly?

12. What technological assumptions underlie the Recess Appointments Clause? What about the Twenty-Fifth Amendment? Should these issues affect our interpretations?

13. As the Court notes, Congress did not take significant intra-session breaks until 1867. Is this change in congressional practice likely explained is part by changes in technology, such as the invention of the telegraph in 1838, which made it much easier to notify congressmen of the need to return to Washington? How worried should we be about the fact that the inapplicability of the Recess Appointments Clause to long intra-session breaks would "frustrate its purpose," if the same technological changes that made such intra-session breaks possible also render the Clause itself somewhat obsolete?

14. How would a broader recess-appointments power for the President affect the structure of executive power? Is it surprising to see Justice Scalia, the foremost proponent of a unitary executive in cases like *Morrison*, advocating a smaller recess-appointment power here?

D. PRESIDENTIAL COUNTERMANDING AUTHORITY

Free Enterprise Fund, building on earlier cases, derived the (qualified) presidential right to remove subordinates from his right to control them more generally. If a President may not, or does not, *fire* a lower-level executive official or agency, may he instead simply tell the official what to do? When may the President countermand other executive officials' decisions?

The independent counsel statute upheld in *Morrison v. Olson* was enacted following President Nixon's perceived abuse of the power to fire prosecutors and tell them what to do. On October 20, 1973 (the "Saturday Night Massacre") President Nixon fired his Attorney General Elliot Richardson and Deputy Attorney General William Ruckelhaus when they refused to fire Archibald Cox, the prosecutor investigating Watergate. Solicitor General (and Acting Attorney General) Robert Bork, later famous as a failed nominee to the Supreme Court for the seat now held by Justice Kennedy, agreed to fire Cox. Cox's replacement, Leon Jaworski, crossed swords with President Nixon as well. Jaworski's attempt to require the President to turn over his recordings of Oval Office conversations led to *United States v. Nixon*.

Nixon involved two very important issues of presidential power related to Jaworski's request. The first issue, considered here, was whether Nixon could simply *countermand* Jaworski's request by telling Jaworski not to ask for the tapes; this argument would have applied equally to Jaworski's attempt to get information from a private party with no particular claim to secrecy. We might call this an "internal" issue of executive power: within the executive branch, who is in charge? This is the sort of issue with which this Chapter has been concerned: the relationships of authority and relative autonomy among different executive officials. The second issue in *Nixon*, considered in Chapter 2, was whether Nixon could keep these conversations secret as part of "executive privilege"; this argument would have applied equally to the attempt by a private party, not subject to the President, to get information from the President, and could apply to the efforts of lower-level executive officials, not just the President, to keep secrets. This is an "external" issue of executive power: what can other branches do to extract information from the executive branch? First, however, the internal issues.

UNITED STATES v. NIXON

418 U.S. 683 (1974)

MR. CHIEF JUSTICE BURGER delivered the opinion of the Court.

This litigation presents for review the denial of a motion, filed in the District Court on behalf of the President of the United States ... to quash a third-party subpoena *duces tecum* issued by the United States District Court for the District of Columbia ... The subpoena directed the President to produce certain tape recordings and documents relating to his conversations with aides and advisers....

II. *JUSTICIABILITY*

In the District Court, the President's counsel argued that the court lacked jurisdiction to issue the subpoena because the matter was an intra-branch dispute between a subordinate and superior officer of the Executive Branch, and hence not subject to judicial resolution. That argument has been renewed in this Court with emphasis on the contention that the dispute does not present a "case" or "controversy" which can be adjudicated in the federal courts. The President's counsel argues that the federal courts should not intrude into areas committed to the other branches of Government.

He views the present dispute as essentially a "jurisdictional" dispute within the Executive Branch which he analogizes to a dispute between two congressional committees. Since the Executive Branch has exclusive authority and absolute discretion to decide whether to prosecute a case, *Confiscation Cases,* 7 Wall. [74 U.S.] 454 (1869); *United States v. Cox,* 342 F.2d 167, 171 (CA5), cert. *denied sub nom. Cox v. Hauber,* 381 U.S. 935 (1965), it is contended that a President's decision is final in determining what evidence is to be used in a given criminal case....

Under the authority of Art. II, §2, Congress has vested in the Attorney General the power to conduct the criminal litigation of the United States Government. 28 U.S.C. §516. It has also vested in him the power to appoint subordinate officers to assist him in the discharge of his duties. 28 U.S.C. §§509, 510, 515, 533. Acting pursuant to those statutes, the Attorney General has delegated the authority to represent the United States in these particular matters to a Special Prosecutor with unique authority and tenure.[8] The regulation gives the Special Prosecutor explicit power to contest the invocation of executive privilege in the process of seeking evidence deemed relevant to the performance of these specially delegated duties.

So long as this regulation is extant, it has the force of law. In *United States ex rel. Accardi v. Shaughnessy,* 347 U. S. 260 (1954), regulations of the Attorney General delegated certain of his discretionary powers to the Board of Immigration Appeals and required that Board to exercise its own discretion on appeals in deportation cases. The Court held that, so long as the Attorney General's regulations remained operative, he denied himself the authority to exercise the discretion delegated to the Board even though the original authority was his and he could reassert it by amending the regulations.

Here, as in *Accardi,* it is theoretically possible for the Attorney General to amend or revoke the regulation defining the Special Prosecutor's authority. But he has not done so.[10] So long as this regulation remains in force, the Executive Branch is bound by it, and indeed the United States, as the sovereign composed of the three branches, is bound to respect and to enforce it. Moreover, the delegation of authority to the Special Prosecutor in this case is not an ordinary delegation by the Attorney General to a subordinate officer: with the authorization of the President, the Acting Attorney General provided in the regulation that the Special Prosecutor was not to be removed without the "consensus" of eight designated leaders of Congress.

---

8. The regulation issued by the Attorney General pursuant to his statutory authority vests in the Special Prosecutor plenary authority to control the course of investigations and litigation related to "all offenses arising out of the 1972 Presidential Election for which the Special Prosecutor deems it necessary and appropriate to assume responsibility, allegations involving the President, members of the White House staff, or Presidential appointees, and any other matters which he consents to have assigned to him by the Attorney General." In particular, the Special Prosecutor was given full authority, *inter alia,* "to contest the assertion of *Executive Privilege' . . . and handl[e] all aspects of any cases within his jurisdiction." The regulation then goes on to provide:* "In exercising this authority, the Special Prosecutor will have the greatest degree of independence that is consistent with the Attorney General's statutory accountability for all matters falling within the jurisdiction of the Department of Justice. The Attorney General will not countermand or interfere with the Special Prosecutor's decisions or actions. The Special Prosecutor will determine whether and to what extent he will inform or consult with the Attorney General about the conduct of his duties and responsibilities. In accordance with assurances given by the President to the Attorney General that the President will not exercise his Constitutional powers to effect the discharge of the Special Prosecutor or to limit the independence that he is hereby given, the Special Prosecutor will not be removed from his duties except for extraordinary improprieties on his part and without the President's first consulting the Majority and the Minority Leaders and Chairmen and ranking Minority Members of the Judiciary Committees of the Senate and House of Representatives and ascertaining that their consensus is in accord with his proposed action."

10. At his confirmation hearings, Attorney General William Saxbe testified that he agreed with the regulation adopted by Acting Attorney General Bork, and would not remove the Special Prosecutor except for "gross impropriety." There is no contention here that the Special Prosecutor is guilty of any such impropriety.

EXERCISE 11:

Consider the following questions in connection with *United States v. Nixon*:

1. Why is the President required to repeal regulations in order to countermand the Special Counsel? Why should his request to be free from the duty to disclose the tapes not be deemed to amend those regulations?

2. The Court in footnote 10 relies in part on the Attorney General's statements during his confirmation hearing that "gross impropriety" would be required for removal of the special prosecutor. Do these promises have the "force of law"? Why not, if the regulations regarding the special prosecutor do?

3. Is the President allowed to delegate decisionmaking regarding the removal of prosecutors to members of Congress? As described in footnote 8, do the regulations do that? Constitutional restrictions on congressional exercise of executive power are covered in Chapter 3 below.

4. Does the Court in effect approve of the entrenchment of presidential decision-making? The President at time 1 seems to be allowed, under the Court's holding, to require the President at time 2 to exercise his executive power only by using particular words, i.e., words that would repeal the regulation at time 1. Entrenchment is generally not allowed in a legislative context. *See, e.g., United States v. Winstar*, 518 U.S. 839 (1996). Is there a good reason to allow a different rule for intertemporal exercises of *executive* power than for intertemporal exercises of *legislative* power?

5. The Court relies heavily on *United States ex rel. Accardi v. Shaughnessy*, a 1954 immigration case. The case involved some complications that the *Nixon* Court does not mention, but which might have been used to distinguish the holding. The regulations in *Accardi* involved a procedures with which the Attorney General was accused of interfering. Either the immigration statute or the Fifth Amendment— the *Accardi* Court referred briefly in its conclusion to "due process"—could have been construed to give the deportable individuals in the case an interest in the stability of procedures over time, a factor not present in *Nixon*. *Accardi* was also itself a 5–4 case; Justice Jackson in dissent would have held that even under the regulations at issue in the case, the Attorney General retained full discretion under the immigration statute to determine whether to suspend deportation.

6. What do you make of this argument by Gary Lawson?

No modern judicial decision specifically addresses the President's power either directly to make all discretionary decisions within the executive department or to nullify the actions of insubordinate subordinates. Instead, debate has focused almost exclusively on whether and when the President must have unlimited power to remove subordinate executive officials. That is an interesting and important question, but it does not address the central issue concerning the executive power. Even if the President has a constitutionally unlimited power to remove certain executive officials, that power alone does not satisfy the Article II Vesting Clause. If an official exercises power contrary to the President's directives and is then removed, one must still determine whether the official's exercise of power is legally valid. If the answer is "no," then the President necessarily has the power to nullify discretionary actions of subordinates, and removal is therefore not the President's sole power of control. If the answer is "yes," then the insubordinate ex-official will have effectively exercised executive power contrary to the President's wishes, which contravenes the vesting of that power in the President. A presidential removal power, even an unlimited removal power, is thus either constitutionally superfluous or constitutionally inadequate. [Footnote:] It is therefore constitutionally nonexistent as well.

The Rise and Rise of the Administrative State, 107 HARV. L. REV. 1231, 1244 & n.74 (1994). What is the relationship between removal power and countermanding power?

7. What duties do lower-level executive officials have when the President acts illegally? In Chapter 3 (particularly Exercise 23, Question 6) we will consider the idea of "executive review," analogous to "judicial review." *Marbury* roots judicial review in the Article VI oath. That oath, however, is taken by all officials. Do lower-level officials have a duty to disobey the President in cases of illegal conduct, or are they instead obliged to resign? What if the illegality is particularly clear?

Chapter 2

THE SCOPE OF EXECUTIVE POWER

A. INTRODUCTION

While **Chapter 1** concerned the internal structure of executive power—the President's relationship to subordinates within the executive branch—this chapter concerns the external boundary of executive power: what it does and does not encompass, particularly in relation to the powers of Congress.

Americans inherited from Britain a system that had fought over the boundary between legislative and executive power at least since 1215, when King John submitted to limits on his executive powers in the Magna Charta. Other limits over the monarch's powers—his ability to raise money in various ways, his power over subordinates like judges, his ability to detain subjects, and on and on—were imposed over time. Writing shortly before the American Revolution, Sir William Blackstone described the legislative power of Parliament as theoretically omnipotent. The king had a great many powers, but this was only because the legislative power had not (yet) been exerted to restrain them. If Parliament wanted to, Blackstone explained, it could reduce the king's powers as much as it liked. Because the king could veto legislation, however—and without any possibility of override—any reduction in royal power could only happen with his (or a predecessor's) consent. 1 WILLIAM BLACKSTONE, COMMENTARIES ON THE LAW OF ENGLAND 156 (1765) (Parliament can do "everything that is not naturally impossible"); JEAN LOUIS DE LOLME, THE CONSTITUTION OF ENGLAND 101 (2007) (orig. 1771) ("[I]t is a fundamental principle with the English Lawyers, that Parliament can do every thing, *except* making a Woman a Man, or a Man a Woman.").

Unlike Parliament, which had a general legislative power, the federal Congress was limited in Article I, section 1 to those legislative powers "herein granted." Many of these powers were, however, powers traditionally exercised by the British monarch: the power to declare war and the power to create offices, for instance. Many Founders interpreted the grant of "executive power"—without any "herein granted" qualifier"—to refer to the prerogative powers of the British monarch minus these powers given to Congress. Even Madison, who opposed extensive presidential power in many ways, wrote to Edmund Pendleton in 1789 that "the Executive power being in general terms vested in the President, all power of an Executive nature, not particularly taken away must belong to that department." Among those with this broad perspective, however, there were still enormous disagreement among the Framers about exactly what "power of an Executive nature" encompassed, as well as the extent of those powers "particularly taken away" and given to Congress.

The foundational case in this area, *Youngstown Sheet & Tube Co. v. Sawyer*, 343 U.S. 579 (1952), also known as *The Steel Seizure Cases*, poses the question of whether the President has only *express* executive power, or whether the President also possesses *inherent* executive power, and if so, how much. This long-standing question in constitutional law is caused by a number of factors: first, Article II, unlike Article I, is thin; second, the primary model for the President, the British King, performed a number of tasks not (clearly) enumerated in Article II, such as removal from office; third, it is difficult to define, a priori, what "executive Power" is; and, fourth, practical pressures, such as the President acting internationally, have tended to push toward recognition of inherent presidential power. Debates over the existence and extent of inherent executive power date to the beginning of the Republic, when Alexander Hamilton debated James Madison for and against expansive interpretations of executive power. *The Steel Seizure Cases* presented an attractive opportunity for the Supreme Court to acknowledge, and clarify the extent of, inherent president power — the President prosecuting a war. Did the Court do so?

The Steel Seizure Cases also provided the (default) governing analysis for the exercise of executive power in, surprisingly, Justice Jackson's *concurrence*. For most questions of executive power other than appointment and removal, you should use the Jackson's analysis. As you will see, this analysis will usually require you to determine whether the President's actions are justified by an enumerated or inherent executive power. The remainder of this Chapter covers these enumerated and inherent powers.

B. EMERGENCY EXECUTIVE POWER?

YOUNGSTOWN SHEET & TUBE CO. v. SAWYER

343 U.S. 579 (1952)

Justice Black delivered the opinion of the Court.

We are asked to decide whether the President was acting within his constitutional power when he issued an order directing the Secretary of Commerce to take possession of and operate most of the Nation's steel mills. The mill owners argue that the President's order amounts to lawmaking, a legislative function which the Constitution has expressly confided to the Congress and not to the President. The Government's position is that the order was made on findings of the President that his action was necessary to avert a national catastrophe which would inevitably result from a stoppage of steel production, and that in meeting this grave emergency the President was acting within the aggregate of his constitutional powers as the Nation's Chief

Executive and the Commander in Chief of the Armed Forces of the United States. The issue emerges here from the following series of events:

In the latter part of 1951, a dispute arose between the steel companies and their employees over terms and conditions that should be included in new collective bargaining agreements. Long-continued conferences failed to resolve the dispute. The Federal Mediation and Conciliation Service then intervened in an effort to get labor and management to agree. On April 4, 1952, the Union gave notice of a nation-wide strike called to begin at 12:01 a.m. April 9. The indispensability of steel as a component of substantially all weapons and other war materials led the President to believe that the proposed work stoppage would immediately jeopardize our national defense and that governmental seizure of the steel mills was necessary in order to assure the continued availability of steel. Reciting these considerations for his action, the President, a few hours before the strike was to begin, issued Executive Order 10340 The order directed the Secretary of Commerce to take possession of most of the steel mills and keep them running. The Secretary immediately issued his own possessory orders, calling upon the presidents of the various seized companies to serve as operating managers for the United States. They were directed to carry on their activities in accordance with regulations and directions of the Secretary. The next morning the President sent a message to Congress reporting his action. Twelve days later he sent a second message. Congress has taken no action.

Obeying the Secretary's orders under protest, the companies brought proceedings against him in the District Court. Their complaints charged that the seizure was not authorized by an act of Congress or by any constitutional provisions. The District Court was asked to declare the orders of the President and the Secretary invalid and to issue preliminary and permanent injunctions restraining their enforcement. Opposing the motion for preliminary injunction, the United States asserted that a strike disrupting steel production for even a brief period would so endanger the well-being and safety of the Nation that the President had "inherent power" to do what he had done — power "supported by the Constitution, by historical precedent, and by court decisions." Holding against the Government on all points, the District Court on April 30 issued a preliminary injunction restraining the Secretary from "continuing the seizure and possession of the plants . . . and from acting under the purported authority of Executive Order No. 10340." [T]he Court of Appeals stayed the District Court's injunction. Deeming it best that the issues raised be promptly decided by this Court, we granted certiorari on May 3 and set the cause for argument on May 12.

The President's power, if any, to issue the order must stem either from an act of Congress or from the Constitution itself. There is no statute that expressly authorizes the President to take possession of property as he did here. Nor is there any act of Congress to which our attention has been directed from which such a power can fairly be implied. Indeed, we do not understand the Government to rely on statutory authorization for this seizure. There are two statutes which do authorize the President to take both personal and real property under certain conditions. However, the Government admits that these conditions were not met and that the President's order was not rooted in either of the statutes.

Moreover, the use of the seizure technique to solve labor disputes in order to prevent work stoppages was not only unauthorized by any congressional enactment; prior to this controversy, Congress had refused to adopt that method of settling labor disputes. When the Taft-Hartley Act was under consideration in 1947, Congress rejected an amendment which would have authorized such governmental seizures in cases of emergency. Apparently it was thought that the technique of seizure, like that of compulsory arbitration, would interfere with the process of collective bargaining. Consequently, the plan Congress adopted in that Act did not provide for seizure under any circumstances. Instead, the plan sought to bring about settlements by use of the customary devices of mediation, conciliation, investigation by boards of inquiry, and public reports. In some instances temporary injunctions were authorized to provide cooling-off periods. All this failing, unions were left free to strike after a secret vote by employees as to whether they wished to accept their employers' final settlement offer.

It is clear that if the President had authority to issue the order he did, it must be found in some provision of the Constitution. And it is not claimed that express constitutional language grants this power to the President. The contention is that presidential power should be implied from the aggregate of his powers under the Constitution. Particular reliance is placed on provisions in Article II which say that "The executive Power shall be vested in a President"; that "he shall take Care that the Laws be faithfully executed"; and that he "shall be Commander in Chief of the Army and Navy of the United States."

The order cannot properly be sustained as an exercise of the President's military power as Commander in Chief of the Armed Forces. The Government attempts to do so by citing a number of cases upholding broad powers in military commanders engaged in day-to-day fighting in a theater of war. Such cases need not concern us here. Even though "theater of war" be an expanding concept, we cannot with faithfulness to our constitutional system hold that the Commander in Chief of the Armed Forces has the ultimate power as such to take possession of private property in order to keep labor disputes from stopping production. This is a job for the Nation's lawmakers, not for its military authorities.

Nor can the seizure order be sustained because of the several constitutional provisions that grant executive power to the President. In the framework of our Constitution, the President's power to see that the laws are faithfully executed refutes the idea that he is to be a lawmaker. The Constitution limits his functions in the lawmaking process to the recommending of laws he thinks wise and the vetoing of laws he thinks bad. And the Constitution is neither silent nor equivocal about who shall make laws which the President is to execute. The first section of the first article says that "All legislative Powers herein granted shall be vested in a Congress of the United States . . . ."

The President's order does not direct that a congressional policy be executed in a manner prescribed by Congress—it directs that a presidential policy be executed in a manner prescribed by the President. The preamble of the order itself, like that of many statutes, sets out reasons why the President believes certain policies should be adopted, proclaims these policies as rules of conduct to be followed, and again, like a statute, authorizes a government official to promulgate additional rules and regulations consistent with the policy proclaimed and needed to carry that policy into execution. The power of Congress to adopt such public policies as those proclaimed by the order is beyond question. The Constitution does not subject this law-making power of Congress to presidential or military supervision or control.

It is said that other Presidents without congressional authority have taken possession of private business enterprises in order to settle labor disputes. But even if this be true, Congress has not thereby lost its exclusive constitutional authority to make laws necessary and proper to carry out the powers vested by the Constitution "in the Government of the United States, or in any Department or Officer thereof."

The Founders of this Nation entrusted the law making power to the Congress alone in both good and bad times. It would do no good to recall the historical events, the fears of power and the hopes for freedom that lay behind their choice. Such a review would but confirm our holding that this seizure order cannot stand.

The judgment of the District Court is affirmed.

JUSTICE FRANKFURTER, concurring.

[The Framers] rested the structure of our central government on the system of checks and balances. For them the doctrine of separation of powers was not mere theory; it was a felt necessity. Not so long ago it was fashionable to find our system of checks and balances obstructive to effective government. It was easy to ridicule that system as outmoded—too easy. The experience through which the world has passed in our own day has made vivid the realization that the Framers of our Constitution were not inexperienced doctrinaires. These long-headed statesmen had no illusion that our people enjoyed biological or psychological or sociological immunities from the hazards of concentrated power. It is absurd to see a dictator in a representative product of the sturdy democratic traditions of the Mississippi Valley. The accretion of dangerous power does not come in a day. It does come, however slowly, from the generative force of unchecked disregard of the restrictions that fence in even the most disinterested assertion of authority.

The Framers, however, did not make the judiciary the overseer of our government. They were familiar with the revisory functions entrusted to judges in a few of the States and refused to lodge such powers in this Court. Judicial power can be exercised only as to matters that were the traditional concern of the courts at Westminster, and only if they arise in ways that to the expert feel of lawyers constitute "Cases" or "Controversies."

It is in this mood and with this perspective that the issue before the Court must be approached. We must therefore put to one side consideration of what powers the

President would have had if there had been no legislation whatever bearing on the authority asserted by the seizure, or if the seizure had been only for a short, explicitly temporary period, to be terminated automatically unless Congressional approval were given. These and other questions, like or unlike, are not now here. I would exceed my authority were I to say anything about them.

The question before the Court comes in this setting. Congress has frequently—at least 16 times since 1916—specifically provided for executive seizure of production, transportation, communications, or storage facilities. In every case it has qualified this grant of power with limitations and safeguards. In formulating legislation for dealing with industrial conflicts, Congress could not more clearly and emphatically have withheld authority than it did in 1947. Previous seizure legislation had subjected the powers granted to the President to restrictions of varying degrees of stringency. Instead of giving him even limited powers, Congress in 1947 deemed it wise to require the President, upon failure of attempts to reach a voluntary settlement, to report to Congress if he deemed [seizure necessary].

By the Labor Management Relations Act of 1947, Congress said to the President, "You may not seize. Please report to us and ask for seizure power if you think it is needed in a specific situation." This of course calls for a report on the unsuccessful efforts to reach a voluntary settlement, as a basis for discharge by Congress of its responsibility—which it has unequivocally reserved—to fashion further remedies than it provided. Absence of authority in the President to deal with a crisis does not imply want of power in the Government. Conversely the fact that power exists in the Government does not vest it in the President. The need for new legislation does not enact it. Nor does it repeal or amend existing law.

It is one thing to draw an intention of Congress from general language and to say that Congress would have explicitly written what is inferred, where Congress has not addressed itself to a specific situation. It is quite impossible, however, when Congress did specifically address itself to a problem, as Congress did to that of seizure, to find secreted in the interstices of legislation the very grant of power which Congress consciously withheld. To find authority so explicitly withheld is not merely to disregard in a particular instance the clear will of Congress. It is to disrespect the whole legislative process and the constitutional division of authority between President and Congress.

Apart from his vast share of responsibility for the conduct of our foreign relations, the embracing function of the President is that "he shall take Care that the Laws be faithfully executed . . . ." Art. II, § 3. The nature of that authority has for me been comprehensively indicated by Justice Holmes. "The duty of the President to see that the laws be executed is a duty that does not go beyond the laws or require him to achieve more than Congress sees fit to leave within his power." *Myers v. United States*, 272 U.S. 52, 177 (1926). The powers of the President are not as particularized as are those of Congress. But unenumerated powers do not mean undefined powers. The separation of powers built into our Constitution gives essential content to undefined provisions in the frame of our government.

To be sure, the content of the three authorities of government is not to be derived from an abstract analysis. The areas are partly interacting, not wholly disjointed. The Constitution is a framework for government. Therefore the way the framework has consistently operated fairly establishes that it has operated according to its true nature. Deeply embedded traditional ways of conducting government cannot supplant the Constitution or legislation, but they give meaning to the words of a text or supply them. It is an inadmissibly narrow conception of American constitutional law to confine it to the words of the Constitution and to disregard the gloss which life has written upon them. In short, a systematic, unbroken, executive practice, long pursued to the knowledge of the Congress and never before questioned, engaged in by Presidents who have also sworn to uphold the Constitution, making as it were such exercise of power part of the structure of our government, may be treated as a gloss on "executive Power" vested in the President by [Article II, § 1].

A scheme of government like ours no doubt at times feels the lack of power to act with complete, all-embracing, swiftly moving authority. No doubt a government with distributed authority, subject to be challenged in the courts of law, at least long enough to consider and adjudicate the challenge, labors under restrictions from which other governments are free. It has not been our tradition to envy such governments. In any event our government was designed to have such restrictions. The price was deemed not too high in view of the safeguards which these restrictions afford.

JUSTICE DOUGLAS, concurring.

We cannot decide this case by determining which branch of government can deal most expeditiously with the present crisis. The answer must depend on the allocation of powers under the Constitution. That in turn requires an analysis of the conditions giving rise to the seizure and of the seizure itself.

The legislative nature of the action taken by the President seems to me to be clear. When the United States takes over an industrial plant to settle a labor controversy, it is condemning property. But there is a duty to pay for all property taken by the Government. The command of the Fifth Amendment is that no "private property be taken for public use, without just compensation." That constitutional requirement has an important bearing on the present case.

The President has no power to raise revenues. That power is in the Congress by Article I, Section 8 of the Constitution. The President might seize and the Congress by subsequent action might ratify the seizure. But until and unless Congress acted, no condemnation would be lawful. The branch of government that has the power to pay compensation for a seizure is the only one able to authorize a seizure or make lawful one that the President had effected. That seems to me to be the necessary result of the condemnation provision in the Fifth Amendment.

JUSTICE JACKSON, concurring in the judgment and opinion of the Court.

[A]s we approach the question of presidential power, we half overcome mental hazards by recognizing them. The opinions of judges, no less than executives and publicists, often suffer the infirmity of confusing the issue of a power's validity with the cause it is invoked to promote, of confounding the permanent executive office with its temporary occupant. The tendency is strong to emphasize transient results upon policies—such as wages or stabilization—and lose sight of enduring consequences upon the balanced power structure of our Republic.

A judge, like an executive adviser, may be surprised at the poverty of really useful and unambiguous authority applicable to concrete problems of executive power as they actually present themselves. Just what our forefathers did envision, or would have envisioned had they foreseen modern conditions, must be divined from materials almost as enigmatic as the dreams Joseph was called upon to interpret for Pharaoh. A century and a half of partisan debate and scholarly speculation yields no net result but only supplies more or less apt quotations from respected sources on each side of any question. They largely cancel each other. And court decisions are indecisive because of the judicial practice of dealing with the largest questions in the most narrow way.

The actual art of governing under our Constitution does not and cannot conform to judicial definitions of the power of any of its branches based on isolated clauses or even single Articles torn from context. While the Constitution diffuses power the better to secure liberty, it also contemplates that practice will integrate the dispersed powers into a workable government. It enjoins upon its branches separateness but interdependence, autonomy but reciprocity. Presidential powers are not fixed but fluctuate, depending upon their disjunction or conjunction with those of Congress. We may well begin by a somewhat over-simplified grouping of practical situations in which a President may doubt, or others may challenge, his powers, and by distinguishing roughly the legal consequences of this factor of relativity.

1. When the President acts pursuant to an express or implied authorization of Congress, his authority is at its maximum, for it includes all that he possesses in his own right plus all that Congress can delegate. In these circumstances, and in these only, may he be said (for what it may be worth) to personify the federal sovereignty. If his act is held unconstitutional under these circumstances, it usually means that the Federal Government as an undivided whole lacks power. A seizure executed by the President pursuant to an Act of Congress would be supported by the strongest of presumptions and the widest latitude of judicial interpretation, and the burden of persuasion would rest heavily upon any who might attack it.

2. When the President acts in absence of either a congressional grant or denial of authority, he can only rely upon his own independent powers, but there is a zone of twilight in which he and Congress may have concurrent authority, or in which its distribution is uncertain. Therefore, congressional inertia, indifference or quiescence may sometimes, at least as a practical matter, enable, if not invite, measures on independent presidential responsibility. In this area, any actual test of power is likely to depend on the imperatives of events and contemporary imponderables rather than on abstract theories of law.

3. When the President takes measures incompatible with the expressed or implied will of Congress, his power is at its lowest ebb, for then he can rely only upon his

own constitutional powers minus any constitutional powers of Congress over the matter. Courts can sustain exclusive presidential control in such a case only by disabling the Congress from acting upon the subject. Presidential claim to a power at once so conclusive and preclusive must be scrutinized with caution, for what is at stake is the equilibrium established by our constitutional system.

Into which of these classifications does this executive seizure of the steel industry fit? It is eliminated from the first by admission, for it is conceded that no congressional authorization exists for this seizure. That takes away also the support of the many precedents and declarations which were made in relation, and must be confined, to this category.

Can it then be defended under flexible tests available to the second category? It seems clearly eliminated from that class because Congress has not left seizure of private property an open field but has covered it by three statutory policies inconsistent with this seizure. In cases where the purpose is to supply needs of the Government itself, two courses are provided: one, seizure of a plant which fails to comply with obligatory orders placed by the Government; another, condemnation of facilities, including temporary use under the power of eminent domain. The third is applicable where it is the general economy of the country that is to be protected rather than exclusive governmental interests. None of these were invoked. In choosing a different and inconsistent way of his own, the President cannot claim that it is necessitated or invited by failure of Congress to legislate upon the occasions, grounds and methods for seizure of industrial properties.

This leaves the current seizure to be justified only by the severe tests under the third grouping, where it can be supported only by any remainder of executive power after subtraction of such powers as Congress may have over the subject. In short, we can sustain the President only by holding that seizure of such strike-bound industries is within his domain and beyond control by Congress. Thus, this Court's first review of such seizures occurs under circumstances which leave presidential power most vulnerable to attack and in the least favorable of possible constitutional postures.

I did not suppose, and I am not persuaded, that history leaves it open to question, at least in the courts, that the executive branch, like the Federal Government as a whole, possesses only delegated powers. The purpose of the Constitution was not only to grant power, but to keep it from getting out of hand. However, because the President does not enjoy unmentioned powers does not mean that the mentioned ones should be narrowed by a niggardly construction. Some clauses could be made almost unworkable, as well as immutable, by refusal to indulge some latitude of interpretation for changing times. I have heretofore, and do now, give to the enumerated powers the scope and elasticity afforded by what seem to be reasonable, practical implications instead of the rigidity dictated by a doctrinaire textualism.

The Solicitor General seeks the power of seizure in three clauses of the Executive Article, the first reading, "The executive Power shall be vested in a President of the United States of America." Lest I be thought to exaggerate, I quote the interpretation which his brief puts upon it: "In our view, this clause constitutes a grant of all the executive powers of which the Government is capable." If that be true, it is difficult to see why the forefathers bothered to add several specific items, including some trifling ones.

The example of such unlimited executive power that must have most impressed the forefathers was the prerogative exercised by George III, and the description of its evils in the Declaration of Independence leads me to doubt that they were creating their new Executive in his image. And if we seek instruction from our own times, we can match it only from the executive powers in those governments we disparagingly describe as totalitarian. I cannot accept the view that this clause is a grant in bulk of all conceivable executive power but regard it as an allocation to the presidential office of the generic powers thereafter stated.

The clause on which the Government next relies is that "The President shall be Commander in Chief of the Army and Navy of the United States . . . ." These cryptic words have given rise to some of the most persistent controversies in our constitutional history. Of course, they imply something more than an empty title. But just what authority goes with the name has plagued presidential advisers who would not waive or narrow it by nonassertion yet cannot say where it begins or ends. It undoubtedly puts the Nation's armed forces under presidential command. Hence, this loose appellation is sometimes advanced as support for any presidential action, internal or external, involving use of force, the idea being that it vests power to do anything, anywhere, that can be done with an army or navy. That seems to be the logic of an argument tendered at our bar—that the President having, on his own responsibility, sent American troops abroad derives from that act "affirmative power" to seize the means of producing a supply of steel for them.

I cannot foresee all that it might entail if the Court should indorse this argument. Nothing in our Constitution is plainer than that declaration of a war is entrusted only to Congress. Assuming that we are in a war *de facto*, whether it is or is not a war *de jure*, does that empower the Commander-in-Chief to seize industries he thinks necessary to supply our army? The Constitution expressly places in Congress power "to raise and *support* Armies" and "to *provide* and *maintain* a Navy." This certainly lays upon Congress primary responsibility for supplying the armed forces.

There are indications that the Constitution did not contemplate that the title Commander-in-Chief *of the Army and Navy* will constitute him also Commander-in-Chief of the country, its industries and its inhabitants. He has no monopoly of "war powers," whatever they are. While Congress cannot deprive the President of the command of the army and navy, only Congress can provide him an army or navy to command. It is also empowered to make rules for the "Government and Regulation of land and naval Forces," by which it may to some unknown extent impinge upon even command functions.

That military powers of the Commander-in-Chief were not to supersede representative government of internal affairs seems obvious from the Constitution and from elementary American history. Time out of mind, and even now in many parts of the world, a military commander can seize private housing to shelter his troops. Not so, however, in the United States, for the Third Amendment says, "No Soldier shall, in time of peace be quartered in any house, without the consent of the Owner, nor in time of war, but in a manner to be prescribed by law." Thus, even in war time, his seizure of needed military housing must be authorized by Congress. It also was expressly left to Congress to "provide for calling forth the Militia to execute the Laws of the Union, suppress Insurrections and repel Invasions . . . ." [Art. I, §8, cl. 15.] Such a limitation on the command power, written at a time when the militia rather than a standing army was contemplated as the military weapon of the Republic, underscores the Constitution's policy that Congress, not the Executive, should control utilization of the war power as an instrument of domestic policy.

The third clause in which the Solicitor General finds seizure powers is that "he shall take Care that the Laws be faithfully executed." That authority must be matched against words of the Fifth Amendment that "No person shall be . . . deprived of life, liberty, or property, without due process of law." One gives a governmental authority that reaches so far as there is law, the other gives a private right that authority shall go no farther. These signify about all there is of the principle that ours is a government of laws, not of men, and that we submit ourselves to rulers only if under rules.

The Solicitor General lastly grounds support of the seizure upon nebulous, inherent powers never expressly granted but said to have accrued to the office from the customs and claims of preceding administrations. The plea is for a resulting power to deal with a crisis or an emergency according to the necessities of the case, the unarticulated assumption being that necessity knows no law. The vagueness and generality of the clauses that set forth presidential powers afford a plausible basis for pressures within and without an administration for presidential action beyond that supported by those whose responsibility it is to defend his actions in court.

The Solicitor General, acknowledging that Congress has never authorized the seizure here, says practice of prior Presidents has authorized it. He seeks color of legality from claimed executive precedents, chief of which is President Roosevelt's seizure of June 9, 1941, of the California plant of the North American Aviation Company. Its superficial similarities with the present case, upon analysis, yield to distinctions so decisive that it cannot be regarded as even a precedent, much less an authority for the present seizure.

In view of the ease, expedition and safety with which Congress can grant and has granted large emergency powers, certainly ample to embrace this crisis, I am quite unimpressed with the argument that we should affirm possession of them without statute. Such power either has no beginning or it has no end. If it exists, it need submit to no legal restraint. I am not alarmed that it would plunge us straightway into dictatorship, but it is at least a step in that wrong direction.

As to whether there is imperative necessity for such powers, it is relevant to note the gap that exists between the President's paper powers and his real powers. The

Constitution does not disclose the measure of the actual controls wielded by the modern presidential office. That instrument must be understood as an Eighteenth-Century sketch of a government hoped for, not as a blueprint of the Government that is. Vast accretions of federal power, eroded from that reserved by the States, have magnified the scope of presidential activity. Subtle shifts take place in the centers of real power that do not show on the face of the Constitution.

Executive power has the advantage of concentration in a single head in whose choice the whole Nation has a part, making him the focus of public hopes and expectations. In drama, magnitude and finality his decisions so far overshadow any others that almost alone he fills the public eye and ear. No other personality in public life can begin to compete with him in access to the public mind through modern methods of communications. By his prestige as head of state and his influence upon public opinion he exerts a leverage upon those who are supposed to check and balance his power which often cancels their effectiveness.

Moreover, rise of the party system has made a significant extraconstitutional supplement to real executive power. No appraisal of his necessities is realistic which overlooks that he heads a political system as well as a legal system. Party loyalties and interests, sometimes more binding than law, extend his effective control into branches of government other than his own and he often may win, as a political leader, what he cannot command under the Constitution.

The Executive, except for recommendation and veto, has no legislative power. The executive action we have here originates in the individual will of the President and represents an exercise of authority without law. No one, perhaps not even the President, knows the limits of the power he may seek to exert in this instance and the parties affected cannot learn the limit of their rights. We do not know today what powers over labor or property would be claimed to flow from Government possession if we should legalize it, what rights to compensation would be claimed or recognized, or on what contingency it would end. With all its defects, delays and inconveniences, men have discovered no technique for long preserving free government except that the Executive be under the law, and that the law be made by parliamentary deliberations.

Such institutions may be destined to pass away. But it is the duty of the Court to be last, not first, to give them up.

Justice Burton, concurring in both the opinion and judgment of the Court.

For the purposes of this case the most significant feature of that Act is its omission of authority to seize an affected industry. The debate preceding its passage demonstrated the significance of that omission. Collective bargaining, rather than governmental seizure, was to be relied upon. Seizure was not to be resorted to without specific congressional authority. Congress reserved to itself the opportunity to authorize seizure to meet particular emergencies.

The foregoing circumstances distinguish this emergency from one in which Congress takes no action and outlines no governmental policy. In the case before us,

Congress authorized a procedure which the President declined to follow. Instead, he followed another procedure which he hoped might eliminate the need for the first. Upon its failure, he issued an executive order to seize the steel properties in the face of the reserved right of Congress to adopt or reject that course as a matter of legislative policy.

This brings us to a further crucial question. Does the President, in such a situation, have inherent constitutional power to seize private property which makes congressional action in relation thereto unnecessary? We find no such power available to him under the present circumstances. The present situation is not comparable to that of an imminent invasion or threatened attack. We do not face the issue of what might be the President's constitutional power to meet such catastrophic situations. Nor is it claimed that the current seizure is in the nature of a military command addressed by the President, as Commander-in-Chief, to a mobilized nation waging, or imminently threatened with, total war.

JUSTICE CLARK, concurring in the judgment of the Court.

The limits of presidential power are obscure. I conclude that where Congress has laid down specific procedures to deal with the type of crisis confronting the President, he must follow those procedures in meeting the crisis; but that in the absence of such action by Congress, the President's independent power to act depends upon the gravity of the situation confronting the nation. Congress had prescribed methods to be followed by the President in meeting the emergency at hand. [The Defense Production Act of 1950, the Labor-Management Relations Act also called the Taft-Hartley Act, and the Selective Service Act of 1948] furnish the guideposts for decision in this case. [T]he hard fact remains that neither the Defense Production Act nor Taft-Hartley authorized the seizure challenged here, and the Government made no effort to comply with the procedures established by the Selective Service Act of 1948, a statute which expressly authorizes seizures when producers fail to supply necessary defense materiel.

CHIEF JUSTICE VINSON, with whom JUSTICES REED and MINTON join, dissenting.

The President of the United States directed the Secretary of Commerce to take temporary possession of the Nation's steel mills during the existing emergency because "a work stoppage would immediately jeopardize and imperil our national defense and the defense of those joined with us in resisting aggression, and would add to the continuing danger of our soldiers, sailors and airmen engaged in combat in the field." Because we cannot agree that affirmance is proper on any ground, and because of the transcending importance of the questions presented not only in this critical litigation but also to the powers the President and of future Presidents to act in time of crisis, we are compelled to register this dissent.

Those who suggest that this is a case involving extraordinary powers should be mindful that these are extraordinary times. A world not yet recovered from the devastation of World War II has been forced to face the threat of another and more terrifying global conflict.

The whole of the "executive Power" is vested in the President. Before entering office, the President swears that he "will faithfully execute the Office of President of the United States, and will to the best of [his] Ability, preserve, protect and defend the Constitution of the United States." Art. II, § 1.

In passing upon the grave constitutional question presented in this case, we must never forget, as Chief Justice Marshall admonished, that the Constitution is "intended to endure for ages to come, and, consequently, to be adapted to the various *crises* of human affairs," and that "[i]ts means are adequate to its ends."[28] Cases do arise presenting questions which could not have been foreseen by the Framers. In such cases, the Constitution has been treated as a living document adaptable to new situations. But we are not called upon today to expand the Constitution to meet a new situation. For, in this case, we need only look to history and time-honored principles of constitutional law—principles that have been applied consistently by all branches of the Government throughout our history. It is those who assert the invalidity of the Executive Order who seek to amend the Constitution in this case.

A review of executive action demonstrates that our Presidents have on many occasions exhibited the leadership contemplated by the Framers when they made the President Commander in Chief, and imposed upon him the trust to "take Care that the Laws be faithfully executed." With or without explicit statutory authorization, Presidents have at such times dealt with national emergencies by acting promptly and resolutely to enforce legislative programs, at least to save those programs until Congress could act. Congress and the courts have responded to such executive initiative with consistent approval.

Our first President displayed at once the leadership contemplated by the Framers. When the national revenue laws were openly flouted in some sections of Pennsylvania, President Washington, without waiting for a call from the state government, summoned the militia and took decisive steps to secure the faithful execution of the laws.[30] When international disputes engendered by the French revolution threatened to involve this country in war, and while congressional policy remained uncertain, Washington issued his Proclamation of Neutrality. Hamilton, whose defense of the Proclamation has endured the test of time, invoked the argument that the Executive has the duty to do that which will preserve the peace until Congress acts and, in addition, pointed to the need for keeping the Nation informed of the requirements of existing laws and treaties as part of the faithful execution of the laws.

President John Adams issued a warrant for the arrest of Jonathan Robbins in order to execute the extradition provisions of a treaty. Jefferson's initiative in the Louisiana Purchase, the Monroe Doctrine, and Jackson's removal of Government deposits from the Bank of the United States further serve to demonstrate by deed what the

---

28. *McCulloch v. Maryland*, 17 U.S. 316, 415, 424 (1819).

30. 4 Annals of Congress 1411, 1413 (1794).

Framers described by word when they vested the whole of the executive power in the President.

Without declaration of war, President Lincoln took energetic action with the outbreak of the War Between the States. He summoned troops and paid them out of the Treasury without appropriation therefor. He proclaimed a naval blockade of the Confederacy and seized ships violating that blockade. Congress, far from denying the validity of these acts, gave them express approval. The most striking action of President Lincoln was the Emancipation Proclamation, issued in aid of the successful prosecution of the War Between the States, but wholly without statutory authority.

In an action furnishing a most apt precedent for this case, President Lincoln without statutory authority directed the seizure of rail and telegraph lines leading to Washington. Many months later, Congress recognized and confirmed the power of the President to seize railroads and telegraph lines and provided criminal penalties for interference with Government operation. This Act did not confer on the President any additional powers of seizure. Congress plainly rejected the view that the President's acts had been without legal sanction until ratified by the legislature. Sponsors of the bill declared that its purpose was only to confirm the power which the President already possessed. Opponents insisted a statute authorizing seizure was unnecessary and might even be construed as limiting existing Presidential powers.

President Hayes authorized the wide-spread use of federal troops during the Railroad Strike of 1877. President Cleveland also used the troops in the Pullman Strike of 1895 and his action is of special significance. No statute authorized this action.

President Theodore Roosevelt seriously contemplated seizure of Pennsylvania coal mines if a coal shortage necessitated such action. In his autobiography, President Roosevelt expounded the "Stewardship Theory" of Presidential power, stating that "the executive is subject only to the people, and, under the Constitution, bound to serve the people affirmatively in cases where the Constitution does not explicitly forbid him to render the service." Because the contemplated seizure of the coal mines was based on this theory, then ex-President Taft criticized President Roosevelt in a passage in his book relied upon by the District Court in this case. WILLIAM HOWARD TAFT, OUR CHIEF MAGISTRATE AND HIS POWERS 139–47 (1916). In the same book, however, President Taft agreed that such powers of the President as the duty "to take Care that the Laws be faithfully executed" could not be confined to "express Congressional statutes." *Id.* at 88. *In re Neagle*, 135 U.S. 1 (1890), and *In re Debs*, 158 U.S. 564 (1895), were cited as conforming with Taft's concept of the office, as they were later to be cited with approval in his opinion as Chief Justice in *Myers v. United States*, 272 U.S. 52, 133 (1926).

In 1909, President Taft was informed that government-owned oil lands were being patented by private parties at such a rate that public oil lands would be depleted in a matter of months. Although Congress had explicitly provided that these lands were open to purchase by United States citizens, the President nevertheless ordered the lands withdrawn from sale "[i]n aid of proposed legislation." In *United States v. Midwest*

Oil Co., 236 U.S. 459 (1915), the President's action was sustained as consistent with executive practice throughout our history. [T]he situation confronting President Taft was described as "an emergency; there was no time to wait for the action of Congress."

During World War I, President Wilson established a War Labor Board without awaiting specific direction by Congress. [T]he Board had as its purpose the prevention of strikes and lockouts interfering with the production of goods needed to meet the emergency. Effectiveness of War Labor Board decision was accomplished by Presidential action, including seizure of industrial plants. Seizure of the Nation's railroads was also ordered by President Wilson.

Beginning with the Bank Holiday Proclamation and continuing through World War II, executive leadership and initiative were characteristic of President Franklin D. Roosevelt's administration. In 1941, President Roosevelt acted to protect Iceland from attack by Axis powers, when British forces were withdrawn, by sending our forces to occupy Iceland. Congress was informed of this action on the same day that our forces reached Iceland. The occupation of Iceland was but one of "at least 125 incidents" in our history in which Presidents, "without congressional authorization, and in the absence of a declaration of war, [have] ordered the Armed Forces to take action or maintain positions abroad."

Some six months before Pearl Harbor, a dispute at a single aviation plant at Inglewood, California, interrupted a segment of the production of military aircraft. In spite of the comparative insignificance of this work stoppage to total defense production as contrasted with the complete paralysis now threatened by a shutdown of the entire basic steel industry, and even though our armed forces were not then engaged in combat, President Roosevelt ordered the seizure of the plant "pursuant to the powers vested in [him] by the Constitution and laws of the United States, as President of the United States of America and Commander in Chief of the Army and Navy of the United States." The Attorney General (Jackson) vigorously proclaimed that the President had the moral duty to keep this Nation's defense effort a "going concern." His ringing moral justification was coupled with a legal justification equally well stated: "The Presidential proclamation rests upon the aggregate of the Presidential powers derived from the Constitution itself and from statutes enacted by the Congress . . . ."

This is but a cursory summary of executive leadership. But it amply demonstrates that Presidents have taken prompt action to enforce the laws and protect the country whether or not Congress happened to provide in advance for the particular method of execution. At the minimum, the executive actions reviewed herein sustain the action of the President in this case. And many of the cited examples of Presidential practice go far beyond the extent of power necessary to sustain the President's order to seize the steel mills. The fact that temporary executive seizures of industrial plants to meet an emergency have not been directly tested in this Court furnishes not the slightest suggestion that such actions have been illegal. Rather, the fact that

Congress and the courts have consistently recognized and given their support to such executive action indicates that such a power of seizure has been accepted throughout our history.

The broad executive power granted by Article II to an officer on duty 365 days a year cannot, it is said, be invoked to avert disaster. Instead, the President must confine himself to sending a message to Congress recommending action. Under this messenger-boy concept of the Office, the President cannot even act to preserve legislative programs from destruction so that Congress will have something left to act upon. There is no judicial finding that the executive action was unwarranted because there was in fact no basis for the President's finding of the existence of an emergency for, under this view, the gravity of the emergency and the immediacy of the threatened disaster are considered irrelevant as a matter of law.

Seizure of plaintiffs' property is not a pleasant undertaking. Similarly unpleasant to a free country are the draft which disrupts the home and military procurement which causes economic dislocation and compels adoption of price controls, wage stabilization and allocation of materials. The President informed Congress that even a temporary Government operation of plaintiffs' properties was "thoroughly distasteful" to him, but was necessary to prevent immediate paralysis of the mobilization program. Presidents have been in the past, and any man worthy of the Office should be in the future, free to take at least interim action necessary to execute legislative programs essential to survival of the Nation. A sturdy judiciary should not be swayed by the unpleasantness or unpopularity of necessary executive action, but must independently determine for itself whether the President was acting, as required by the Constitution, to "take Care that the Laws be faithfully executed."

[J]udicial, legislative and executive precedents throughout our history demonstrate that in this case the President acted in full conformity with his duties under the Constitution. Accordingly, we would reverse the order of the District Court.

EXERCISE 12:

Consider the following questions in connection with *Youngstown Sheet & Tube Co. v. Sawyer*:

1. Did the President have any statutory authority for his Executive Order?

2. What inference, if any, can reasonably be drawn from the rejection by Congress of an amendment to the Taft-Hartley Act which would have authorized the President to make seizures in the event of emergencies?

3. What argument, if any, is there that the Constitution *expressly* granted the President authority for his Executive Order? What textual provisions are pertinent to that analysis?

4. Justice Black noted: "It is said that other Presidents without congressional authority have taken possession of private business enterprises in order to settle labor disputes." Should that matter? Why or why not?

5. Justice Jackson identified three classes of cases spanning the spectrum of the "fluctuat[ing]" Presidential powers. What are the classes? From where did Justice Jackson draw these categories?

6. Into which of the three classes did the case at bar properly fall? Why?

7. Is Justice Jackson's analysis useful? What value does it add to evaluating whether the President possesses the power he claims in particular cases?

8. Justice Jackson asserted that the clause vesting the "executive Power" in the President must be read narrowly in order to preserve the meaning of "several specific items" addressed in Article II. Is that a fair reading of the Clause and/or of Article II as a whole? Could the specific items be explained in any other way? Is Justice Jackson's construction consistent with the view of this text articulated by the Court in *Myers* and/or *Humphrey's Executor*?

9. What textual argument, if any, is there against finding extraordinary executive authority in times of crisis? What policy argument, if any, is there against such powers?

10. Justice Jackson asserted that the "real powers" of the President include "[v]ast accretions of federal power, eroded from that reserved by the States." Are such accretions "that do not show on the face of the Constitution" proper? Why or why not?

11. Did Justices Douglas and Frankfurter, in their separate opinions, open the door to future Presidents to engage in seizures?

12. What is the "gloss" on the terms of the Constitution that Justice Frankfurter identified? Should that gloss control judicial construction of the Constitution? Why or why not? What are the criteria Justice Frankfurter implicitly applied to distinguish such gloss from routine, continuing disputes among the branches of government over the respective scopes of their authority?

13. Which approach presented by the different opinions best fits the role of the judiciary?

14. The dissenters asserted that there was a long history, dating back to the administration of President Washington, of executive action without prior legislative authorization. In contrast, Justice Jackson asserted that the only pertinent history consisted of a few examples in 1941. Do they disagree on the historical facts or only about the inferences to be drawn from the facts?

15. None of the opinions cited any prior judicial precedent. What conclusion should be drawn from the paucity of prior court opinions regarding the constitutionality of executive seizures in the absence of statutory authorization?

16. Was there a majority of justices who concluded that the President possesses inherent executive power (whether or not President Truman possessed inherent power in this case)?

17. What are the implications of this case for other claims of "inherent" authority of the President, or authority "implied" by (but not express in) the Constitution? How

should the Court respond to a claim that the President has inherent or implied authority to remove from office non-judicial officers without limitation? Are there some such officers as to whom the claimed power is stronger than with respect to other officers?

C. EXECUTIVE PRIVILEGE

A brief excerpt from *United States v. Nixon*, concerning the extent of the President's control over the special counsel, appeared in Chapter 1. Here, a longer excerpt from the case considers the extent of the President's right to keep his conversations secret. Because this is the sort of question that could arise even if all executive officials were in agreement, it does not relate only to relationships within the executive branch, but to the boundaries of the concept of "executive power." However, unlike the cases in Sections B and D, in which the President or other executive officials claimed the affirmative power to do something—the sort of case in which Justice Jackson's three categories are most paradigmatically relevant—executive privilege concerns the executive branch's power to shield itself from other branches' exercises of power.

UNITED STATES v. NIXON

418 U.S. 683 (1974)

MR. CHIEF JUSTICE BURGER delivered the opinion of the Court.

This litigation presents for review the denial of a motion, filed in the District Court on behalf of the President of the United States to quash a third-party subpoena *duces tecum* issued by the United States District Court for the District of Columbia . . . The subpoena directed the President to produce certain tape recordings and documents relating to his conversations with aides and advisers.

The District Court held that the judiciary, not the President, was the final arbiter of a claim of executive privilege. The court concluded that, under the circumstances of this case, the presumptive privilege was overcome by the Special Prosecutor's *prima facie* "demonstration of need sufficiently compelling to warrant judicial examination in chambers."

IV. *THE CLAIM OF PRIVILEGE*

A

[W]e turn to the claim that the subpoena should be quashed because it demands "confidential conversations between a President and his close advisors that it would be inconsistent with the public interest to produce." The first contention is a broad claim that the separation of powers doctrine precludes judicial review of a President's claim of privilege. The second contention is that, if he does not prevail on the claim of absolute privilege, the court should hold as a matter of constitutional law that the privilege prevails over the subpoena *duces tecum*.

In the performance of assigned constitutional duties, each branch of the Government must initially interpret the Constitution, and the interpretation of its powers by any branch is due great respect from the others. The President's counsel, as we have noted, reads the Constitution as providing an absolute privilege of confidentiality for all Presidential communications. Many decisions of this Court, however, have unequivocally reaffirmed the holding of Marbury v. Madison, 1 Cranch [5 U.S.] 137 (1803), that "[i]t is emphatically the province and duty of the judicial department to say what the law is." No holding of the Court has defined the scope of judicial power specifically relating to the enforcement of a subpoena for confidential Presidential communications for use in a criminal prosecution, but other exercises of power by the Executive Branch and the Legislative Branch have been found invalid as in conflict with the Constitution.

B

In support of his claim of absolute privilege, the President's counsel urges two grounds, one of which is common to all governments and one of which is peculiar to our system of separation of powers. The first ground is the valid need for protection of communications between high Government officials and those who advise and assist them in the performance of their manifold duties; the importance of this confidentiality is too plain to require further discussion. Human experience teaches that those who expect public dissemination of their remarks may well temper candor with a concern for appearances and for their own interests to the detriment of the decisionmaking process. Whatever the nature of the privilege of confidentiality of Presidential communications in the exercise of Art. II powers, the privilege can be said to derive from the supremacy of each branch within its own assigned area of constitutional duties. Certain powers and privileges flow from the nature of enumerated powers; the protection of the confidentiality of Presidential communications has similar constitutional underpinnings.

The second ground asserted by the President's counsel in support of the claim of absolute privilege rests on the doctrine of separation of powers. Here it is argued that the independence of the Executive Branch within its own sphere, *Humphrey's Executor v. United States*, 295 U. S. 602, 295 U. S. 629–630 (1935); *Kilbourn v. Thompson*, 103 U. S. 168, 103 U. S. 190–191 (1881), insulates a President from a judicial subpoena in an ongoing criminal prosecution, and thereby protects confidential Presidential communications.

However, neither the doctrine of separation of powers nor the need for confidentiality of high-level communications, without more, can sustain an absolute, unqualified Presidential privilege of immunity from judicial process under all circumstances. The President's need for complete candor and objectivity from advisers calls for great deference from the courts. However, when the privilege depends solely on the broad, undifferentiated claim of public interest in the confidentiality of such conversations, a confrontation with other values arises. Absent a claim of need to protect military, diplomatic, or sensitive national security secrets, we find it difficult to accept the argument that even the very important interest in confidentiality of Presidential communications is significantly diminished by production of such material for *in camera* inspection with all the protection that a district court will be obliged to provide.

The impediment that an absolute, unqualified privilege would place in the way of the primary constitutional duty of the Judicial Branch to do justice in criminal prosecutions would plainly conflict with the function of the courts under Art. III. In designing the structure of our Government and dividing and allocating the sovereign power among three co-equal branches, the Framers of the Constitution sought to provide a comprehensive system, but the separate powers were not intended to operate with absolute independence.

"While the Constitution diffuses power the better to secure liberty, it also contemplate that practice will integrate the dispersed powers into a workable government. It enjoins upon its branches separateness but interdependence, autonomy but reciprocity." *Youngstown Sheet & Tube Co. v. Sawyer,* 343 U.S. at 343 U. S. 635 (Jackson, J., concurring). To read the Art. II powers of the President as providing an absolute privilege as against a subpoena essential to enforcement of criminal statutes on no more than a generalized claim of the public interest in confidentiality of nonmilitary and nondiplomatic discussions would upset the constitutional balance of "a workable government" and gravely impair the role of the courts under Art. III.

C.

The expectation of a President to the confidentiality of his conversations and correspondence, like the claim of confidentiality of judicial deliberations, for example, has all the values to which we accord deference for the privacy of all citizens and, added to those values, is the necessity for protection of the public interest in candid, objective, and even blunt or harsh opinions in Presidential decisionmaking. A President and those who assist him must be free to explore alternatives in the process of shaping policies and making decisions, and to do so in a way many would be unwilling to express except privately. These are the considerations justifying a presumptive privilege for Presidential communications. The privilege is fundamental to the operation of Government, and inextricably rooted in the separation of powers under the Constitution.

But this presumptive privilege must be considered in light of our historic commitment to the rule of law. We have elected to employ an adversary system of criminal justice in which the parties contest all issues before a court of law. The need to develop all relevant facts in the adversary system is both fundamental and comprehensive. The ends of criminal justice would be defeated if judgments were to be founded on a partial or speculative presentation of the facts. The very integrity of the judicial system and public confidence in the system depend on full disclosure of all the facts, within the framework of the rules of evidence. To ensure that justice is done, it is imperative to the function of courts that compulsory process be available for the production of evidence needed either by the prosecution or by the defense.

[T]he Fifth Amendment to the Constitution provides that no man "shall be compelled in any criminal case to be a witness against himself." And, generally, an attorney or a priest may not be required to disclose what has been revealed in professional confidence. These and other interests are recognized in law by privileges against forced disclosure, established in the Constitution, by statute, or at common law. Whatever their origins, these exceptions to the demand for every man's evidence are not lightly created nor expansively construed, for they are in derogation of the search for truth.

In this case, the President challenges a subpoena served on him as a third party requiring the production of materials for use in a criminal prosecution; he does so on the claim that he has a privilege against disclosure of confidential communications. He does not place his claim of privilege on the ground they are military or diplomatic secrets.

No case of the Court has extended this high degree of deference to a President's generalized interest in confidentiality. Nowhere in the Constitution, as we have noted earlier, is there any explicit reference to a privilege of confidentiality, yet to the extent this interest relates to the effective discharge of a President's powers, it is constitutionally based.

The right to the production of all evidence at a criminal trial similarly has constitutional dimensions. The Sixth Amendment explicitly confers upon every defendant in a criminal trial the right "to be confronted with the witnesses against him" and "to have compulsory process for obtaining witnesses in his favor." Moreover, the Fifth Amendment also guarantees that no person shall be deprived of liberty without due process of law. It is the manifest duty of the courts to vindicate those guarantees, and to accomplish that it is essential that all relevant and admissible evidence be produced.

In this case, we must weigh the importance of the general privilege of confidentiality of Presidential communications in performance of the President's responsibilities against the inroads of such a privilege on the fair administration of criminal justice. The interest in preserving confidentiality is weighty indeed, and entitled to great respect. However, we cannot conclude that advisers will be moved to temper the candor of their remarks by the infrequent occasions of disclosure because of the possibility that such conversations will be called for in the context of a criminal prosecution.

On the other hand, the allowance of the privilege to withhold evidence that is demonstrably relevant in a criminal trial would cut deeply into the guarantee of due process of law and gravely impair the basic function of the court. A President's acknowledged need for confidentiality in the communications of his office is general in nature, whereas the constitutional need for production of relevant evidence in a criminal proceeding is specific and central to the fair adjudication of a particular criminal case in the administration of justice. Without access to specific facts, a criminal prosecution may be totally frustrated. The President's broad interest in confidentiality of communications will not be vitiated by disclosure of a limited number of conversations preliminarily shown to have some bearing on the pending criminal cases.

We conclude that, when the ground for asserting privilege as to subpoenaed materials sought for use in a criminal trial is based only on the generalized interest in confidentiality, it cannot prevail over the fundamental demands of due process of law in the fair administration of criminal justice. The generalized assertion of privilege must yield to the demonstrated, specific need for evidence in a pending criminal trial.

Affirmed.

Mr. Justice Rehnquist took no part in the consideration or decision of these cases.

EXERCISE 13:

1. What is the holding of the Court?

2. Did the Court recognize the existence of executive privilege? Given that the President lost the case, would the executive branch ever have a reason to cite it? Does the Court give a convincing explanation for its holding here?

3. What does the Constitution say explicitly about the flow of information within the executive branch? What inference should we draw from this provision?

4. What does the Constitution say explicitly about the flow of information between within the branches? What inference should we draw from this provision?

5. The Court does not delve significantly into historical materials. They give some support to an absolute claim of privilege. The Federalist no. 70, for instance, refers to "secrecy and dispatch" as executive characteristics. Does that make sense if Congress or the courts can learn the President's secrets? While *Nixon* cites *Marbury*'s holding on judicial review, the issue of executive-branch communications was also discussed by the Court, according to the court reporter in *Marbury*. "Confidential" executive information was outside the scope of proper judicial inquiry, but other information was not. "The court said that if Mr. Lincoln wished time to consider what answers he should make, they would give him time; but they had no doubt he ought to answer. There was nothing confidential required to be disclosed. If there had been, he was not obliged to answer it; and if he thought that any thing was communicated to him in confidence he was not bound to disclose it; nor was he obliged to state anything which would criminate himself; but that the fact whether such commissions had been in the office or not, could not be a confidential fact; it is a fact which all the world have a right to know." *Marbury v. Madison*, 5 U.S. 137, 144–45 (1803).

6. Does the Court give a convincing explanation for why the executive-privilege claim fails in this case? Would these arguments work in the context of the privilege against self-incrimination or the attorney-client privilege? Lawyers may not divulge their client's communications even if it means that an innocent man is in jail as a

result. Alton Logan, for instance, spent twenty-six years in prison for murder because the real killer, Andrew Wilson, had authorized his lawyers to make Wilson's guilt public only after Wilson had died. Legal ethics experts approved Wilson's lawyers' decision. See http://www.cbsnews.com/news/26-year-secret-kept-innocent-man -in-prison/ (60 Minutes report). Attorney-client privilege, that is, requires layers to "withhold evidence that is demonstrably relevant in a criminal trial." Why should executive privilege be different?

7. The President and other executive officials have made other claims for special rights. The President himself is absolutely immune from liability for official acts he takes as President under *Nixon v. Fitzgerald*, 457 U.S. 731 (1982), but under *Harlow v. Fitzgerald*, 457 U.S. 800 (1982), lower-level executive officials receive only "qualified immunity," i.e., immunity as long as they act reasonably. The President may be sued civilly during his tenure in office under *Clinton v. Jones*, 520 U.S. 681 (1997). Whether he may be prosecuted criminally while in office has long been unclear. What inference should we draw from the reference to criminal liability following impeachment in Art. I, § 3, cl. 7?

8. Even if the President is free from prosecution, would others be allowed to detain him forcibly if, say, he went insane and was killing people in the streets? Senator William Maclay records a discussion he had in the Senate on September 26, 1789, with Vice President John Adams, Senator Oliver Ellsworth (later Chief Justice), and Senator Philip Schuyler (also Alexander Hamilton's father-in-law):

> [Adams and Ellsworth contended that] the President, personally, was not the subject to any process whatever; could have no action whatever brought against him; was above the power of all judges, justices, etc. For what, said they, would you put it in the power of a common justice to exercise any authority over him and stop the whole machine of Government? I said that, although President, he is not above the laws. Both of them declared you could only impeach him, and no other process whatever lay against him. I put the case: "Suppose the President committed murder in the street. Impeach him? But you can only remove him from office on impeachment. Why, when he is no longer President you can indict him. But in the meantime he runs away. But I will put up another case. Suppose he continues his murders daily, and neither House is sitting to impeach him. Oh, the people would rise and restrain him. Very well, you will allow the mob to do what legal justice must abstain from." Mr. Adams said I was arguing from cases nearly impossible. There had been some hundreds of crowned heads within these two centuries in Europe, and there was no instance of any of them having committed murder. Very true, in the retail way, Charles IX of France excepted. They generally do these things on a great scale. I am, however, certainly within the bounds of possibility, though it may be improbable. General Schuyler joined us. "What think you, General?" said I, by way of giving the matter a different turn. "I am not a good civilian, but I think the President a kind of sacred person." Bravo,

my "jure divino" man! Not a word of the above is worth minuting, but it shows clearly how amazingly fond of the old leaven many people are. I needed no index, however, of this kind with respect to John Adams.

JOURNAL OF WILLIAM MACLAY 167 (1890). Which side had the better of this argument?

9. If the President had prevailed on his executive-privilege claim, would Congress have had any remedy? Would it have been permitted to draw an adverse inference about the President's guilt in an impeachment proceeding? The Constitution gives the House the "sole power of impeachment" in Art. I, § 2, ¶ 5 and the Senate "the sole Power to try all Impeachments" in Art. I, § 3, ¶ 6. Art. I, § 3, ¶ 7 provides that "Judgment in Cases of Impeachment shall not extend further than to removal from Office, and disqualification to hold and enjoy any Office of honor, Trust or Profit under the United States: but the Party convicted shall nevertheless be liable and subject to Indictment, Trial, Judgment and Punishment, according to Law." Art. II, § 4 provides: "The President, Vice President and all Civil Officers of the United States, shall be removed from Office on Impeachment for, and Conviction of, Treason, Bribery, or other high Crimes and Misdemeanors." Is the President's refusal to answer judicial or congressional questions about his conversations impeachable? There are no judicial precedents on what counts as an impeachable offense, but the practice of impeachments is of some interpretive or precedential relevance. In 1798, Senator William Blount was impeached, but the Senate removed him under Art. I, § 5, cl. 2 rather than try the impeachment. One cabinet official, two presidents, and 15 federal judges have been impeached, most recently Samuel Kent in 2009 and Thomas Porteous in 2010. Charles Black, Impeachment: A Handbook (1974), gives and extensive analysis of what offenses count as impeachable, and the central chapter of the book has been placed online at goo.gl/4fF5mX.

10. In 1804, Justice Samuel Chase was impeached in part for his conduct in enforcing the Alien and Sedition Acts. The Senate's failure to convict him has generally been taken to mean that judges cannot be removed merely for erroneous judicial decisions. Does this seem plausible to you? What if judges' incorrect decisions manifest disregard for their oaths?

11. In 1998, President Clinton was impeached for perjury and obstruction of justice related to his testimony in a sexual-harassment lawsuit. He argued that only official acts as President were impeachable, and the Senate refused to convict him. Does this sort of limit on impeachment make sense?

12. If a majority of the House and two-thirds of the Senate had the power to remove officers simply based on disagreements with their policy decisions — that is, if "bad decisionmaking" were deemed a high crime or misdemeanor — would that be absurd? How important is it to our constitutional scheme that officers be removable only for particularly serious offenses?

13. May an officer be impeached for acts before taking office? Judge Porteous's impeachment and removal in 2010 was apparently the first impeachment that

involved behavior before taking office. If a President says openly before taking officer that he will do things that members of Congress deem impeachable, but people elect him anyway, are they estopped from impeaching him based on those promises?

14. Are merely bad tendencies or character traits impeachable? Judge John Pickering was impeached and removed in 1803 in part for habitual drunkenness. Was that a mistake?

15. The Twenty-Fifth Amendment allows the President to be suspended from acting as President if he is "unable to discharge the powers and duties of his office." What does that mean? Does gross incompetence amount to such a disability? Note that two-thirds of each house is required to suspend the President, a higher threshold than impeachment, which only requires a majority of the House and two-thirds of the Senate. Should these impeachment or suspension thresholds be lowered? Raised?

D. EXECUTIVE POWER IN FOREIGN POLICY

The primary forum for claims of expansive, inherent executive power is the context of foreign policy. The Constitution identifies numerous powers related to foreign affairs, in both Articles I and II. For instance, Article I, § 8, cl. 11, grants Congress the power to "declare War," and Article II, § 2, cl. 2, identifies that the President has the power to "appoint Ambassadors, other public Ministers and Consuls." However, neither Article I nor Article II, individually or collectively, expressly grants all the powers the federal government exercises in the context of foreign affairs. Many scholars have argued that the grant of "executive Power" to the President is itself a grant of power to the President over foreign affairs. *See, e.g.,* Saikrishna B. Prakash & Michael D. Ramsey, *The Executive Power over Foreign Affairs*, 111 YALE L.J. 231, 234 (2001) (concluding that the grant of "executive Power" gave the President "a 'residual' foreign affairs power," but disagreeing with scholars who interpreted "executive Power" more capaciously).

Fans of the Hamilton musical will no doubt remember the second cabinet-meeting rap battle between Alexander Hamilton and Thomas Jefferson over whether the United States should honor its treaty with France following the French Revolution. In the musical, President George Washington announces, "Remember, my decision on this matter is not subject to congressional approval. The only person you have to convince is me." This was indeed Washington's position (and Hamilton's), but it was vigorously disputed by others, most notably James Madison. Madison and Hamilton's essays back and forth, with Madison taking the name "Helvidius" and Hamilton "Pacificus," are the most extensive and most valuable early exposition of early views on executive power. While Hamilton and Madison disagreed about many things, their areas of agreement are especially compelling evidence of the original meaning of Articles I and II. Both Madison and Hamilton, for instance, held that Article II gave the President all powers generally understood as executive, subtracting out those powers explicitly given to Congress in Article I. Despite their agreement on the basic relationship between Articles I and II, Hamilton and Madison disagreed fiercely over the scope of the particular exceptions, particularly the scope of Congress's power to "declare War." As this Section displays, these boundary-line disagreements have persisted throughout American history.

1. Traditional Delegation of Foreign Policy Power to the Executive

Since the beginning of the Republic, Presidents have claimed and exercised relatively broad powers in the international relations context. *Curtiss-Wright*, below, heavily relied on this practice to support its conclusion that the President possesses inherent power in the context of foreign policy. The Court upheld legislation which gave the President extremely broad latitude to conduct foreign policy: the sort of latitude that in other contexts would have been characteristic of legislative power.

UNITED STATES v. CURTISS-WRIGHT EXPORT CORPORATION
299 U.S. 304 (1936)

MR. JUSTICE SUTHERLAND delivered the opinion of the Court.

On January 27, 1936, an indictment was returned in the court below, the first count of which charges that appellees, beginning with the 29th day of May, 1934, conspired to sell in the United States certain arms of war, namely, fifteen machine guns, to Bolivia, a country then engaged in armed conflict in the Chaco, in violation of the Joint Resolution of Congress approved May 28, 1934, and the provisions of a proclamation issued on the same day by the President of the United States pursuant to authority conferred by section 1 of the resolution. The Joint Resolution (48 Stat. 811) follows:

> 'Resolved by the Senate and House of Representatives of the United States of America in Congress assembled, That if the President finds that the prohibition of the sale of arms and munitions of war in the United States to those countries now engaged in armed conflict in the Chaco may contribute to the reestablishment of peace between those countries, and if he makes proclamation to that effect, it shall be unlawful to sell, except under such limitations and exceptions as the President prescribes, any arms or munitions of war in any place in the United States to the countries now engaged in that armed conflict, or to any person, company, or association acting in

the interest of either country, until otherwise ordered by the President or by Congress.

'Sec. 2. Whoever sells any arms or munitions of war in violation of section 1 shall, on conviction, be punished by a fine not exceeding $10,000 or by imprisonment not exceeding two years, or both.'

The President's proclamation (48 Stat. 1744, No. 2087), after reciting the terms of the Joint Resolution, declares:

'Now, Therefore, I, Franklin D. Roosevelt, President of the United States of America, acting under and by virtue of the authority conferred in me by the said joint resolution of Congress, do hereby declare and proclaim that I have found that the prohibition of the sale of arms and munitions of war in the United States to those countries now engaged in armed conflict in the Chaco may contribute to the reestablishment of peace between those countries; and I do hereby admonish all citizens of the United States and every person to abstain from every violation of the provisions of the joint resolution above set forth, hereby made applicable to Bolivia and Paraguay, and I do hereby warn them that all violations of such provisions will be rigorously prosecuted.

'And I do hereby delegate to the Secretary of State the power of prescribing exceptions and limitations to the application of the said joint resolution of May 28, 1934, as made effective by this my proclamation issued thereunder.'

On November 14, 1935, this proclamation was revoked (49 Stat. 3480), in the following terms:

'Now, therefore, I, Franklin D. Roosevelt, President of the United States of America, do hereby declare and proclaim that I have found that the prohibition of the sale of arms and munitions of war in the United States to Bolivia or Paraguay will no longer be necessary as a contribution to the reestablishment of peace between those countries, and the above-mentioned Proclamation of May 28, 1934, is hereby revoked as to the sale of arms and munitions of war to Bolivia or Paraguay from and after November 29, 1935, provided, however, that this action shall not have the effect of releasing or extinguishing any penalty, forfeiture or liability incurred under the aforesaid Proclamation of May 28, 1934, or the Joint Resolution of Congress approved by the President on the same date; and that the said Proclamation and Joint Resolution shall be treated as remaining in force for the purpose of sustaining any proper action or prosecution for the enforcement of such penalty, forfeiture or liability.'

Appellees severally demurred to the first count of the indictment on the ground that it did not charge facts sufficient to show the commission by appellees of any offense against any law of the United States. The points urged in support of the demurrer were, first, that the Joint Resolution effects an invalid delegation of legislative power to the executive; [and] second, that the Joint Resolution never became effective because of the failure of the President to find essential jurisdictional facts. The court below sustained the demurrer upon the first point.

First. It is contended that by the Joint Resolution Congress abdicated its essential functions and delegated them to the Executive. Whether, if the Joint Resolution had related solely to internal affairs, it would be open to the challenge that it constituted an unlawful delegation of legislative power to the Executive, we find it unnecessary to determine. The whole aim of the resolution is to affect a situation entirely external to the United States, and falling within the category of foreign affairs. The determination which we are called to make, therefore, is whether the Joint Resolution, as applied to that situation, is vulnerable to attack under the rule that forbids a delegation of the lawmaking power. In other words, assuming (but not deciding) that the challenged delegation, if it were confined to internal affairs, would be invalid, may it nevertheless be sustained on the ground that its exclusive aim is to afford a remedy for a hurtful condition within foreign territory?

It will contribute to the elucidation of the question if we first consider the differences between the powers of the federal government in respect of foreign or external affairs and those in respect of domestic or internal affairs. That there are differences between them, and that these differences are fundamental, may not be doubted.

The two classes of powers are different, both in respect of their origin and their nature. The broad statement that the federal government can exercise no powers except those specifically enumerated in the Constitution, and such implied powers as are necessary and proper to carry into effect the enumerated powers, is categorically true only in respect of our internal affairs. In that field, the primary purpose of the Constitution was to carve from the general mass of legislative powers then possessed by the states such portions as it was thought desirable to vest in the federal government, leaving those not included in the enumeration still in the states. *Carter v. Carter Coal Co.*, 298 U.S. 238, 294 [(1936)]. That this doctrine applies only to powers which the states had is self-evident. And since the states severally never possessed international powers, such powers could not have been carved from the mass of state powers but obviously were transmitted to the United States from some other source. During the Colonial period, those powers were possessed exclusively by and were entirely under the control of the Crown. By the Declaration of Independence, 'the Representatives of the United States of America' declared the United (not the several) Colonies to be free and independent states, and as such to have 'full Power to levy War, conclude Peace, contract Alliances, establish Commerce and to do all other Acts and Things which Independent States may of right do.'

As a result of the separation from Great Britain by the colonies, acting as a unit, the powers of external sovereignty passed from the Crown not to the colonies severally, but to the colonies in their collective and corporate capacity as the United States of America. Even before the Declaration, the colonies were a unit in foreign affairs, acting through a common agency—namely, the Continental Congress, composed of delegates from the thirteen colonies. That agency exercised the powers of war and peace, raised an army, created a navy, and finally adopted the Declaration of Independence. Rulers come and go; governments end and forms of government change; but sovereignty survives. A political society cannot endure without a supreme will somewhere. Sovereignty is never held in suspense. When, therefore, the external sovereignty of Great Britain in respect of the colonies ceased, it immediately passed to the Union. That fact was given practical application almost at once. The treaty of peace, made on September 3, 1783, was concluded between his Brittanic Majesty and the 'United States of America.'

The Union existed before the Constitution, which was ordained and established among other things to form 'a more perfect Union.' Prior to that event, it is clear that the Union, declared by the Articles of Confederation to be 'perpetual,' was the sole possessor of external sovereignty, and in the Union it remained without change save in so far as the Constitution in express terms qualified its exercise. The Framers' Convention was called and exerted its powers upon the irrefutable postulate that though the states were several their people in respect of foreign affairs were one. In that convention, the entire absence of state power to deal with those affairs was thus forcefully stated by Rufus King:

> 'The states were not 'sovereigns' in the sense contended for by some. They did not possess the peculiar features of sovereignty,—they could not make war, nor peace, nor alliances, nor treaties. Considering them as political beings, they were dumb, for they could not speak to any foreign sovereign whatever. They were deaf, for they could not hear any propositions from such sovereign. They had not even the organs or faculties of defence or offence, for they could not of themselves raise troops, or equip vessels, for war.'

5 ELLIOT'S DEBATES, 212.

It results that the investment of the federal government with the powers of external sovereignty did not depend upon the affirmative grants of the Constitution. The powers to declare and wage war, to conclude peace, to make treaties, to maintain diplomatic relations with other sovereignties, if they had never been mentioned in the Constitution, would have vested in the federal government as necessary concomitants of nationality. Neither the Constitution nor the laws passed in pursuance of it have any force in foreign territory unless in respect of our own citizens; and operations of the nation in such territory must be governed by treaties, international understandings and compacts, and the principles of international law. As a member of the family of nations, the right and power of the United States in that field are equal to the right and power of the other members of the international family. Otherwise, the United States is not completely sovereign. The power to acquire territory by discovery and occupation; the power to expel undesirable aliens, the power to make such international agreements as do not constitute treaties in the constitutional sense, none of which is expressly affirmed by the Constitution, nevertheless exist as inherently inseparable from the conception of nationality. This the court recognized, and in each of the cases cited found the warrant for its conclusions not in the provisions of the Constitution, but in the law of nations.

Not only, as we have shown, is the federal power over external affairs in origin and essential character different from that over internal affairs, but participation in the exercise of the power is significantly limited. In this vast external realm, with its important, complicated, delicate and manifold problems, the President alone has the power to speak or listen as a representative of the nation. He makes treaties with the advice and consent of the Senate; but he alone negotiates. Into the field of negotiation the Senate cannot intrude; and Congress itself is powerless to invade it. As Marshall said in his great argument of March 7, 1800, in the House of Representatives, 'The President is the sole organ of the nation in its external relations, and its sole representative with foreign nations.' Annals, 6th Cong., col. 613. The Senate Committee on Foreign Relations at a very early day in our history (February 15, 1816), reported to the Senate, among other things, as follows:

> 'The President is the constitutional representative of the United States with regard to foreign nations. He manages our concerns with foreign nations and must necessarily be most competent to determine when, how, and upon what subjects negotiation may be urged with the greatest prospect of success. For his conduct he is responsible to the Constitution. The committee considers this responsibility the surest pledge for the faithful discharge of his duty. They think the interference of the Senate in the direction of foreign negotiations calculated to diminish that responsibility and thereby to impair the best security for the national safety. The nature of transactions with foreign nations, moreover, requires caution and unity of design, and their success frequently depends on secrecy and dispatch.'

8 U.S. Sen. Reports Comm. on Foreign Relations, p. 24.

It is important to bear in mind that we are here dealing not alone with an authority vested in the President by an exertion of legislative power, but with such an authority plus the very delicate, plenary and exclusive power of the President as the sole organ of the federal government in the field of international relations—a power which does not require as a basis for its exercise an act of Congress, but which, of course, like every other governmental power, must be exercised in subordination to the applicable provisions of the Constitution. It is quite apparent that if, in the maintenance of our international relations, embarrassment—perhaps serious embarrassment—is to be avoided and success for our aims achieved, congressional legislation which is to be made effective through negotiation and inquiry within the international field must often accord to the President a degree of discretion and freedom from statutory restriction which would not be admissible were domestic affairs alone involved. Moreover, he, not Congress, has the better opportunity of knowing the conditions which prevail in foreign countries, and especially is this true in time of war. He has his confidential sources of information. He has his agents in the form of diplomatic, consular and other officials. Secrecy in respect of information gathered by them may be highly necessary, and the premature disclosure of it productive of harmful results. Indeed, so clearly is this true that the first President refused to accede to a request to lay before the House of Representatives the instructions, correspondence and documents relating to the negotiation of the Jay Treaty—a refusal the wisdom of which was recognized by the House itself and has never since been doubted. In his reply to the request, President Washington said:

> 'The nature of foreign negotiations requires caution, and their success must often depend on secrecy; and even when brought to a conclusion a full disclosure of all the measures, demands, or eventual concessions which may have been proposed or contemplated would be extremely impolitic; for this might have a pernicious influence on future negotiations, or produce immediate inconveniences, perhaps danger and mischief, in relation to other powers. The necessity of such caution and secrecy was one cogent reason for vesting the power of making treaties in the President, with the advice and consent of the Senate, the principle on which that body was formed confining it to a small number of members. To admit, then, a right in the House of Representatives to demand and to have as a matter of course all the papers respecting a negotiation with a foreign power would be to establish a dangerous precedent.'

1 MESSAGES AND PAPERS OF THE PRESIDENTS, p. 194.

The marked difference between foreign affairs and domestic affairs in this respect is recognized by both houses of Congress in the very form of their requisitions for information from the executive departments. In the case of every department except the Department of State, the resolution directs the official to furnish the information. In the case of the State Department, dealing with foreign affairs, the President is requested to furnish the information 'if not incompatible with the public interest.' A statement that to furnish the information is not compatible with the public interest rarely, if ever, is questioned.

In the light of the foregoing observations, it is evident that this court should not be in haste to apply a general rule which will have the effect of condemning legislation like that under review as constituting an unlawful delegation of legislative power. The principles which justify such legislation find overwhelming support in the unbroken legislative practice which has prevailed almost from the inception of the national government to the present day.

Let us examine, in chronological order, the acts of legislation which warrant this conclusion:

The Act of June 4, 1794, authorized the President to lay, regulate and revoke embargoes. He was 'authorized' 'whenever, in his opinion, the public safety shall so require,' to lay the embargo upon all ships and vessels in the ports of the United States, including those of foreign nations, 'under such regulations as the circumstances of the case may require, and to continue or revoke the same, whenever he shall think proper.' 1 Stat. 372. The Act of March 3, 1795 (1 Stat. 444), gave the President authority to permit the exportation of arms, cannon and military stores, the law prohibiting such exports to the contrary notwithstanding, the only prescribed guide for his action being that such exports should be in 'cases connected with the security of the commercial interest of the United States, and for public purposes only.' [The Court reviewed a number of similar statutes from the late-eighteenth, and early-nineteenth century.]

Practically every volume of the United States Statutes contains one or more acts or joint resolutions of Congress authorizing action by the President in respect of subjects affecting foreign relations, which either leave the exercise of the power to his unrestricted judgment, or provide a standard far more general than that which has always been considered requisite with regard to domestic affairs. The result of holding that the joint resolution here under attack is void and unenforceable as constituting an unlawful delegation of legislative power would be to stamp this multitude of comparable acts and resolutions as likewise invalid. The uniform, long-continued and undisputed legislative practice just disclosed rests upon an admissible view of the Constitution which, even if the practice found far less support in principle than we think it does, we should not feel at liberty at this late day to disturb.

We deem it unnecessary to consider, seriatim, the several clauses which are said to evidence the unconstitutionality of the Joint Resolution as involving an unlawful delegation of legislative power. It is enough to summarize by saying that, both upon principle and in accordance with precedent, we conclude there is sufficient warrant for the broad discretion vested in the President. The judgment of the court below must be reversed and the cause remanded for further proceedings in accordance with the foregoing opinion.

It is so ordered.

MR. JUSTICE MCREYNOLDS does not agree. He is of opinion that the court below reached the right conclusion and its judgment ought to be affirmed.

MR. JUSTICE STONE took no part in the consideration or decision of this case.

EXERCISE 14:

1. What were the sources of evidence for the Court's claim that the President possessed inherent executive power in the context of foreign affairs? What role did the text, structure, historical context, tradition, and precedent play in the Court's analysis? For example, how did the Court account for the fact that many foreign policy powers are expressly enumerated?

2. On what basis did the Supreme Court distinguish the President's executive power in the domestic context from the foreign context? Is the Court's distinction correct? Keep *Curtiss-Wright* in mind when you read *Schechter Poultry*, in **Chapter 3**, which struck down an excessive delegation to President Roosevelt in the domestic sphere.

3. How is the Court's holding consistent with the constitutional principle of limited and enumerated powers and the textual, structural, and historical evidence supporting that principle? If, as many believe, *Curtiss-Wright* significantly narrowed the principle of limited and enumerated powers in the foreign affairs context, that move is analogous to one you will see in Volumes 3 and 4, where the Court moved toward not judicially enforcing the principle in the domestic context as well. Is this an example of a "slippery slope"?

4. Typically, the principle of limited and enumerated powers is justified on policy grounds as preventing a concentration of governmental power in one branch of government, which, in turn, prevents tyranny, and which therefore preserves individual liberty. How, if at all, does this rationale apply in the *Curtiss-Wright* context?

5. What conception of sovereignty did the Court utilize? Is that conception compatible with the conceptions of sovereignty displayed in *Chisholm v. Georgia*, covered in Volume 1?

6. What policy arguments did the Court utilize to support its conclusion?

7. Are there limits to the President's foreign affairs executive power, under the Court's rationale?

8. What implications for federalism—for the federal-state balance—do the holding and reasoning have, if any?

9. Using what you learned in Volume 1 regarding the Political Question Doctrine, determine whether the Court should have refused to entertain this suit under that doctrine.

2. Executive Agreements

A related context is treaties and executive agreements. The Constitution expressly laid out the process by which treaties were to be entered in Article II, §2, cl. 2. However, that text left many important questions unanswered. For example, may the President unilaterally rescind a treaty? *See Goldwater v. Carter*, 444 U.S. 996 (1979) (dismissing a challenge by a U.S. Senator to President Carter's unilateral rescission of a treaty with the Republic of China (Taiwan), though without explanation). Also, may the President enter into international agreements—commonly called executive agreements—without the Senate's approval? This latter question was answered affirmatively by the Supreme Court below.

DAMES & MOORE v. REGAN
453 U.S. 654 (1981)

Justice Rehnquist delivered the opinion of the Court.

The questions presented by this case touch fundamentally upon the matter in which our Republic is to be governed. Throughout the nearly two centuries of our

Nation's existence under the Constitution, this subject has generated considerable debate. We have had the benefit of commentators such as John Jay, Alexander Hamilton, and James Madison writing in The Federalist Papers at the Nation's very inception, the benefit of astute foreign observers of our system such as Alexis deTocqueville and James Bryce writing during the first century of the Nation's existence, and the benefit of many other treatises as well as more than 400 volumes of reports of decisions of this Court. As these writings reveal it is doubtless both futile and perhaps dangerous to find any epigrammatical explanation of how this country has been governed. Indeed, as Justice Jackson noted, "[a] judge . . . may be surprised at the poverty of really useful and unambiguous authority applicable to concrete problems of executive power as they actually present themselves." *Youngstown Sheet & Tube Co. v. Sawyer*, 343 U.S. 579 (1952) (concurring opinion).

Our decision today will not dramatically alter this situation. We are confined to a resolution of the dispute presented to us. That dispute involves various Executive Orders and regulations by which the President nullified attachments and liens on Iranian assets in the United States, directed that these assets be transferred to Iran, and suspended claims against Iran that may be presented to an International Claims Tribunal. This action was taken in an effort to comply with an Executive Agreement between the United States and Iran. We granted certiorari before judgment in this case, and set an expedited briefing and argument schedule, because lower courts had reached conflicting conclusions on the validity of the President's actions and, as the Solicitor General informed us, unless the Government acted by July 19, 1981, Iran could consider the United States to be in breach of the Executive Agreement.

But before turning to the facts and law which we believe determine the result in this case, we stress that the expeditious treatment of the issues involved by all of the courts which have considered the President's actions makes us acutely aware of the necessity to rest decision on the narrowest possible ground capable of deciding the case. *Ashwander v. TVA*, 297 U.S. 288, 347 (1936) (Brandeis, J., concurring). This does not mean that reasoned analysis may give way to judicial fiat. It does mean that the statement of Justice Jackson—that we decide difficult cases presented to us by virtue of our commissions, not our competence—is especially true here. We attempt to lay down no general "guidelines" covering other situations not involved here, and attempt to confine the opinion only to the very questions necessary to decision of the case.

Perhaps it is because it is so difficult to reconcile the foregoing definition of Art. III judicial power with the broad range of vitally important day-to-day questions regularly decided by Congress or the Executive, without either challenge or interference by the Judiciary, that the decisions of the Court in this area have been rare, episodic, and afford little precedential value for subsequent cases. The tensions present in any exercise of executive power under the tri-partite system of Federal Government established by the Constitution have been reflected in opinions by Members of this Court more than once. The Court stated in *United States v. Curtiss-Wright Export Corp.*, 299 U.S. 304, 319–320 (1936):

> "[W]e are here dealing not alone with an authority vested in the President by an exertion of legislative power, but with such an authority plus the very delicate, plenary and exclusive power of the President as the sole organ of the federal government in the field of international relations—a power which does not require as a basis for its exercise an act of Congress, but which, of course, like every other governmental power, must be exercised in subordination to the applicable provisions of the Constitution."

And yet 16 years later, Justice Jackson in his concurring opinion in *Youngstown*, which both parties agree brings together as much combination of analysis and common sense as there is in this area, focused not on the "plenary and exclusive power of the President" but rather responded to a claim of virtually unlimited powers for the Executive by noting:

> "The example of such unlimited executive power that must have most impressed the forefathers was the prerogative exercised by George III, and the description of its evils in the Declaration of Independence leads me to doubt that they were creating their new Executive in his image."

I

On November 4, 1979, the American Embassy in Tehran was seized and our diplomatic personnel were captured and held hostage. In response to that crisis, President Carter, acting pursuant to the International Emergency Economic Powers Act (hereinafter IEEPA), declared a national emergency on November 14, 1979, and blocked the removal or transfer of "all property and interests in property of the Government of Iran, its instrumentalities and controlled entities and the Central Bank of Iran which are or become subject to the jurisdiction of the United States . . . ." Exec. Order No. 12170, 3 CFR 457 (1980). President Carter authorized the Secretary of the Treasury to promulgate regulations carrying out the blocking order. On November 15, 1979, the Treasury Department's Office of Foreign Assets Control issued a regulation providing that "[u]nless licensed or authorized . . . any attachment, judgment, decree, lien, execution, garnishment, or other judicial process is null and void with respect to any property in which on or since [November 14, 1979,] there existed an interest of Iran." 31 CFR § 535.203(e) (1980).

On November 26, 1979, the President granted a general license authorizing certain judicial proceedings against Iran but which did not allow the "entry of any judgment or of any decree or order of similar or analogous effect . . . ." § 535.504(a). On December 19, 1979, a clarifying regulation was issued stating that "the general authorization for judicial proceedings contained in § 535.504(a) includes pre-judgment attachment." § 535.418.

On December 19, 1979, petitioner Dames & Moore filed suit in the United States District Court for the Central District of California against the Government of Iran, the Atomic Energy Organization of Iran, and a number of Iranian banks. In its complaint, petitioner alleged that its wholly owned subsidiary, Dames & Moore International, S. R. L., was a party to a written contract with the Atomic Energy Organization, and that the subsidiary's entire interest in the contract had been assigned to petitioner. Under the contract, the subsidiary was to conduct site studies for a proposed nuclear power plant in Iran. As provided in the terms of the contract, the Atomic Energy Organization terminated the agreement for its own convenience on June 30, 1979. Petitioner contended, however, that it was owed $3,436,694.30 plus interest for services performed under the contract prior to the date of termination. The District Court issued orders of attachment directed against property of the defendants, and the property of certain Iranian banks was then attached to secure any judgment that might be entered against them.

On January 20, 1981, the Americans held hostage were released by Iran pursuant to an Agreement entered into the day before. The Agreement stated that "[i]t is the purpose of [the United States and Iran] . . . to terminate all litigation as between the Government of each party and the nationals of the other, and to bring about the settlement and termination of all such claims through binding arbitration." In furtherance of this goal, the Agreement called for the establishment of an Iran-United States Claims Tribunal which would arbitrate any claims not settled within six months. Awards of the Claims Tribunal are to be "final and binding" and "enforceable . . . in the courts of any nation in accordance with its laws." Under the Agreement, the United States is obligated

> "to terminate all legal proceedings in United States courts involving claims of United States persons and institutions against Iran and its state enterprises, to nullify all attachments and judgments obtained therein, to prohibit all further litigation based on such claims, and to bring about the termination of such claims through binding arbitration."

In addition, the United States must "act to bring about the transfer" by July 19, 1981, of all Iranian assets held in this country by American banks. One billion dollars of these assets will be deposited in a security account in the Bank of England and used to satisfy awards rendered against Iran by the Claims Tribunal.

On January 19, 1981, President Carter issued a series of Executive Orders implementing the terms of the agreement. Exec. Orders Nos. 12276–12285, 46 Fed. Reg. 7913–7932. These Orders revoked all licenses permitting the exercise of "any right, power, or privilege" with regard to Iranian funds, securities, or deposits; "nullified" all non-Iranian interests in such assets acquired subsequent to the blocking order of November 14, 1979; and required those banks holding Iranian assets to transfer them "to the Federal Reserve Bank of New York, to be held or transferred as directed by the Secretary of the Treasury." Exec. Order No. 12279, 46 Fed. Reg. 7919.

On February 24, 1981, President Reagan issued an Executive Order in which he "ratified" the January 19th Executive Orders. Exec. Order No. 12294, 46 Fed. Reg. 14111. Moreover, he "suspended" all "claims which may be presented to the . . .

Tribunal" and provided that such claims "shall have no legal effect in any action now pending in any court of the United States." The suspension of any particular claim terminates if the Claims Tribunal determines that it has no jurisdiction over that claim; claims are discharged for all purposes when the Claims Tribunal either awards some recovery and that amount is paid, or determines that no recovery is due.

Meanwhile, on January 27, 1981, petitioner moved for summary judgment in the District Court against the Government of Iran and the Atomic Energy Organization, but not against the Iranian banks. The District Court granted petitioner's motion and awarded petitioner the amount claimed under the contract plus interest. Thereafter, petitioner attempted to execute the judgment by obtaining writs of garnishment and execution in state court in the State of Washington, and a sheriff's sale of Iranian property in Washington was noticed to satisfy the judgment. However, by order of May 28, 1981, as amended by order of June 8, the District Court stayed execution of its judgment pending appeal by the Government of Iran and the Atomic Energy Organization. The District Court also ordered that all prejudgment attachments obtained against the Iranian defendants be vacated and that further proceedings against the bank defendants be stayed in light of the Executive Orders discussed above.

On April 28, 1981, petitioner filed this action in the District Court for declaratory and injunctive relief against the United States and the Secretary of the Treasury, seeking to prevent enforcement of the Executive Orders and Treasury Department regulations implementing the Agreement with Iran. In its complaint, petitioner alleged that the actions of the President and the Secretary of the Treasury implementing the Agreement with Iran were beyond their statutory and constitutional powers and, in any event, were unconstitutional to the extent they adversely affect petitioner's final judgment against the Government of Iran and the Atomic Energy Organization, its execution of that judgment in the State of Washington, its prejudgment attachments, and its ability to continue to litigate against the Iranian banks. On May 28, 1981, the District Court denied petitioner's motion for a preliminary injunction and dismissed petitioner's complaint for failure to state a claim upon which relief could be granted. Prior to the District Court's ruling, the United States Courts of Appeals for the First and the District of Columbia Circuits upheld the President's authority to issue the Executive Orders and regulations challenged by petitioner.

On June 3, 1981, petitioner filed a notice of appeal from the District Court's order, and the appeal was docketed in the United States Court of Appeals for the Ninth Circuit. On June 4, the Treasury Department amended its regulations to mandate "the transfer of bank deposits and certain other financial assets of Iran in the United States to the Federal Reserve Bank of New York by noon, June 19." The District Court, however, entered an injunction pending appeal prohibiting the United States from requiring the transfer of Iranian property that is subject to "any writ of attachment, garnishment, judgment, levy, or other judicial lien" issued by any court in favor of petitioner. Arguing that this is a case of "imperative public importance," petitioner then sought a writ of certiorari before judgment. Because the issues presented here are of great significance and demand prompt resolution, we granted the petition for the writ, adopted an expedited briefing schedule, and set the case for oral argument on June 24, 1981.

II

The parties and the lower courts, confronted with the instant questions, have all agreed that much relevant analysis is contained in *Youngstown Sheet & Tube Co. v. Sawyer*, 343 U.S. 579 (1952). Justice Jackson's concurring opinion elaborated in a general way the consequences of different types of interaction between the two democratic branches in assessing Presidential authority to act in any given case. Although we have in the past found and do today find Justice Jackson's classification of executive actions into three general categories analytically useful, we should be mindful that "[t]he great ordinances of the Constitution do not establish and divide fields of black and white." Justice Jackson himself recognized that his three categories represented "a somewhat over-simplified grouping," 343 U.S., at 635, and it is doubtless the case that executive action in any particular instance falls, not neatly in one of three pigeonholes, but rather at some point along a spectrum running from explicit congressional authorization to explicit congressional prohibition.

IV

Although we have concluded that the IEEPA constitutes specific congressional authorization to the President to nullify the attachments and order the transfer of Iranian assets, there remains the question of the President's authority to suspend claims pending in American courts. Such claims have, of course, an existence apart from the attachments which accompanied them. In terminating these claims through Executive Order No. 12294 the President purported to act under authority of both the IEEPA and 22 U.S.C. § 1732, the so-called "Hostage Act."7 46 Fed. Reg. 14111 (1981).

We conclude that although the IEEPA authorized the nullification of the attachments, it cannot be read to authorize the suspension of the claims. The claims of American citizens against Iran are not in themselves transactions involving Iranian property or efforts to exercise any rights with respect to such property. An *in personam* lawsuit, although it might eventually be reduced to judgment and that judgment might be executed upon, is an effort to establish liability and fix damages and does not focus on any particular property within the jurisdiction. The terms of the IEEPA therefore do not authorize the President to suspend claims in American courts. This is the view of all the courts which have considered the question.

The Hostage Act, passed in 1868, provides:

> "Whenever it is made known to the President that any citizen of the United States has been unjustly deprived of his liberty by or under the authority of any foreign government, it shall be the duty of the President forthwith to demand of that government the reasons of such imprisonment; and if it appears to be wrongful and in violation of the rights of American citizenship, the President shall forthwith demand the release of such citizen, and if

the release so demanded is unreasonably delayed or refused, the President shall use such means, not amounting to acts of war, as he may think necessary and proper to obtain or effectuate the release; and all the facts and proceedings relative thereto shall as soon as practicable be communicated by the President to Congress."

22 U.S.C. § 1732.

We are reluctant to conclude that this provision constitutes specific authorization to the President to suspend claims in American courts. Although the broad language of the Hostage Act suggests it may cover this case, there are several difficulties with such a view. The legislative history indicates that the Act was passed in response to a situation unlike the recent Iranian crisis. Congress in 1868 was concerned with the activity of certain countries refusing to recognize the citizenship of naturalized Americans traveling abroad, and repatriating such citizens against their will. See, e. g., Cong. Globe, 40th Cong., 2d Sess., 4331 (1868) (Sen. Fessenden); id., at 4354 (Sen. Conness). These countries were not interested in returning the citizens in exchange for any sort of ransom. This also explains the reference in the Act to imprisonment "in violation of the rights of American citizenship." Although the Iranian hostage-taking violated international law and common decency, the hostages were not seized out of any refusal to recognize their American citizenship—they were seized precisely *because of* their American citizenship. The legislative history is also somewhat ambiguous on the question whether Congress contemplated Presidential action such as that involved here or rather simply reprisals directed against the offending foreign country and *its* citizens. See, e. g., Cong. Globe, 40th Cong., 2d Sess., 4205 (1868).

Concluding that neither the IEEPA nor the Hostage Act constitutes specific authorization of the President's action suspending claims, however, is not to say that these statutory provisions are entirely irrelevant to the question of the validity of the President's action. We think both statutes highly relevant in the looser sense of indicating congressional acceptance of a broad scope for executive action in circumstances such as those presented in this case. As noted in Part III, *supra*, the IEEPA delegates broad authority to the President to act in times of national emergency with respect to property of a foreign country. The Hostage Act similarly indicates congressional willingness that the President have broad discretion when responding to the hostile acts of foreign sovereigns. As Senator Williams, draftsman of the language eventually enacted as the Hostage Act, put it:

"If you propose any remedy at all, you must invest the Executive with some discretion, so that he may apply the remedy to a case as it may arise. As to England or France he might adopt one policy to relieve a citizen imprisoned by either one of those countries; as to the Barbory powers, he might adopt another policy; as to the islands of the ocean, another. With different countries that have different systems of government he might adopt different means."

Cong. Globe, 40th Cong., 2d Sess., 4359 (1868).

Although we have declined to conclude that the IEEPA or the Hostage Act directly authorizes the President's suspension of claims for the reasons noted, we cannot ignore the general tenor of Congress' legislation in this area in trying to determine whether the President is acting alone or at least with the acceptance of Congress. As we have noted, Congress cannot anticipate and legislate with regard to every possible action the President may find it necessary to take or every possible situation in which he might act. Such failure of Congress specifically to delegate authority does not, "especially . . . in the areas of foreign policy and national security," imply "congressional disapproval" of action taken by the Executive. On the contrary, the enactment of legislation closely related to the question of the President's authority in a particular case which evinces legislative intent to accord the President broad discretion may be considered to "invite" "measures on independent presidential responsibility," *Youngstown*, 343 U.S., at 637 (Jackson, J., concurring). At least this is so where there is no contrary indication of legislative intent and when, as here, there is a history of congressional acquiescence in conduct of the sort engaged in by the President. It is to that history which we now turn.

Not infrequently in affairs between nations, outstanding claims by nationals of one country against the government of another country are "sources of friction" between the two sovereigns. *United States v. Pink*, 315 U.S. 203, 225 (1942). To resolve these difficulties, nations have often entered into agreements settling the claims of their respective nationals. As one treatise writer puts it, international agreements settling claims by nationals of one state against the government of another "are established international practice reflecting traditional international theory." L. Henkin, Foreign Affairs and the Constitution 262 (1972). Consistent with that principle, the United States has repeatedly exercised its sovereign authority to settle the claims of its nationals against foreign countries. Though those settlements have sometimes been made by treaty, there has also been a longstanding practice of settling such claims by executive agreement without the advice and consent of the Senate.[8] Under such agreements, the President has agreed to renounce or extinguish claims of United States nationals against foreign governments in return for lump-sum payments or the establishment of arbitration procedures. To be sure, many of these settlements were encouraged by the United States claimants themselves, since a claimant's only hope of obtaining any payment at all might lie in having his Government negotiate a diplomatic settlement on his behalf. But it is also undisputed that the "United States has sometimes disposed of the claims of its citizens without their consent, or even without consultation with them, usually without exclusive regard for their interests, as distinguished from those of the nation as a whole." Henkin, *supra*, at 262–263. It is clear that the practice of settling claims continues today. Since 1952, the President has entered into at least 10 binding settlements with foreign nations.

---

8. At least since the case of the "Wilmington Packet" in 1799, Presidents have exercised the power to settle claims of United States nationals by executive agreement. In fact, during the period of 1817–1917, "no fewer than eighty executive agreements were entered into by the United States looking toward the liquidation of claims of its citizens."

Crucial to our decision today is the conclusion that Congress has implicitly approved the practice of claim settlement by executive agreement. This is best demonstrated by Congress' enactment of the International Claims Settlement Act of 1949, 64 Stat. 13, as amended, 22 U.S.C. § 1621 *et seq.* The Act had two purposes: (1) to allocate to United States nationals funds received in the course of an executive claims settlement with Yugoslavia, and (2) to provide a procedure whereby funds resulting from future settlements could be distributed. To achieve these ends Congress created the International Claims Commission, now the Foreign Claims Settlement Commission, and gave it jurisdiction to make final and binding decisions with respect to claims by United States nationals against settlement funds. 22 U.S.C. § 1623(a). By creating a procedure to implement future settlement agreements, Congress placed its stamp of approval on such agreements. Indeed, the legislative history of the Act observed that the United States was seeking settlements with countries other than Yugoslavia and that the bill contemplated settlements of a similar nature in the future. H.R. Rep. No. 770, 81st Cong., 1st Sess., 4, 8 (1949).

Over the years Congress has frequently amended the International Claims Settlement Act to provide for particular problems arising out of settlement agreements, thus demonstrating Congress' continuing acceptance of the President's claim settlement authority. With respect to the Executive Agreement with the People's Republic of China, for example, Congress established an allocation formula for distribution of the funds received pursuant to the Agreement. 22 U.S.C. § 1627(f). As with legislation involving other executive agreements, Congress did not question the fact of the settlement or the power of the President to have concluded it. Finally, the legislative history of the IEEPA further reveals that Congress has accepted the authority of the Executive to enter into settlement agreements. Though the IEEPA was enacted to provide for some limitation on the President's emergency powers, Congress stressed that "[n]othing in this act is intended . . . to interfere with the authority of the President to [block assets], or to impede the settlement of claims of U. S. citizens against foreign countries." S. Rep. No. 95-466, p. 6 (1977), U. S. Code Cong. & Admin. News, 1977, pp. 4540, 4544; 50 U.S.C. § 1706(a)(1).[10]

In addition to congressional acquiescence in the President's power to settle claims, prior cases of this Court have also recognized that the President does have some measure of power to enter into executive agreements without obtaining the advice and consent of the Senate. In *United States v. Pink*, 315 U.S. 203 (1942), for example, the Court upheld the validity of the Litvinov Assignment, which was part of an Executive Agreement whereby the Soviet Union assigned to the United States amounts owed to it by American nationals so that outstanding claims of other American nationals could be paid. The Court explained that the resolution of such claims was integrally connected with normalizing United States' relations with a foreign state:

---

10. Indeed, Congress has consistently failed to object to this longstanding practice of claim settlement by executive agreement, even when it has had an opportunity to do so.

"Power to remove such obstacles to full recognition as settlement of claims of our nationals . . . certainly is a modest implied power of the President . . . . No such obstacle can be placed in the way of rehabilitation of relations between this country and another nation, unless the historic conception of the powers and responsibilities . . . is to be drastically revised."

In light of all of the foregoing—the inferences to be drawn from the character of the legislation Congress has enacted in the area, such as the IEEPA and the Hostage Act, and from the history of acquiescence in executive claims settlement—we conclude that the President was authorized to suspend pending claims pursuant to Executive Order No. 12294. As Justice Frankfurter pointed out in *Youngstown*, 343 U.S., at 610–611, "a systematic, unbroken, executive practice, long pursued to the knowledge of the Congress and never before questioned . . . may be treated as a gloss on 'Executive Power' vested in the President by § 1 of Art. II." Past practice does not, by itself, create power, but "long-continued practice, known to and acquiesced in by Congress, would raise a presumption that the [action] had been [taken] in pursuance of its consent . . . ." *United States v. Midwest Oil Co.*, 236 U.S. 459, 474 (1915). Such practice is present here and such a presumption is also appropriate. In light of the fact that Congress may be considered to have consented to the President's action in suspending claims, we cannot say that action exceeded the President's powers.

Congress has not disapproved of the action taken here. Though Congress has held hearings on the Iranian Agreement itself, Congress has not enacted legislation, or even passed a resolution, indicating its displeasure with the Agreement. Quite the contrary, the relevant Senate Committee has stated that the establishment of the Tribunal is "of vital importance to the United States." S. Rep. No. 97-71, p. 5 (1981).[13] We are thus clearly not confronted with a situation in which Congress has in some way resisted the exercise of Presidential authority.

Finally, we re-emphasize the narrowness of our decision. We do not decide that the President possesses plenary power to settle claims, even as against foreign governmental entities. But where, as here, the settlement of claims has been determined to be a necessary incident to the resolution of a major foreign policy dispute between our country and another, and where, as here, we can conclude that Congress acquiesced in the President's action, we are not prepared to say that the President lacks the power to settle such claims.

V

The judgment of the District Court is accordingly affirmed, and the mandate shall issue forthwith.

---

13. Contrast congressional reaction to the Iranian Agreements with congressional reaction to a 1973 Executive Agreement with Czechoslovakia. There the President sought to settle over $105 million in claims against Czechoslovakia for $20.5 million. Congress quickly demonstrated its displeasure by enacting legislation requiring that the Agreement be renegotiated. Though Congress has shown itself capable of objecting to executive agreements, it has rarely done so and has not done so in this case.

It is so ordered.

Justice Stevens, concurring in part. [Opinion omitted.]

Justice Powell, concurring and dissenting in part. [Opinion omitted.]

EXERCISE 15:

1. What is the Supreme Court's holding in this case?

2. What analysis did the Supreme Court utilize to resolve the issues it faced?

3. From what sources did the Court draw to ascertain Congress' will in the case? Into what Justice Jackson category did the Court put this case? What challenges did the Court face doing so? Did the Court come to the correct conclusion?

4. The Court was reluctant to rely on inherent executive power; why?

5. What limits, if any, are there to the President's power to enter into executive agreements?

6. Justice Rehnquist explained that, in this case in particular, and the general area of constitutional power in foreign affairs, it has been difficult for the Supreme Court to reach clarity. Why is that? Why is this context more difficult than other, substantively as or more contentious areas, such as substantive due process (covered in Volume 5)?

7. What power does the President have to *exit* executive agreements? President Obama entered into an agreement with Iran regarding its nuclear program that many, including President Trump, have criticized. Does one President have the right to bind a successor? Recall the issues of entrenchment discussed above in Exercise 11 Question 4. Does that issue depend on international law? Or does international law depend on this issue of domestic international law? *Compare* Emer de Vattel, The Law of Nations § 154, at 192–93 (1797) ("But all rulers of states have not a power to make public treaties by their own authority alone: some are obliged to take the advice of a senate, or of the representatives of the nation. It is from the fundamental laws of each state that we must learn where resides the authority that is capable of contracting with validity in the name of the state.") with Carol Morello, Iran Warns Congress It Can't Stop a Nuclear Deal, Washington Post, April 19, 2015 (quoting Iranian Foreign Minister Javad Zarif: "Whether you have a Democratic or Republican president, the United States is bound by international law, whether some senators like it or not. And international law requires the United States live up to the terms of an agreement it enters into.").

MEDELLÍN v. TEXAS

552 U.S. 491 (2008)

Chief Justice Roberts delivered the opinion of the Court.

The International Court of Justice (ICJ), located in the Hague, is a tribunal established pursuant to the United Nations Charter to adjudicate disputes between member states. In the *Case Concerning Avena and Other Mexican Nationals (Mex. v. U.S.)*, 2004 I.C.J. 12 (Judgment of Mar. 31) (*Avena*), that tribunal considered a claim brought by Mexico against the United States. The ICJ held that, based on violations of the Vienna Convention, 51 named Mexican nationals were entitled to review and reconsideration of their state-court convictions and sentences in the United States. After the *Avena* decision, President George W. Bush determined, through a Memorandum for the Attorney General (Feb. 28, 2005), (Memorandum or President's Memorandum), that the United States would "discharge its international obligations" under *Avena* "by having State courts give effect to the decision."

Petitioner José Ernesto Medellín, who had been convicted and sentenced in Texas state court for murder, is one of the 51 Mexican nationals named in the *Avena* decision. Relying on the ICJ's decision and the President's Memorandum, Medellín filed an application for a writ of habeas corpus in state court. The Texas Court of Criminal Appeals dismissed Medellín's application as an abuse of the writ under state law [because of procedural default]. We granted certiorari to decide two questions. *First*, is the ICJ's judgment in *Avena* directly enforceable as domestic law in a state court in the United States? *Second*, does the President's Memorandum independently require the States to provide review and reconsideration of the claims of the 51 Mexican nationals named in *Avena* without regard to state procedural default rules? We conclude that neither *Avena* nor the President's Memorandum constitutes directly enforceable federal law that pre-empts state limitations on the filing of successive habeas petitions. We therefore affirm the decision below.

II

Medellín first contends that the ICJ's judgment in *Avena* constitutes a "binding" obligation on the state and federal courts of the United States. He argues that "by virtue of the Supremacy Clause, the treaties requiring compliance with the *Avena* judgment are *already* the 'Law of the Land' by which all state and federal courts in this country are 'bound.'" Accordingly, Medellín argues, *Avena* is a binding federal rule of decision that pre-empts contrary state limitations on successive habeas petitions.

[The Supreme Court determined that the Vienna Convention was not a self-executing treaty and thus], while the ICJ's judgment in *Avena* creates an international law obligation on the part of the United States, it does not of its own force constitute binding federal law that pre-empts state restrictions on the filing of successive habeas petitions.

III

Medellín next argues that the ICJ's judgment in *Avena* is binding on state courts by virtue of the President's February 28, 2005 Memorandum. The United States contends that while the *Avena* judgment does not of its own force require domestic courts to set aside ordinary rules of procedural default, that judgment became the law of the land with precisely that effect pursuant to the President's Memorandum and his power "to establish binding rules of decision that preempt contrary state law."

A

The United States maintains that the President's constitutional role "uniquely qualifies" him to resolve the sensitive foreign policy decisions that bear on compliance with an ICJ decision and "to do so expeditiously." We do not question these propositions. See, *e.g., American Ins. Assn. v. Garamendi*, 539 U.S. 396, 414 (2003) (Article II of the Constitution places with the President the " 'vast share of responsibility for the conduct of our foreign relations' " (quoting *Youngstown Sheet & Tube Co. v. Sawyer*, 343 U.S. 579, 610–611 (1952) (Frankfurter, J., concurring))). In this case, the President seeks to vindicate United States interests in ensuring the reciprocal observance of the Vienna Convention, protecting relations with foreign governments, and demonstrating commitment to the role of international law. These interests are plainly compelling.

Such considerations, however, do not allow us to set aside first principles. The President's authority to act, as with the exercise of any governmental power, "must stem either from an act of Congress or from the Constitution itself." *Youngstown, supra,* at 585; *Dames & Moore v. Regan*, 453 U.S. 654, 668 (1981). Justice Jackson's familiar tripartite scheme provides the accepted framework for evaluating executive action in this area.

B

The United States marshals two principal arguments in favor of the President's authority "to establish binding rules of decision that preempt contrary state law." The Solicitor General first argues that the relevant treaties give the President the authority to implement the *Avena* judgment and that Congress has acquiesced in the exercise of such authority. The United States also relies upon an "independent" international dispute-resolution power wholly apart from the asserted authority based on the pertinent treaties.

1

The United States maintains that the President's Memorandum is authorized by the Optional Protocol and the U.N. Charter. That is, because the relevant treaties "create an obligation to comply with *Avena*," they "*implicitly* give the President authority to implement that treaty-based obligation." (emphasis added). As a result, the President's Memorandum is well grounded in the first category of the *Youngstown* framework.

We disagree. The President has an array of political and diplomatic means available to enforce international obligations, but unilaterally converting a non-self-executing treaty into a self-executing one is not among them. The responsibility for transforming an international obligation arising from a non-self-executing treaty into domestic law falls to Congress.

The requirement that Congress, rather than the President, implement a non-self-executing treaty derives from the text of the Constitution, which divides the treaty-making power between the President and the Senate. The Constitution vests the President with the authority to "make" a treaty. Art. II, § 2. If the Executive determines that a treaty should have domestic effect of its own force, that determination may be implemented in "mak[ing]" the treaty, by ensuring that it contains language plainly providing for domestic enforceability. If the treaty is to be self-executing in this respect, the Senate must consent to the treaty by the requisite two-thirds vote, *ibid.*, consistent with all other constitutional restraints.

Once a treaty is ratified without provisions clearly according it domestic effect, however, whether the treaty will ever have such effect is governed by the fundamental constitutional principle that "'[t]he power to make the necessary laws is in Congress; the power to execute in the President.'" *Hamdan v. Rumsfeld*, 548 U.S. 557, 591 (2006) (quoting *Ex parte Milligan*, 4 Wall. 2, 139 (1866) (opinion of Chase, C. J.)); see U.S. Const., Art. I, § 1 ("All legislative Powers herein granted shall be vested in a Congress of the United States"). The terms of a non-self-executing treaty can become domestic law only in the same way as any other law—through passage of legislation by both Houses of Congress, combined with either the President's signature or a congressional override of a Presidential veto. See Art. I, § 7. Indeed, "the President's power to see that the laws are faithfully executed refutes the idea that he is to be a lawmaker." *Youngstown*, 343 U.S., at 587.

A non-self-executing treaty, by definition, is one that was ratified with the understanding that it is not to have domestic effect of its own force. That understanding precludes the assertion that Congress has implicitly authorized the President—acting on his own—to achieve precisely the same result. We therefore conclude, given the absence of congressional legislation, that the non-self-executing treaties at issue here did not "express[ly] or implied[ly]" vest the President with the unilateral authority to make them self-executing. See *id.*, at 635 (Jackson, J., concurring). Accordingly, the President's Memorandum does not fall within the first category of the *Youngstown* framework.

Indeed, the preceding discussion should make clear that the non-self-executing character of the relevant treaties not only refutes the notion that the ratifying parties vested the President with the authority to unilaterally make treaty obligations binding on domestic courts, but also implicitly prohibits him from doing so. When the President asserts the power to "enforce" a non-self-executing treaty by unilaterally creating domestic law, he acts in conflict with the implicit understanding of the ratifying Senate. His assertion of authority, insofar as it is based on the pertinent non-self-executing treaties, is therefore within Justice Jackson's third category, not the first or even the second. See *id.*, at 637–638.

The United States nonetheless maintains that the President's Memorandum should be given effect as domestic law because "this case involves a valid Presidential action in the context of Congressional 'acquiescence.'" Under the *Youngstown* tripartite framework, congressional acquiescence is pertinent when the President's action falls within the second category—that is, when he "acts in absence of either a congressional grant or denial of authority." 343 U.S., at 637 (Jackson, J., concurring). Here, however, as we have explained, the President's effort to accord domestic effect to the *Avena* judgment does not meet that prerequisite.

In any event, even if we were persuaded that congressional acquiescence could support the President's asserted authority to create domestic law pursuant to a non-self-executing treaty, such acquiescence does not exist here. * * *

2

We thus turn to the United States' claim that — independent of the United States' treaty obligations — the Memorandum is a valid exercise of the President's foreign affairs authority to resolve claims disputes with foreign nations. The United States relies on a series of cases in which this Court has upheld the authority of the President to settle foreign claims pursuant to an executive agreement. See *Dames & Moore*, 453 U.S., at 679–680; *United States v. Pink*, 315 U.S. 203, 229 (1942). In these cases this Court has explained that, if pervasive enough, a history of congressional acquiescence can be treated as a "gloss on 'Executive Power' vested in the President by § 1 of Art. II." *Dames & Moore, supra*, at 686.

This argument is of a different nature than the one rejected above. Rather than relying on the United States' treaty obligations, the President relies on an independent source of authority in ordering Texas to put aside its procedural bar to successive habeas petitions. Nevertheless, we find that our claims-settlement cases do not support the authority that the President asserts in this case.

The claims-settlement cases involve a narrow set of circumstances: the making of executive agreements to settle civil claims between American citizens and foreign governments or foreign nationals. They are based on the view that "a systematic, unbroken, executive practice, long pursued to the knowledge of the Congress and never before questioned," can "raise a presumption that the [action] had been [taken] in pursuance of its consent." *Dames & Moore, supra*, at 686. Even still, the limitations on this source of executive power are clearly set forth and the Court has been careful to note that "[p]ast practice does not, by itself, create power." *Dames & Moore, supra*, at 686.

The President's Memorandum is not supported by a "particularly longstanding practice" of congressional acquiescence, but rather is what the United States itself has described as "unprecedented action[.]" Indeed, the Government has not identified a single instance in which the President has attempted (or Congress has acquiesced in) a Presidential directive issued to state courts, much less one that reaches deep into the heart of the State's police powers and compels state courts to reopen final criminal judgments and set aside neutrally applicable state laws. The Executive's narrow and strictly limited authority to settle international claims disputes pursuant to an executive agreement cannot stretch so far as to support the current Presidential Memorandum.

The judgment of the Texas Court of Criminal Appeals is affirmed.

It is so ordered.

Justice Stevens, concurring in the judgment. [Opinion omitted.]

Justice Breyer, with whom Justice Souter and Justice Ginsburg join, dissenting. [Opinion omitted.]

EXERCISE 16:

1. What analysis did the Supreme Court utilize to evaluate whether President Bush possessed the authority to cause the Vienna Convention to displace Texas' procedural law? Into what Justice Jackson category did the Court conclude this case fell, and for what reasons?

2. What textual, structural, traditional, and precedential arguments did the Court utilize in its analysis?

3. *Medellín* was (partly) a case about federal executive power, but what role did the constitutional principle of federalism play in the Court's reasoning?

4. What evidence did Chief Justice Roberts rely on to ascertain Congress' intent? Was that evidence sufficient? What did it show (according to the Chief Justice)?

5. How did the Court distinguish *Medellín* from *Dames & Moore*? Was the Court's distinction fair? After *Medellín*, for what proposition does *Dames & Moore* stand?

3. Recognition Power

ZIVOTOFSKY v. KERRY

135 S.Ct. 2076 (2015)

Justice Kennedy delivered the opinion of the Court.

A delicate subject lies in the background of this case. That subject is Jerusalem. Questions touching upon the history of the ancient city and its present legal and international status are among the most difficult and complex in international affairs. In our constitutional system these matters are committed to the Legislature and the Executive, not the Judiciary. As a result, in this opinion the Court does no more, and must do no more, than note the existence of international debate and tensions respecting Jerusalem. Those matters are for Congress and the President to discuss and consider as they seek to shape the Nation's foreign policies.

The Court addresses two questions to resolve the interbranch dispute now before it. First, it must determine whether the President has the exclusive power to grant formal recognition to a foreign sovereign. Second, if he has that power, the Court must determine whether Congress can command the President and his Secretary of State to issue a formal statement that contradicts the earlier recognition. The statement in question here is a congressional mandate that allows a United States citizen born in Jerusalem to direct the President and Secretary of State, when issuing his passport, to state that his place of birth is "Israel."

I

A

Jerusalem's political standing has long been, and remains, one of the most sensitive issues in American foreign policy, and indeed it is one of the most delicate issues in current international affairs. In 1948, President Truman formally recognized Israel in a signed statement of "recognition." That statement did not recognize Israeli sovereignty over Jerusalem. Over the last 60 years, various actors have sought to assert full or partial sovereignty over the city, including Israel, Jordan, and the Palestinians. Yet, in contrast to a consistent policy of formal recognition of Israel, neither President Truman nor any later United States President has issued an official statement or declaration acknowledging any country's sovereignty over Jerusalem. Instead, the Executive Branch has maintained that "the status of Jerusalem . . . should be decided not unilaterally but in consultation with all concerned."

In 2002, Congress passed the Act at issue here, the Foreign Relations Authorization Act, Fiscal Year 2003, 116 Stat. 1350. Section 214 of the Act is titled "United States Policy with Respect to Jerusalem as the Capital of Israel." The subsection that lies at the heart of this case, §214(d), addresses passports. That subsection seeks to override the FAM [Foreign Affairs Manual] by allowing citizens born in Jerusalem to list their place of birth as "Israel."

When he signed the Act into law, President George W. Bush issued a statement declaring his position that §214 would, "if construed as mandatory rather than advisory, impermissibly interfere with the President's constitutional authority to formulate the position of the United States, speak for the Nation in international affairs, and determine the terms on which recognition is given to foreign states."

B

In 2002, petitioner Menachem Binyamin Zivotofsky was born to United States citizens living in Jerusalem. In December 2002, Zivotofsky's mother visited the American Embassy in Tel Aviv to request both a passport and a consular report of birth abroad for her son. She asked that his place of birth be listed as "Jerusalem, Israel." The Embassy clerks explained that, pursuant to State Department policy, the passport would list only "Jerusalem."

II

In considering claims of Presidential power this Court refers to Justice Jackson's familiar tripartite framework from *Youngstown Sheet & Tube Co. v. Sawyer*, 343 U.S. 579, 635–638 (1952) (concurring opinion). In this case the Secretary contends that §214(d) infringes on the President's exclusive recognition power by "requiring the President to contradict his recognition position regarding Jerusalem in official communications with foreign sovereigns." In so doing the Secretary acknowledges the President's power is "at its lowest ebb." *Youngstown*, 343 U.S., at 637.

To determine whether the President possesses the exclusive power of recognition the Court examines the Constitution's text and structure, as well as precedent and history bearing on the question.

A

Recognition is a "formal acknowledgement" that a particular "entity possesses the qualifications for statehood" or "that a particular regime is the effective government of a state." RESTATEMENT (THIRD) OF FOREIGN RELATIONS LAW OF THE UNITED STATES § 203, Comment a, p. 84 (1986).

Despite the importance of the recognition power in foreign relations, the Constitution does not use the term "recognition," either in Article II or elsewhere. The Secretary asserts that the President exercises the recognition power based on the Reception Clause, which directs that the President "shall receive Ambassadors and other public Ministers." Art. II, § 3. Alexander Hamilton claimed that the power to receive ambassadors was "more a matter of dignity than of authority," a ministerial duty largely "without consequence." THE FEDERALIST No. 69.

At the time of the founding, however, prominent international scholars suggested that receiving an ambassador was tantamount to recognizing the sovereignty of the sending state. . . . It is a logical and proper inference, then, that a Clause directing the President alone to receive ambassadors would be understood to acknowledge his power to recognize other nations. This in fact occurred early in the Nation's history when President Washington recognized the French Revolutionary Government by receiving its ambassador. See A. Hamilton, PACIFICUS No. 1, in THE LETTERS OF PACIFICUS AND HELVIDIUS 5, 13–14 (1845) (reprint 1976) (President "acknowledged the republic of France, by the reception of its minister"). After this incident the import of the Reception Clause became clear—causing Hamilton to change his earlier view.

The inference that the President exercises the recognition power is further supported by his additional Article II powers. It is for the President, "by and with the Advice and Consent of the Senate," to "make Treaties, provided two thirds of the Senators present concur." Art. II, § 2, cl. 2. In addition, "he shall nominate, and by and with the Advice and Consent of the Senate, shall appoint Ambassadors" as well as "other public Ministers and Consuls." As a matter of constitutional structure, these additional powers give the President control over recognition decisions. At international law, recognition may be effected by different means, but each means is dependent upon Presidential power. The President, too, nominates the Nation's ambassadors and dispatches other diplomatic agents. Congress may not send an ambassador without his involvement. Beyond that, the President himself has the power to open diplomatic channels simply by engaging in direct diplomacy with foreign heads of state and their ministers. The Constitution thus assigns the President means to effect recognition on his own initiative. Congress, by contrast, has no constitutional power that would enable it to initiate diplomatic relations with a foreign nation. Because these specific Clauses confer the recognition power on the President, the Court need not consider whether or to what extent the Vesting Clause, which provides that the "executive Power" shall be vested in the President, provides further support for the President's action here.

The text and structure of the Constitution grant the President the power to recognize foreign nations and governments. The question then becomes whether that power is exclusive. The various ways in which the President may unilaterally effect recognition — and the lack of any similar power vested in Congress — suggest that it is. So, too, do functional considerations. Put simply, the Nation must have a single policy regarding which governments are legitimate in the eyes of the United States and which are not. Foreign countries need to know, before entering into diplomatic relations or commerce with the United States, whether their ambassadors will be received; whether their officials will be immune from suit in federal court; and whether they may initiate lawsuits here to vindicate their rights. These assurances cannot be equivocal.

Recognition is a topic on which the Nation must "speak . . . with one voice." That voice must be the President's.

It remains true, of course, that many decisions affecting foreign relations — including decisions that may determine the course of our relations with recognized countries — require congressional action. In addition, the President cannot make a treaty or appoint an ambassador without the approval of the Senate. Art. II, §2, cl. 2. The President, furthermore, could not build an American Embassy abroad without congressional appropriation of the necessary funds. Art. I, §8, cl. 1. Under basic separation-of-powers principles, it is for the Congress to enact the laws, including "all Laws which shall be necessary and proper for carrying into Execution" the powers of the Federal Government. §8, cl. 18.

In foreign affairs, as in the domestic realm, the Constitution "enjoins upon its branches separateness but interdependence, autonomy but reciprocity." Youngstown, 343 U. S., at 635 (Jackson, J., concurring). Although the President alone effects the formal act of recognition, Congress' powers, and its central role in making laws, give it substantial authority regarding many of the policy determinations that precede and follow the act of recognition itself. If Congress disagrees with the President's recognition policy, there may be consequences. Formal recognition may seem a hollow act if it is not accompanied by the dispatch of an ambassador, the easing of trade restrictions, and the conclusion of treaties. And those decisions require action by the Senate or the whole Congress.

In practice, then, the President's recognition determination is just one part of a political process that may require Congress to make laws. The President's exclusive recognition power encompasses the authority to acknowledge, in a formal sense, the legitimacy of other states and governments, including their territorial bounds. Albeit limited, the exclusive recognition power is essential to the conduct of Presidential duties. The formal act of recognition is an executive power that Congress may not qualify. If the President is to be effective in negotiations over a formal recognition determination, it must be evident to his counterparts abroad that he speaks for the Nation on that precise question.

A clear rule that the formal power to recognize a foreign government subsists in the President therefore serves a necessary purpose in diplomatic relations. All this, of course, underscores that Congress has an important role in other aspects of foreign policy, and the President may be bound by any number of laws Congress enacts. In this way ambition counters ambition, ensuring that the democratic will of the people is observed and respected in foreign affairs as in the domestic realm. See THE FEDERALIST No. 51 (J. Madison).

B

No single precedent resolves the question whether the President has exclusive recognition authority and, if so, how far that power extends.

* * *

C

Having examined the Constitution's text and this Court's precedent, it is appropriate to turn to accepted understandings and practice. In separation-of-powers cases this Court has often "put significant weight upon historical practice." *NLRB v. Noel Canning*, 573 U. S. ___, ___ (2014). Here, history is not all on one side, but on balance it provides strong support for the conclusion that the recognition power is the President's alone.

As Zivotofsky argues, certain historical incidents can be interpreted to support the position that recognition is a shared power. But the weight of historical evidence supports the opposite view, which is that the formal determination of recognition is a power to be exercised only by the President. . . . [E]ven a brief survey of the major historical examples, with an emphasis on those said to favor Zivotofsky, establishes no more than that some Presidents have chosen to cooperate with Congress, not that Congress itself has exercised the recognition power.

This history confirms the Court's conclusion in the instant case that the power to recognize or decline to recognize a foreign state and its territorial bounds resides in the President alone. For the most part, Congress has respected the Executive's policies and positions as to formal recognition. At times, Congress itself has defended the President's constitutional prerogative. Over the last 100 years, there has been scarcely any debate over the President's power to recognize foreign states. In this respect the Legislature, in the narrow context of recognition, on balance has acknowledged the importance of speaking "with one voice." The weight of historical evidence indicates Congress has accepted that the power to recognize foreign states and governments and their territorial bounds is exclusive to the Presidency.

III

The problem with § 214(d) . . . lies in how Congress exercised its authority over passports. It was an improper act for Congress to "aggrandiz[e] its power at the expense of another branch" by requiring the President to contradict an earlier recognition determination in an official document issued by the Executive Branch. To allow Congress to control the President's communication in the context of a formal recognition determination is to allow Congress to exercise that exclusive power itself. As a result, the statute is unconstitutional.

The judgment of the Court of Appeals for the District of Columbia Circuit is Affirmed.

[Justice Breyer's concurrence, which would prefer to defer to the President on political-question grounds, rather than exclusive recognition power, is omitted.]

Justice Thomas, concurring in the judgment in part and dissenting in part.

Our Constitution allocates the powers of the Federal Government over foreign affairs in two ways. First, it expressly identifies certain foreign affairs powers and vests them in particular branches, either individually or jointly. Second, it vests the residual foreign affairs powers of the Federal Government—i.e., those not specifically enumerated in the Constitution—in the President by way of Article II's Vesting Clause.

I

B

[T]hose who ratified the Constitution understood the "executive Power" vested by Article II to include those foreign affairs powers not otherwise allocated in the Constitution. James Iredell, for example, told the North Carolina ratifying convention that, under the new Constitution, the President would "regulate all intercourse with foreign powers" and act as the "primary agent" of the United States, though no specific allocation of foreign affairs powers in the document so provided. 4 Elliot['s Debates], 127, 128. And Alexander Hamilton presumed as much when he argued that the "[e]nergy" created in the Constitution's Executive would be "essential to the protection of the community against foreign attacks," even though no specific allocation of foreign affairs powers provided for the Executive to repel such assaults. See The Federalist No. 70. These statements confirm that the "executive Power" vested in the President by Article II includes the residual foreign affairs powers of the Federal Government not otherwise allocated by the Constitution.

C

Early practice of the founding generation also supports this understanding of the "executive Power."

II

A

2

b

The argument that § 214(d), as applied to passports, could be an exercise of Congress' power to carry into execution its foreign commerce or naturalization powers falters because this aspect of § 214(d) is directed at neither of the ends served by these powers. Although at a high level of generality, a passport could be related to foreign commerce and naturalization, that attenuated relationship is insufficient. The law in question must be "directly link[ed]" to the enumerated power. [*United States v. Comstock*, 560 U.S. 126,] 169, n. 8 [(2010) (Thomas, J., dissenting)].

As applied to passports, § 214(d) fails that test because it does not " 'carr[y] into Execution' " Congress' foreign commerce or naturalization powers. *Id.*, at 160. At most, it bears a tertiary relationship to an activity Congress is permitted to regulate: It directs the President's formulation of a document, which, in turn, may be used to facilitate travel, which, in turn, may facilitate foreign commerce. And the distinctive history of the passport as a travel rather than citizenship document makes its connection to naturalization even more tenuous.

Nor can this aspect of § 214(d) be justified as an exercise of Congress' power to enact laws to carry into execution the President's residual foreign affairs powers. Simply put, § 214(d)'s passport directive is not a "proper" means of carrying this power into execution.

To be "proper," a law must fall within the peculiar competence of Congress under the Constitution. Though "proper" was susceptible of several definitions at the time of the founding, only two are plausible candidates for use in the Necessary and Proper Clause — (1) "[f]it; accommodated; adapted; suitable; qualified" and (2) "[p]eculiar; not belonging to more; not common." See [Samuel Johnson's Dictionary] at 1537. Because the former would render the word "necessary" superfluous, *McCulloch* [*v. Maryland*, 17 U.S. 316,] 413 [(1819)], and we ordinarily attempt to give effect "to each word of the Constitution," the latter is the more plausible. That is particularly true because the Constitution elsewhere uses the term "proper" by itself, Art. I, § 9, Art. II, §§ 2, 3; the term "necessary" by itself, Art. I, § 7; Art. V; and the term "necessary" as part of the phrase "necessary and expedient," Art. II, § 3. Thus, the best interpretation of "proper" is that a law must fall within the peculiar jurisdiction of Congress.

Our constitutional structure imposes three key limitations on that jurisdiction: It must conform to (1) the allocation of authority within the Federal Government, (2) the allocation of power between the Federal Government and the States, and (3) the protections for retained individual rights under the Constitution. See Lawson & Granger, *The "Proper" Scope of Federal Power: A Jurisdictional Interpretation of the Sweeping Clause*, 43 DUKE L. J. 267, 291, 297 (1993). In other words, to be "proper," a law "must be consistent with principles of separation of powers, principles of federalism, and individual rights." *Id.*, at 297.

d

Justice Scalia characterizes my interpretation of the executive power, the naturalization power, and the Necessary and Proper Clause as producing "a presidency more reminiscent of George III than George Washington." But he offers no competing interpretation of either the Article II Vesting Clause or the Necessary and Proper Clause. And his decision about the Constitution's resolution of conflict among the branches could itself be criticized as creating a supreme legislative body more reminiscent of the Parliament in England than the Congress in America.

Justice Scalia, with whom The Chief Justice and Justice Alito join, dissenting.

Before this country declared independence, the law of England entrusted the King with the exclusive care of his kingdom's foreign affairs. The royal prerogative included the "sole power of sending ambassadors to foreign states, and receiving them at home," the sole authority to "make treaties, leagues, and alliances with foreign states and princes," "the sole prerogative of making war and peace," and the "sole power of raising and regulating fleets and armies." 1 W. Blackstone, Commentaries *253, *257, *262. The People of the United States had other ideas when they organized our Government. They considered a sound structure of balanced powers essential to the preservation of just government, and international relations formed no exception to that principle.

The People therefore adopted a Constitution that divides responsibility for the Nation's foreign concerns between the legislative and executive departments. The Constitution gave the President the "executive Power," authority to send and responsibility to receive ambassadors, power to make treaties, and command of the Army and Navy — though they qualified some of these powers by requiring consent of the Senate. Art. II, §§ 1–3. At the same time, they gave Congress powers over war, foreign commerce, naturalization, and more. Art. I, § 8. "Fully eleven of the powers that Article I, § 8 grants Congress deal in some way with foreign affairs." L. Tribe, American Constitutional Law, § 5–18, p. 965. This case arises out of a dispute between the Executive and Legislative Branches about whether the United States should treat Jerusalem as a part of Israel. The Constitution contemplates that the political branches will make policy about the territorial claims of foreign nations the same way they make policy about other international matters: The President will exercise his powers on the basis of his views, Congress its powers on the basis of its views. That is just what has happened here.

III

Even if the Constitution gives the President sole power to extend recognition, it does not give him sole power to make all decisions relating to foreign disputes over sovereignty. To the contrary, a fair reading of Article I allows Congress to decide for itself how its laws should handle these controversies. Read naturally, power to "regulate Commerce with foreign Nations," § 8, cl. 3, includes power to regulate imports from Gibraltar as British goods or as Spanish goods. Read naturally, power to "regulate the Value . . . of foreign Coin," § 8, cl. 5, includes power to honor (or not) currency issued by Taiwan. And so on for the other enumerated powers. These are not airy hypotheticals. A trade statute from 1800, for example, provided that "the whole of the island of Hispaniola" — whose status was then in controversy — "shall for purposes of [the] act be considered as a dependency of the French Republic." § 7, 2 Stat. 10. In 1938, Congress allowed admission of the Vatican City's public records in federal courts, decades before the United States extended formal recognition. ch.

682, 52 Stat. 1163. The Taiwan Relations Act of 1979 grants Taiwan capacity to sue and be sued, even though the United States does not recognize it as a state. 22 U. S. C. §3303(b)(7). Section 214(d) continues in the same tradition.

V

Justice Thomas's concurrence deems §214(d) constitutional to the extent it regulates birth reports, but unconstitutional to the extent it regulates passports. The concurrence finds no congressional power that would extend to the issuance or contents of passports. Including the power to regulate foreign commerce—even though passports facilitate the transportation of passengers, "a part of our commerce with foreign nations," *Henderson v. Mayor of New York*, 92 U. S. 259, 270 (1876). Including the power over naturalization—even though passports issued to citizens, like birth reports, "have the same force and effect as proof of United States citizenship as certificates of naturalization," 22 U. S. C. §2705. Including the power to enforce the Fourteenth Amendment's guarantee that "[a]ll persons born or naturalized in the United States . . . are citizens of the United States"—even though a passport provides evidence of citizenship and so helps enforce this guarantee abroad. Including the power to exclude persons from the territory of the United States, see Art. I, §9, cl. 1—even though passports are the principal means of identifying citizens entitled to entry. Including the powers under which Congress has restricted the ability of various people to leave the country (fugitives from justice, for example, see 18 U. S. C. §1073)—even though passports are the principal means of controlling exit. Including the power to "make all needful Rules and Regulations respecting the Territory or other Property belonging to the United States," Art. IV, §3, cl. 2—even though "[a] passport remains at all times the property of the United States," 7 FAM §1317 (2013). The concurrence's stingy interpretation of the enumerated powers forgets that the Constitution does not "partake of the prolixity of a legal code," that "only its great outlines [are] marked, its important objects designated, and the minor ingredients which compose those objects [left to] be deduced from the nature of the objects themselves." McCulloch, 4 Wheat. [17 U.S. 316,], 407 [(1819)]. It forgets, in other words, "that it is a *constitution* we are expounding." *Ibid*.

Whereas the Court's analysis threatens congressional power over foreign affairs with gradual erosion, the concurrence's approach shatters it in one stroke. The combination of (a) the concurrence's assertion of broad, unenumerated "residual powers" in the President; (b) its parsimonious interpretation of Congress's enumerated powers; and (c) its even more parsimonious interpretation of Congress's authority to enact laws "necessary and proper for carrying into Execution" the President's executive powers; produces (d) a presidency more reminiscent of George III than George Washington.

EXERCISE 17:

1. Should President Bush have vetoed the resolution, rather than noting his constitutional objections in a signing statement? Remember this issue when we consider "presidential review" in **Chapter 3**.

2. Is *Zivotofsky* a case about Congress's powers under Article I, or the President's powers under Article II? Does it matter?

3. How do the majority and Justice Thomas disagree?

4. To what extent is the debate among the members of the Court the same as the debate between Madison and Hamilton over French neutrality?

5. Many observers worried that the statute at issue here, if enforced, would have antagonized the Arab world. If Congress wants to antagonize another country, but the President does not, what does our Constitution require? If the President does not want to fight a war, can Congress make him do so? Can Congress at least declare that a state of hostility exists between the United States and another country?

4. War Powers

As with international agreements, the Constitution also grants both Congress and the President roles in military conflicts. Article I, § 8, cl. 11, grants Congress the power to "declare War," and subsequent clauses grant it other military-related powers. Article II, § 2, cl. 1, designates the President as the "Commander in Chief of the Army and Navy of the United States."

There are many facets of military affairs including the initiation of hostilities, the conduct of military action, prisoner detention, and cessation of military action. For many of these facets, there are no clear answers to the question of which branch has what authority, and for many reasons. For example, though the Constitution expressly authorized Congress to declare war, many of the conflicts in which the United States has engaged, including many major ones, such as the Korean War, did not involve formal declarations of war. *See also Ludecke v. Watkins*, 335 U.S. 160, 168 (1948) (stating that "'[t]he state of war' may be terminated by treaty or legislation or Presidential proclamation.").

One clear statement about the respective roles of Congress and the President is found in the War Powers Resolution, 50 U.S.C. § 1541 *et seq.*, reprinted below. The Resolution's constitutional status, however, is strongly contested.

THE WAR POWERS RESOLUTION (1973)

50 U.S.C.A. § 1541 *et seq.*

§ 1541. Purpose and policy

(a) Congressional declaration

It is the purpose of this chapter to fulfill the intent of the framers of the Constitution of the United States and insure that the collective judgment of both the Congress and the President will apply to the introduction of United States Armed Forces into hostilities, or into situations where imminent involvement in hostilities is clearly indicated by the circumstances, and to the continued use of such forces in hostilities or in such situations.

(b) Congressional legislative power under necessary and proper clause

* * *

(c) Presidential executive power as Commander-in-Chief; limitation

The constitutional powers of the President as Commander-in-Chief to introduce United States Armed Forces into hostilities, or into situations where imminent involvement in hostilities is clearly indicated by the circumstances, are exercised only pursuant to (1) a declaration of war, (2) specific statutory authorization, or (3) a national emergency created by attack upon the United States, its territories or 50 possessions, or its armed forces.

§ 1542. Consultation; initial and regular consultations

The President in every possible instance shall consult with Congress before introducing United States Armed Forces into hostilities or into situations where imminent involvement in hostilities is clearly indicated by the circumstances, and after every such introduction shall consult regularly with the Congress until United States Armed Forces are no longer engaged in hostilities or have been removed from such situations.

§ 1543. Reporting requirement

(a) Written report; time of submission; circumstances necessitating submission; information reported

In the absence of a declaration of war, in any case in which United States Armed Forces are introduced —

(1) into hostilities or into situations where imminent involvement in hostilities is clearly indicated by the circumstances;

(2) into the territory, airspace or waters of a foreign nation, while equipped for combat, except for deployments which relate solely to supply, replacement, repair, or training of such forces; or

(3) in numbers which substantially enlarge United States Armed Forces equipped for combat already located in a foreign nation;

the President shall submit within 48 hours to the Speaker of the House of Representatives and to the President pro tempore of the Senate a report, in writing, setting forth —

(A) the circumstances necessitating the introduction of United States Armed Forces;

(B) the constitutional and legislative authority under which such introduction took place; and

(C) the estimated scope and duration of the hostilities or involvement.

(b) Other information reported

The President shall provide such other information as the Congress may request in the fulfillment of its constitutional responsibilities with respect to committing the Nation to war and to the use of United States Armed Forces abroad.

(c) Periodic reports; semiannual requirement

Whenever United States Armed Forces are introduced into hostilities or into any situation described in subsection (a) of this section, the President shall, so long as such armed forces continue to be engaged in such hostilities or situation, report to the Congress periodically on the status of such hostilities or situation as well as on the scope and duration of such hostilities or situation, but in no event shall he report to the Congress less often than once every six months.

§ 1544. Congressional action

(b) Termination of use of United States Armed Forces; exceptions; extension period

Within sixty calendar days after a report is submitted or is required to be submitted pursuant to section 1543(a)(1) of this title, whichever is earlier, the President shall terminate any use of United States Armed Forces with respect to which such report was submitted (or required to be submitted), unless the Congress (1) has declared war or has enacted a specific authorization for such use of United States Armed Forces, (2) has extended by law such sixty-day period, or (3) is physically unable to meet as a result of an armed attack upon the United States. Such sixty-day period shall be extended for not more than an additional thirty days if the President determines and certifies to the Congress in writing that unavoidable military necessity respecting the safety of United States Armed Forces requires the continued use of such armed forces in the course of bringing about a prompt removal of such forces.

(c) Concurrent resolution for removal by President of United States Armed Forces

Notwithstanding subsection (b) of this section, at any time that United States Armed Forces are engaged in hostilities outside the territory of the United States, its possessions and territories without a declaration of war or specific statutory authorization, such forces shall be removed by the President if the Congress so directs by concurrent resolution.

§ 1547. Interpretation of joint resolution

(a) Inferences from any law or treaty

Authority to introduce United States Armed Forces into hostilities or into situations wherein involvement in hostilities is clearly indicated by the circumstances shall not be inferred—

(1) from any provision of law (whether or not in effect before November 7, 1973), including any provision contained in any appropriation Act, unless such provision specifically authorizes the introduction of United States Armed Forces into hostilities or into such situations and states that it is intended to constitute specific statutory authorization within the meaning of this chapter[.]

(c) Introduction of United States Armed Forces

For purposes of this chapter, the term "introduction of United States Armed Forces" includes the assignment of members of such armed forces to command, coordinate, participate in the movement of, or accompany the regular or irregular military forces of any foreign country or government when such military forces are engaged, or there exists an imminent threat that such forces will become engaged, in hostilities.

(d) Constitutional authorities or existing treaties unaffected; construction against grant of Presidential authority respecting use of United States Armed Forces

Nothing in this chapter —

(1) is intended to alter the constitutional authority of the Congress or of the President, or the provisions of existing treaties; or

(2) shall be construed as granting any authority to the President with respect to the introduction of United States Armed Forces into hostilities or into situations wherein involvement in hostilities is clearly indicated by the circumstances which authority he would not have had in the absence of this chapter.

EXERCISE 18:

1. What requirements did the Resolution impose upon the President?

2. Which of the Resolution's requirements are most open to constitutional challenge, and why?

3. Into what Jackson category does the Resolution fall?

4. What powers does Congress reserve for itself or its members in the Resolution? Keep this issue in mind when we discuss *INS v. Chadha* in **Chapter 3**.

5. President Nixon vetoed the Resolution, though Congress overrode his veto, and subsequent Presidents have contested the Resolution's constitutionality, though all or nearly all have ostensibly complied with it. Should this presidential opposition to the Resolution impact the Supreme Court's assessment of its constitutionality?

6. The Supreme Court, and lower federal courts, have studiously refrained from evaluating the Resolution's constitutionality. Assuming that a President violated one or more of the Resolution's strictures, what non-judicial recourse would Congress have?

7. A facet of conducting military conflicts that has frequently arisen, and which has received moderate Supreme Court attention, is whether and, if so, the extent of executive power to detain and try alleged members of enemy forces (and other persons required under the circumstances). These cases intertwine with other areas of law, such as habeas corpus, which makes them complex, and it is therefore difficult to sort out those facets of the cases dealing only with the scope of executive power. The Supreme Court issued a key case, *Ex parte Milligan*, 71 U.S. 2 (1866), immediately after the Civil War, where it ruled that President Lincoln exceeded his executive

power when he ordered a military trial of Milligan, a civilian, because Milligan's alleged wrongdoing occurred in Indiana, where the civilian courts remained in operation. Dicta in the case, however, suggested significant presidential authority in theaters of war even without explicit congressional authorization. During World War II, in *Ex parte Quirin*, 317 U.S. 1 (1942), the Court upheld President Roosevelt's exercise of executive power to use military tribunals to try suspected German saboteurs who were arrested on American soil, though the Court relied heavily on congressional authorization for the tribunals. In *Hamdan v. Rumsfeld*, 548 U.S. 557 (2006), the Court noted regarding *Milligan*: "Whether Chief Justice Chase was correct in suggesting that the President may constitutionally convene military commissions 'without the sanction of Congress' in cases of 'controlling necessity' is a question this Court has not answered definitively, and need not answer today." The Court held that such military necessity was not adequately established.

8. The extent of presidential inherent authority to initiate hostilities has been debated each time the President has used force. For an assessment of recent presidential uses of force and the justifications that have been given, see Michael Ramsey, *Constitutional War Initiation and the Obama Presidency*, 110 Am. J. Int'l L. 701 (2016). In addition to looking in detail at the Obama Administration's justifications for using force in Iraq, Syria, Libya, Yemen, Afghanistan, Pakistan, and Somalia, Ramsey canvasses all significant presidential uses of force from 1975 to 2008. Ramsey argues that presidential practice has been closer to an original meaning requiring congressional approval prior to the initiating war than many other commentators have assumed.

Chapter 3

THE SEPARATION OF EXECUTIVE FROM LEGISLATIVE POWER

A. INTRODUCTION

Chapter 1 concerned the internal structure and relationships among those who exercise executive power, and **Chapter 2** considered its scope and the subjects to which it is applied. This Chapter, however, considers the relationship between that sphere and the sphere of legislative power.

The separation of powers is a fundamental principle of the Constitution and the federal government it created. The separation of powers means that one branch of the federal government may exercise only its delegated power and may not exercise the power of another branch. The separation of powers is both a limit on the federal branches of government and a mechanism to protect the other branches. In doing so, the separation of powers prevents the consolidation of federal power in one branch and thereby protects individual liberty and federalism. **Chapter 1** already introduced you to the separation of powers principle in the context of disputes between the President and Congress over appointments and removal.

James Madison's ode to the separation of powers in *Federalist 51* captures beautifully one of the central aspects of the American experiment:

> But the great security against a gradual concentration of the several powers in the same department, consists in giving to those who administer each department the necessary constitutional means and personal motives to resist encroachments of the others. The provision for defense must in this, as in all other cases, be made commensurate to the danger of attack. Ambition must be made to counteract ambition. The interest of the man must be connected with the constitutional rights of the place. It may be a reflection on human nature, that such devices should be necessary to control the abuses of government. But what is government itself, but the greatest of all reflections on human nature? If men were angels, no government would be necessary. If angels were to govern men, neither external nor internal controls on government would be necessary. In framing a government which is to be

administered by men over men, the great difficulty lies in this: you must first enable the government to control the governed; and in the next place oblige it to control itself. A dependence on the people is, no doubt, the primary control on the government; but experience has taught mankind the necessity of auxiliary precautions. This policy of supplying, by opposite and rival interests, the defect of better motives, might be traced through the whole system of human affairs, private as well as public. We see it particularly displayed in all the subordinate distributions of power, where the constant aim is to divide and arrange the several offices in such a manner as that each may be a check on the other that the private interest of every individual may be a sentinel over the public rights. These inventions of prudence cannot be less requisite in the distribution of the supreme powers of the State.

The separation of powers limits (and protects) *all* three branches of the federal government. You have already seen how the separation of powers protected the judicial branch from congressional encroachment in Volume 1 in *Miller v. French*, 530 U.S. 327 (2000), and how it limited the executive branch's encroachment on the judiciary in the note case *CFTC v. Schor*, 478 U.S. 833 (1986). Below are cases considering the principles that prevent the executive branch from exercising legislative power and the legislative branch from exercising executive power.

A *distinction* between legislative power and executive power is clear simply from the structure of Articles I and II and their separate grants of power. Executive power is one thing, and legislative power is another; Chapter 2 considers the difficult question which is which. To keep these two sorts of powers from being joined together, a separation of *personnel* is also required. A separation of personnel between the legislative and executive branch is most clearly expressed in Art. I, § 6, cl. 2: "No Senator or Representative shall, during the Time for which he was elected, be appointed to any civil Office under the Authority of the United States, which shall have been created, or the Emoluments whereof shall have been increased during such time; and no Person holding any Office under the United States, shall be a Member of either House during his Continuance in Office." No such rule prohibits simultaneous holding of executive and judicial offices. In fact, for a brief time during the run-up to *Marbury v. Madison*, John Marshall served as both Secretary of State and as Chief Justice. In early British practice, judges were generally seen as part of the executive branch, but in the Act of Settlement of 1701, judges received tenure during good behavior and began to be seen as a separate third branch of government. However, mingling of personnel between the legislative and executive branches of British government became quite regular indeed; the king's chief ministers were taken from Parliament. Provisions like Art. I, § 6, cl. 2 mark, of course, a clear break from this British practice. The cases in this Chapter separating legislative from executive power elaborate the broader principles of which that provision is an instance.

B. EXCLUDING THE EXECUTIVE FROM LAWMAKING

1. The Nondelegation of Legislative Power

Article I opens with its Vesting Clause: "All legislative Powers herein granted shall be vested in a Congress of the United States." This Clause is the primary textual source of the Nondelegation Doctrine. The Nondelegation Doctrine is also a key product and component of the separation of powers. It designates one body—Congress— as the recipient of "[a]ll" legislative power granted by the Constitution to the federal government. The Constitution, with limited express exceptions, does not grant legislative power to the executive or judicial branches. The Vesting Clause makes Congress accountable for its legislation, gives Congress power to make important political judgments for the American People, protects Congress from the other branches, and prevents the other branches from aggregating all federal power into their hands.

However, the Supreme Court has struggled, from the beginning of the Republic, with how to follow the Vesting Clause faithfully while, at the same time, enabling (especially) the executive branch to carry out its functions. The reason for this is that the President must exercise at least some discretion when "faithfully execut[ing]" the law, which frequently makes the President's actions seem like legislation. For example, in the tariff context, so long as Congress does not specify the tax for each and every product imported to America's shores, the executive branch will exercise discretion to decide under which congressional tax designation a particular product falls.

This line-drawing problem was largely theoretical until the late-nineteenth century, because Congress rarely exercised the full breadth of its legislative powers over American life, and because it rarely delegated significant discretion to the President, especially in the domestic sphere. However, during the Progressive and New Deal eras, Congress began to robustly regulate American life and, at the same time, give significant discretion to the executive branch. One of the Supreme Court's important attempts to "thread the needle" was *J.W. Hampton, Jr. & Co. v. United States*, 276 U.S. 394, 401 (1928), where Hampton challenged, as an unconstitutional delegation of legislative power, a congressional delegation to the President to "equalize the . . . differences in costs of production in the United States and the principal competing country" by adjusting tariffs. The Court, speaking through Chief Justice—and former President—Taft, ruled that the statute was constitutional because it contained an "intelligible principle" to guide the President's discretion. *Id.* at 409.

> It is conceded by counsel that Congress may use executive officers in the application and enforcement of a policy declared in law by Congress and authorize such officers in the application of the congressional declaration to enforce it by regulation equivalent to law. But it is said that this never has been permitted to be done where Congress has exercised the power to levy taxes and fix customs duties. The authorities make no such distinction. The same principle that permits Congress to exercise its rate-making power in

interstate commerce by declaring the rule which shall prevail in the legislative fixing of rates, and enables it to remit to a rate-making body created in accordance with its provisions the fixing of such rates, justifies a similar provision for the fixing of customs duties on imported merchandise. If Congress shall lay down by legislative act an intelligible principle to which the person or body authorized to fix such rates is directed to conform, such legislative action is not a forbidden delegation of legislative power. If it is thought wise to vary the customs duties according to changing conditions of production at home and abroad, it may authorize the Chief Executive to carry out this purpose

Id.

Of course, a short one year later, the Great Depression set in, and, in 1932, President Franklin Roosevelt was elected on the promise of a New Deal, which he immediately began implementing via an overwhelmingly sympathetic Congress, through the so-called First New Deal. The centerpiece of the First New Deal was the National Industrial Recovery Act (NIRA). 48 Stat. 195 (1933). The NIRA was an unprecedented exercise of federal legislative and executive power. You will cover challenges to Congress' power to enact the NIRA under its Commerce Clause authority in Volume 3. Here, we will review the nondelegation challenges to the NIRA.

The first such case to reach the Supreme Court was *Panama Refining Co. v. Ryan*, 293 U.S. 388 (1935), where the Court, in an eight to one vote, struck down one section, the "hot oil" provisions of the NIRA. However, that left most of the Act intact. Then came the following case.

A.L.A. SCHECHTER POULTRY CORPORATION
v. UNITED STATES
295 U.S. 495 (1935)

Mr. Chief Justice Hughes delivered the opinion of the Court.

[I]

Petitioners were convicted in the District Court of the United States for the Eastern District of New York on eighteen counts of an indictment charging violations of what is known as the 'Live Poultry Code,' and on an additional count for conspiracy to commit such violations. By demurrer to the indictment and appropriate motions on the trial, the defendants contended (1) that the code had been adopted pursuant to an unconstitutional delegation by Congress of legislative power; (2) that it attempted to regulate intrastate transactions which lay outside the authority of Congress; and (3) that in certain provisions it was repugnant to the due process clause of the Fifth Amendment.

The Circuit Court of Appeals sustained the conviction on the conspiracy count and on sixteen counts for violation of the code, but reversed the conviction on two counts which charged violation of requirements as to minimum wages and maximum hours of labor, as these were not deemed to be within the congressional power of regulation. On the respective applications of the defendants and of the government, this Court granted writs of certiorari April 15, 1935.

[II]

New York City is the largest live poultry market in the United States. Ninety-six per cent of the live poultry there marketed comes from other states. Three-fourths of this amount arrives by rail and is consigned to commission men or receivers. Most of these freight shipments (about 75 per cent.) come in at the Manhattan Terminal of the New York Central Railroad, and the remainder at one of the four terminals in New Jersey serving New York City. The commission men transact by far the greater part of the business on a commission basis, representing the shippers as agents, and remitting to them the proceeds of sale, less commissions, freight, and handling charges. Otherwise, they buy for their own account. They sell to slaughterhouse operators who are also called marketmen.

The defendants are slaughterhouse operators of the latter class. A.L.A. Schechter Poultry Corporation and Schechter Live Poultry Market are corporations conducting wholesale poultry slaughterhouse markets in Brooklyn, New York City. Defendants ordinarily purchase their live poultry from commission men at the West Washington Market in New York City or at the railroad terminals serving the city, but occasionally they purchase from commission men in Philadelphia. They buy the poultry for slaughter and resale. After the poultry is trucked to their slaughterhouse markets in Brooklyn, it is there sold, usually within twenty-four hours, to retail poultry dealers and butchers who sell directly to consumers. The poultry purchased from defendants is immediately slaughtered, prior to delivery, by shochtim in defendants' employ. Defendants do not sell poultry in interstate commerce.

The 'Live Poultry Code' was promulgated under section 3 of the National Industrial Recovery Act. That section authorizes the President to approve 'codes of fair competition.' Such a code may be approved for a trade or industry, upon application by one or more trade or industrial associations or groups, if the President finds (1) that such associations or groups 'impose no inequitable restrictions on admission to membership therein and are truly representative,' and (2) that such codes are not designed 'to promote monopolies or to eliminate or oppress small enterprises and will not operate to discriminate against them, and will tend to effectuate the policy' of title 1 of the act. Such codes 'shall not permit monopolies or monopolistic practices.' As a condition of his approval, the President may 'impose such conditions for the protection of consumers, competitors, employees, and others, and in furtherance of the public interest, and may provide such exceptions to and exemptions from the provisions of such code as the President in his discretion deems necessary to effectuate the policy herein declared.' Where such a code has not been approved, the President may prescribe one, either on his own motion or on complaint. Violation of any provision of a code (so approved or prescribed) is made a misdemeanor punishable by a fine of not more than $500 for each offense, and each day the violation continues is to be deemed a separate offense.

The 'Live Poultry Code' was approved by the President on April 13, 1934. The declared purpose is 'To effect the policies of title I of the National Industrial Recovery Act.' The code is established as 'a code for fair competition for the live poultry industry of the metropolitan area in and about the City of New York.'

The code fixes the number of hours for workdays. It provides that no employee, with certain exceptions, shall be permitted to work in excess of forty hours in any one week, and that no employees, save as stated, 'shall be paid in any pay period less than at the rate of fifty (50) cents per hour.' The article containing 'general labor provisions' prohibits the employment of any person under 16 years of age, and declares that employees shall have the right of 'collective bargaining' and freedom of choice with respect to labor organizations. The minimum number of employees, who shall be employed by slaughterhouse operators, is fixed; the number being graduated according to the average volume of weekly sales.

Provision is made for administration through an 'industry advisory committee,' to be selected by trade associations and members of the industry, and a 'code supervisor,' to be appointed, with the approval of the committee, by agreement between the Secretary of Agriculture and the Administrator for Industrial Recovery.

The President approved the code by an executive order (No. 6675-A) in which he found that the application for his approval had been duly made in accordance with the provisions of title 1 of the National Industrial Recover Act; that there had been due notice and hearings; that the code constituted 'a code of fair competition' as contemplated by the act and complied with its pertinent provisions; and that the code would tend 'to effectuate the policy of Congress as declared in section 1 of Title I.'

[III]

The Question of the Delegation of Legislative Power. — We recently had occasion to review the pertinent decisions and the general principles which govern the determination of this question. *Panama Refining Company v. Ryan*, 293 U.S. 388 [(1935)]. The Constitution provides that 'All legislative powers herein granted shall be vested in a Congress of the United States, which shall consist of a Senate and House of Representatives.' Article 1, s 1. And the Congress is authorized 'To make all Laws which shall be necessary and proper for carrying into Execution' its general powers. Article 1, s 8, par. 18. The Congress is not permitted to abdicate or to transfer to others the essential legislative functions with which it is thus vested. We have repeatedly recognized the necessity of adapting legislation to complex conditions involving a host of details with which the national Legislature cannot deal directly. We pointed out in the *Panama Refining Company* Case that the Constitution has never been regarded as denying to Congress the necessary resources of flexibility and practicality, which will enable it to perform its function in laying down policies and establishing standards, while leaving to selected instrumentalities the making of subordinate rules within prescribed limits and the determination of facts to which the policy as declared by the Legislature is to apply. But we said that the constant recognition of the necessity and validity of such provisions, and the wide range of administrative authority which has been developed by means of them, cannot be allowed to obscure the limitations of the authority to delegate, if our constitutional system is to be maintained.

Accordingly, we look to the statute to see whether Congress has overstepped these limitations—whether Congress in authorizing 'codes of fair competition' has itself established the standards of legal obligation, thus performing its essential legislative function, or, by the failure to enact such standards, has attempted to transfer that function to others.

What is meant by 'fair competition' as the term is used in the act? Does it refer to a category established in the law, and is the authority to make codes limited accordingly? Or is it used as a convenient designation for whatever set of laws the formulators of a code for a particular trade or industry may propose and the President may approve (subject to certain restrictions), or the President may himself prescribe, as being wise and beneficent provisions for the government of the trade or industry in order to accomplish the broad purposes of rehabilitation, correction, and expansion which are stated in the first section of title 1?[9]

The act does not define 'fair competition.' 'Unfair competition,' as known to the common law, is a limited concept. Primarily, and strictly, it relates to the palming off of one's goods as those of a rival trader. In recent years, its scope has been extended. It has been held to apply to misappropriation as well as misrepresentation, to the selling of another's goods as one's own—to misappropriation of what equitably belongs to a competitor. Unfairness in competition has been predicated of acts which lie outside the ordinary course of business and are tainted by fraud or coercion or conduct otherwise prohibited by law. But it is evident that in its widest range, 'unfair competition,' as it has been understood in the law, does not reach the objectives of the codes which are authorized by the National Industrial Recovery Act. The codes may, indeed, cover conduct which existing law condemns, but they are not limited to conduct of that sort. The government does not contend that the act contemplates such a limitation.

---

9. That section, under the heading 'Declaration of Policy,' is as follows: 'Section 1. A national emergency productive of widespread unemployment and disorganization of industry, which burdens interstate and foreign commerce, affects the public welfare, and undermines the standards of living of the American people, is hereby declared to exist. It is hereby declared to be the policy of Congress to remove obstructions to the free flow of interstate and foreign commerce which tend to diminish the amount thereof; and to provide for the general welfare by promoting the organization of industry for the purpose of co-operative action among trade groups, to induce and maintain united action of labor and management under adequate governmental sanctions and supervision, to eliminate unfair competitive practices, to promote the fullest possible utilization of the present productive capacity of industries, to avoid undue restriction of production (except as may be temporarily required), to increase the consumption of industrial and agricultural products by increasing purchasing power, to reduce and relieve unemployment, to improve standards of labor, and otherwise to rehabilitate industry and to conserve natural resources.'

It would be opposed both to the declared purposes of the act and to its administrative construction.

For a statement of the authorized objectives and content of the 'codes of fair competition,' we are referred repeatedly to the 'Declaration of Policy' in section 1 of title 1 of the Recovery Act. Thus the approval of a code by the President is conditioned on his finding that it 'will tend to effectuate the policy of this title.' Section 3(a) of the act. But, even if this clause were to be taken to relate to practices which fall under the ban of existing law, either common law or statute, it is still only one of the authorized aims described in section 1. Under section 3, whatever 'may tend to effectuate' these general purposes may be included in the 'codes of fair competition.' We think the conclusion is inescapable that the authority sought to be conferred by section 3 was not merely to deal with 'unfair competitive practices' which offend against existing law, and could be the subject of judicial condemnation without further legislation, or to create administrative machinery for the application of established principles of law to particular instances of violation. Rather, the purpose is clearly disclosed to authorize new and controlling prohibitions through codes of laws which would embrace what the formulators would propose, and what the President would approve or prescribe, as wise and beneficent measures for the government of trades and industries in order to bring about their rehabilitation, correction, and development, according to the general declaration of policy in section 1. Codes of laws of this sort are styled 'codes of fair competition.'

We find no real controversy upon this point and we must determine the validity of the code in question in this aspect. As the government candidly says in its brief: 'The words 'policy of this title' clearly refer to the 'policy' which Congress declared in the section entitled 'Declaration of Policy'—Section 1. All of the policies there set forth point toward a single goal—the rehabilitation of industry and the industrial recovery which unquestionably was the major policy of Congress in adopting the National Industrial Recovery Act.' And that this is the controlling purpose of the code now before us appears both from its repeated declarations to that effect and from the scope of its requirements.

The government urges that the codes will 'consist of rules of competition deemed fair for each industry by representative members of that industry—by the persons most vitally concerned and most familiar with its problems.' But would it be seriously contended that Congress could delegate its legislative authority to trade or industrial associations or groups so as to empower them to enact the laws they deem to be wise and beneficent for the rehabilitation and expansion of their trade or industries? Could trade or industrial associations or groups be constituted legislative bodies for that purpose because such associations or groups are familiar with the problems of their enterprises? And could an effort of that sort be made valid by such a preface of generalities as to permissible aims as we find in section 1 of title 1? The answer is obvious. Such a delegation of legislative power is unknown to our law, and is utterly inconsistent with the constitutional prerogatives and duties of Congress.

The question, then, turns upon the authority which section 3 of the Recovery Act vests in the President to approve or prescribe. If the codes have standing as penal statutes, this must be due to the effect of the executive action. But Congress cannot delegate legislative power to the President to exercise an unfettered discretion to make whatever laws he thinks may be needed or advisable for the rehabilitation and expansion of trade or industry. See *Panama Refining Company v. Ryan.*

Accordingly we turn to the Recovery Act to ascertain what limits have been set to the exercise of the President's discretion: First, the President, as a condition of approval, is required to find that the trade or industrial associations or groups which propose a code 'impose no inequitable restrictions on admission to membership' and are 'truly representative.' That condition, however, relates only to the status of the initiators of the new laws and not to the permissible scope of such laws. Second, the President is required to find that the code is not 'designed to promote monopolies or to eliminate or oppress small enterprises and will not operate to discriminate against them.' And to this is added a proviso that the code 'shall not permit monopolies or monopolistic practices.' But these restrictions leave virtually untouched the field of policy envisaged by section 1, and, in that wide field of legislative possibilities, the proponents of a code, refraining from monopolistic designs, may roam at will, and the President may approve or disapprove their proposals as he may see fit. That is the precise effect of the further finding that the President is to make — that the code 'will tend to effectuate the policy of this title.' While this is called a finding, it is really but a statement of an opinion as to the general effect upon the promotion of trade or industry of a scheme of laws. These are the only findings which Congress has made essential in order to put into operation a legislative code having the aims described in the 'Declaration of Policy.'

Nor is the breadth of the President's discretion left to the necessary implications of this limited requirement as to his findings. As already noted, the President in approving a code may impose his own conditions, adding to or taking from what is proposed, as 'in his discretion' he thinks necessary 'to effectuate the policy' declared by the act. Of course, he has no less liberty when he prescribes a code on his own motion or on complaint, and he is free to prescribe one if a code has not been approved. And this authority relates to a host of different trades and industries, thus extending the President's discretion to all the varieties of laws which he may deem to be beneficial in dealing with the vast array of commercial and industrial activities throughout the country.

To summarize and conclude upon this point: Section 3 of the Recovery Act is without precedent. It supplies no standards for any trade, industry, or activity. It does not undertake to prescribe rules of conduct to be applied to particular states of fact determined by appropriate administrative procedure. Instead of prescribing rules of conduct, it authorizes the making of codes to prescribe them. For that legislative undertaking, section 3 sets up no standards, aside from the statement of the general aims of rehabilitation, correction, and expansion described in section 1. In view of the scope of that broad declaration and of the nature of the few restrictions that are imposed, the discretion of the President in approving or prescribing codes, and thus enacting laws for the government of trade and industry throughout the country, is virtually unfettered. We think that the code-making authority thus conferred is an unconstitutional delegation of legislative power.

[IV]

[The Supreme Court then concluded that the Code was beyond Congress' Commerce Clause authority.]

[V]

On both the grounds we have discussed, the attempted delegation of legislative power and the attempted regulation of intrastate transactions which affect interstate commerce only indirectly, we hold the code provisions here in question to be invalid and that the judgment of conviction must be reversed.

Mr. Justice Cardozo (concurring).

The delegated power of legislation which has found expression in this code is not canalized within banks that keep it from overflowing. It is unconfined and vagrant. Here, in the case before us, is an attempted delegation not confined to any single act nor to any class or group of acts identified or described by reference to a standard. Here in effect is a roving commission to inquire into evils and upon discovery correct them.

I have said that there is no standard, definite or even approximate, to which legislation must conform. Let me make my meaning more precise. The code does not confine itself to the suppression of methods of competition that would be classified as unfair according to accepted business standards or accepted norms of ethics. It sets up a comprehensive body of rules to promote the welfare of the industry, if not the welfare of the nation, without reference to standards, ethical or commercial, that could be known or predicted in advance of its adoption. One of the new rules, the source of ten counts in the indictment, is aimed at an established practice, not unethical or oppressive, the practice of selective buying.

I am authorized to state that Mr. Justice Stone joins in this opinion.

EXERCISE 19:

1. What authority did Congress delegate to the President in the NIRA? On a scale of one to ten, with ten being the most capacious, how much power did Congress delegate to the President?

2. What restrictions or limits did Congress place on the President's exercise of the delegated authority? Do these restrictions change your answer to Question 1?

3. What legal analysis did the unanimous Supreme Court utilize to determine whether the NIRA violated the Nondelegation Doctrine? Did the Court correctly determine that the NIRA failed the test?

4. In what legal materials did the Court root the Nondelegation Doctrine?

5. Is the Court's "intelligible principle" test faithful to the Constitution?

6. Is the Court's "intelligible principle" test one that judges have the capacity to apply in a principled manner? If you answer no, what test do you propose?

———

Following *Schechter,* as you will learn in Volumes 3 and 5, the Supreme Court largely backed out of enforcing the structural limitations on the federal government's power, around 1937. Consequently, the Supreme Court has not ruled that a congressional delegation of discretion to the executive branch has violated Article I since *Schechter.* Below is the modern statement of the nondelegation doctrine.

MISTRETTA v. UNITED STATES
488 U.S. 361 (1989)

JUSTICE BLACKMUN delivered the opinion of the Court.

[W]e granted certiorari in order to consider the constitutionality of the Sentencing Guidelines promulgated by the United States Sentencing Commission. The Commission is a body created under the Sentencing Reform Act of 1984, 18 U.S.C. § 3551 *et seq.*

I

A. *Background*

Historically, federal sentencing never has been thought to be assigned by the Constitution to the exclusive jurisdiction of any one of the three Branches of Government. Congress, of course, has the power to fix the sentence for a federal crime and the scope of judicial discretion with respect to a sentence is subject to congressional control. Congress early abandoned fixed-sentence rigidity, however, and put in place a system of ranges within which the sentencer could choose the precise punishment. Congress delegated almost unfettered discretion to the sentencing judge to determine what the sentence should be within the customarily wide range so selected. This broad discretion was further enhanced by the power later granted the judge to suspend the sentence and by the resulting growth of an elaborate probation system. Also, with the advent of parole, Congress moved toward a "three-way sharing" of sentencing responsibility by granting corrections personnel in the Executive Branch the discretion to release a prisoner before the expiration of the sentence imposed by the judge. Thus, under the indeterminate-sentence system, Congress defined the maximum, the judge imposed a sentence within the statutory range (which he usually could replace with probation), and the Executive Branch's parole official eventually determined the actual duration of imprisonment.

Congress, in 1984, it enacted the sweeping reforms that are at issue here. Helpful in our consideration and analysis of the statute is the Senate Report on the 1984 legislation. It observed that the indeterminate-sentencing system had two unjustifi[ed] and "shameful" consequences. The first was the great variation among sentences imposed by different judges upon similarly situated offenders. The second was the uncertainty as to the time the offender would spend in prison. Each was a serious impediment to an evenhanded and effective operation of the criminal justice system.

B. *The Act*

The Act, as adopted, revises the old sentencing process in several ways: 1. It rejects imprisonment as a means of promoting rehabilitation. 2. It consolidates the power that had been exercised by the sentencing judge and the Parole Commission to decide what punishment an offender should suffer. This is done by creating the United States Sentencing Commission, directing that Commission to devise guidelines to be used for sentencing, and prospectively abolishing the Parole Commission. 3. It makes all sentences basically determinate. 4. It makes the Sentencing Commission's guidelines binding on the courts, although it preserves for the judge the discretion to depart from the guideline applicable to a particular case if the judge finds an aggravating or mitigating factor present that the Commission did not adequately consider when formulating the guidelines. The Act also requires the court to give "the specific reason" for imposing a sentence different from that described in the guideline. 5. It authorizes limited appellate review of the sentence.

C. *The Sentencing Commission*

The Commission is established "as an independent commission in the judicial branch of the United States." 28 U.S.C. § 991(a). It has seven voting members (one of whom is the Chairman) appointed by the President "by and with the advice and consent of the Senate."

II. *This Litigation*

On December 10, 1987, John M. Mistretta (petitioner) and another were indicted in the U.S. District Court for the Western District of Missouri on three counts centering in a cocaine sale. Mistretta moved to have the promulgated Guidelines ruled unconstitutional on the grounds that the Sentencing Commission was constituted in violation of the established doctrine of separation of powers, and that Congress delegated excessive authority to the Commission to structure the Guidelines.

The District Court rejected petitioner's delegation argument on the ground that, despite the language of the statute, the Sentencing Commission "should be judicially characterized as having Executive Branch status," 682 F. Supp. at 1035, and that the Guidelines are similar to substantive rules promulgated by other agencies. *Id.* at 1034–35.

Petitioner was sentenced under the Guidelines to 18 months' imprisonment, to be followed by a 3-year term of supervised release. The court also imposed a $1,000 fine and a $50 special assessment.

Because of the "imperative public importance" of the issue and because of the disarray among the Federal District Courts, we granted [petitions for expedited review].

III. *Delegation of Power*

Petitioner argues that in delegating the power to promulgate sentencing guidelines for every federal criminal offense to an independent Sentencing Commission,

Congress has granted the Commission excessive legislative discretion in violation of the constitutionally based nondelegation doctrine. We do not agree.

The nondelegation doctrine is rooted in the principle of separation of powers that underlies our tripartite system of Government. The Constitution provides that "[a]ll legislative Powers herein granted shall be vested in a Congress of the United States," U.S. Const., Art. I, § 1, and we long have insisted that "the integrity and maintenance of the system of government ordained by the Constitution" mandate that Congress generally cannot delegate its legislative power to another Branch. *Field v. Clark*, 143 U.S. 649, 692 (1892). We also have recognized, however, that the separation-of-powers principle, and the nondelegation doctrine in particular, do not prevent Congress from obtaining the assistance of its coordinate Branches. In a passage now enshrined in our jurisprudence, Chief Justice Taft, writing for the Court, explained our approach to such cooperative ventures: "In determining what [Congress] may do in seeking assistance from another branch, the extent and character of that assistance must be fixed according to common sense and the inherent necessities of the governmental co-ordination." *J.W. Hampton Jr., & Co. v. United States*, 276 U.S. 394, 406 (1928). So long as Congress "shall lay down by legislative act an intelligible principle to which the person or body authorized to [exercise the delegated authority] is directed to conform, such legislative action is not a forbidden delegation of legislative power."

Applying this "intelligible principle" test to congressional delegations, our jurisprudence has been driven by a practical understanding that in our increasingly complex society, replete with ever changing and more technical problems, Congress simply cannot do its job absent an ability to delegate power under broad general directives.

Until 1935, this Court never struck down a challenged statute on delegation grounds. After invalidating in 1935 two statutes as excessive delegations, *see A.L.A. Schechter Poultry Corp. v. United States*, 295 U.S. 495 (1935), and *Panama Refining Co. v. Ryan*, 293 U.S. 388 (1935), we have upheld, again without deviation, Congress' ability to delegate power under broad standards.[1] *See, e.g.*, Lichter v. United States, 334 U.S. 742, 785–86 (1948) (upholding delegation of authority to determine excessive profits); *American Power & Light Co. v. SEC*, 329 U.S. 90, 105 (1946) (upholding delegation of authority to Securities and Exchange Commission to prevent unfair or inequitable distribution of voting power among security holders); *Yakus v. United*

---

1. In *Schechter* and *Panama Refining* the Court concluded that Congress had failed to articulate any policy or standard that would serve to confine the discretion of the authorities to whom Congress had delegated power. No delegation of the kind at issue in those cases is present here. The Act does not make crimes of acts never before criminalized, *see Fahey v. Mallonee*, 332 U.S. 245, 249 (1947) (analyzing *Panama Refining*), or delegate regulatory power to private individuals, *see Yakus v. United States*, 321 U.S. 414, 424 (1944) (analyzing *Schechter*). In recent years, our application of the nondelegation doctrine principally has been limited to the interpretation of statutory texts, and, more particularly, to giving narrow constructions to statutory delegations that might otherwise be thought to be unconstitutional. *See, e.g., Industrial Union Dep't v. American Petroleum Institute*, 448 U.S. 607, 646 (1980).

States, 321 U.S. 414, 426 (1944) (upholding delegation to Price Administrator to fix commodity prices that would be fair and equitable, and would effectuate purposes of Emergency Price Control Act of 1942); *FPC v. Hope Natural Gas Co.*, 320 U.S. 591, 600 (1944) (upholding delegation to Federal Power Commission to determine just and reasonable rates); *National Broadcasting Co. v. United States*, 319 U.S. 190, 225–26 (1943) (upholding delegation to Federal Communication Commission to regulate broadcast licensing "as public interest, convenience, or necessity" require).

In light of our approval of these broad delegations, we harbor no doubt that Congress' delegation of authority to the Sentencing Commission is sufficiently specific and detailed to meet constitutional requirements. Congress charged the Commission with three specific goals: to "assure the meeting of the purposes of sentencing as set forth" in the Act; to "provide certainty and fairness in meeting the purposes of sentencing, avoiding unwarranted sentencing disparities among defendants with similar records . . . while maintaining sufficient flexibility to permit individualized sentences," where appropriate; and to "reflect, to the extent practicable, advancement in knowledge of human behavior as it relates to the criminal justice process." 28 U.S.C. §991(b)(1). Congress further specified four "purposes" of sentencing that the Commission must pursue in carrying out its mandate: "to reflect the seriousness of the offense, to promote respect for the law, and provide just punishment for the offense"; "to afford adequate deterrence to criminal conduct"; "to protect the public from further crimes of the defendant"; and "to provide the defendant with needed . . . correctional treatment." 18 U.S.C. §3553(a)(2).

In addition, Congress prescribed the specific tool—the guidelines system—for the Commission to use in regulating sentencing. More particularly, Congress directed the Commission to develop a system of "sentencing ranges" applicable "for each category of offense involving each category of defendant." 28 U.S.C. §994(b). Congress instructed the Commission that these sentencing ranges must be consistent with the pertinent provisions of Title 18 of the United States Code and could not include sentences in excess of the statutory maxima. Congress also required that for sentences of imprisonment, "the maximum of the range established for such a term shall not exceed the minimum of that range by more than the greater of 25 percent or 6 months, except that, if the minimum term of the range is 30 years or more, the maximum may be life imprisonment." *Id.* §994(b)(2). Moreover, Congress directed the Commission to use current average sentences "as a starting point" for its structuring of the sentencing ranges. *Id.* §994(m).

To guide the Commission in its formulation of offense categories, Congress directed it to consider seven factors. Congress [also] set forth 11 factors for the Commission to consider in establishing categories of defendants. Congress also prohibited the Commission from considering the "race, sex, national origin, creed, and socioeconomic status of offenders," *id.* §994(d), and instructed that the guidelines should reflect the "general inappropriateness" of considering certain other factors, such as current unemployment, that might serve as proxies for forbidden factors, *id.* §994(e).

We cannot dispute petitioner's contention that the Commission enjoys significant discretion in formulating guidelines. The Commission does have discretionary authority to determine the relative severity of federal crimes and to assess the relative weight of the offender characteristics that Congress listed for the Commission to consider. The Commission also has significant discretion to determine which crimes have been punished too leniently, and which too severely.

But our cases do not at all suggest that delegations of this type may not carry with them the need to exercise judgment on matter of policy. In *Yakus v. United States*, 321 U.S. 414 (1944), the Court upheld a delegation to the Price Administrator to fix commodity prices that "in his judgment will be generally fair and equitable and will effectuate the purposes of this Act" to stabilize prices and avert speculation. *See id.* at 420. In *National Broadcasting Co. v. United States*, 319 U.S. 190 (1943), we upheld a delegation to the Federal Communications Commission granting it the authority to promulgate regulations in accordance with its view of the "public interest." The Act sets forth more than merely an "intelligible principle" or minimal standards.

Developing proportionate penalties for hundreds of different crimes by a virtually limitless array of offenders is precisely the sort of intricate, labor-intensive task for which delegation to an expert body is especially appropriate. "Congress is not confined to that method of executing its policy which involves the least possible delegation of discretion to administrative officers." *Yakus v. United States*, 321 U.S. at 435–26.

The judgment of the U.S. District Court for the Western District of Missouri is affirmed.

JUSTICE SCALIA, dissenting.

I dissent from today's decision because I can find no place within our constitutional system for an agency created by Congress to exercise no governmental power other than the making of laws.

I.

There is no doubt that the Sentencing Commission has established significant, legally binding prescriptions governing application of governmental power against private individuals. Congress also gave the Commission discretion to determine whether 7 specified characteristics of offenses, and 11 specified characteristics of offenders, "have any relevance," and should be included among the factors varying the sentence. Of the latter, it included only three among the factors required to be considered, and declared the remainder not ordinarily relevant.

It should be apparent that the decisions made by the Commission are far from technical, but are heavily laden (or ought to be) with value judgments and policy assessments.

Petitioner's most fundamental and far-reaching challenge to the Commission is that Congress' commitment of such broad policy responsibility to any institution is an unconstitutional delegation of legislative power. Our Members of Congress could not, even if they wished, vote all power to the President and adjourn *sine die*.

But while the doctrine of unconstitutional delegation is unquestionably a fundamental element of our constitutional system, it is not an element readily enforceable by the courts. Once it is conceded, as it must be, that no statute can be entirely precise, and that some judgments, even some judgments involving policy considerations, must be left to the officers executing the law and to the judges applying it, the debate over unconstitutional delegation becomes a debate not over a point of principle but over a question of degree. [I]t is small wonder that we have almost never felt qualified to second-guess Congress regarding the permissible degree of policy judgment that can be left to those executing or applying the law. What legislated standard, one must wonder, can possibly be too vague to survive judicial scrutiny, when we have repeatedly upheld, in various contexts, a "public interest" standard?

In short, I fully agree with the Court's rejection of petitioner's contention that the doctrine of unconstitutional delegation of legislative authority has been violated because of the lack of intelligible, congressionally prescribed standards to guide the Commission.

II.

Precisely because the scope of delegation is largely uncontrollable by the courts, we must be particularly rigorous in preserving the Constitution's structural restrictions that deter excessive delegation. The major one, it seems to me, is that the power to make law cannot be exercised by anyone other than Congress, except in conjunction with the lawful exercise of executive or judicial power.

The whole theory of *lawful* congressional "delegation" is not that Congress is sometimes too busy or too divided and can therefore assign its responsibility of making law to someone else; but rather that a certain degree of discretion, and thus of lawmaking, *inheres* in most executive or judicial action, and it is up to Congress, by the relative specificity or generality of its statutory commands, to determine—up to a point—how small or how large that degree shall be. Thus, the courts could be given the power to say precisely what constitutes a "restraint of trade" or to adopt rules of procedure or to prescribe by rule the manner in which their officers shall execute their judgments because that "lawmaking" was ancillary to their exercise of judicial powers. And the Executive could be given the power to adopt policies and rules specifying in detail what radio and television licenses will be in the "public interest, convenience or necessity," because that was ancillary to the exercise of its executive powers in granting and policing licenses and making a "fair and equitable allocation" of the electromagnetic spectrum.

The focus of controversy, in the long line of our so-called excessive delegation cases, has been whether the *degree* of generality contained in the authorization for exercise of executive or judicial powers in a particular field is so unacceptably high as to *amount* to a delegation of legislative powers. I say "so-called excessive delegation" because although that convenient terminology is often used, what is really at issue is whether there has been *any* delegation of legislative power, which occurs (rarely) when Congress authorizes the exercise of executive or judicial power without adequate standards. Strictly speaking, there is *no* acceptable delegation of legislative power. As John Locke put it almost 300 years ago, "[t]he power of the *legislative* being derived from the people by a positive voluntary grant and institution, can be no other, than what the positive grant conveyed, which being only to make *laws*, and not to make *legislators*, the legislative can have no power to transfer their authority of making laws, and place it in other hands." JOHN LOCKE, SECOND TREATISE OF GOVERNMENT 87 (R. Cox. ed. 1982) (emphasis added). Or as we have less epigrammatically said: "That Congress cannot delegate legislative power to the President is a principle universally recognized as vital to the integrity and maintenance of the system of government ordained by the Constitution." *Field v. Clark*, 143 U.S. [649,] at 692 [(1892)]. In the present case, however, a pure delegation of legislative power is precisely what we have before us. It is irrelevant whether the standards are adequate, because they are not standards related to the exercise of executive or judicial powers; they are, plainly and simply, standards for further legislation.

The lawmaking function of the Sentencing Commission is completely divorced from any responsibility for execution of the law or adjudication of private rights under the law. It is divorced from responsibility for execution of the law not only because the Commission is not said to be "located in the Executive Branch" but, more importantly, because the Commission neither exercises any executive power on its own, nor is subject to the control of the President who does. The only functions it performs, apart from prescribing the law, conducting the investigations useful and necessary for prescribing the law, and clarifying the intended application of the law that it prescribes, are data collection and intragovernmental advice giving and education. These latter activities—similar to functions performed by congressional agencies and even congressional staff—neither determine nor affect private rights, and do not constitute an exercise of governmental power. *See Humphrey's Executor v. United States*, 295 U.S. 602 (1935). And the Commission's lawmaking is completely divorced from the exercise of judicial powers since, not being a court, it has no judicial powers itself, nor is it subject to the control of any other body with judicial powers. The power to make law at issue here, in other words, is not ancillary but quite naked.

The delegation of lawmaking authority to the Commission is, in short, unsupported by any legitimating theory to explain why it is not a delegation of legislative power. To disregard structural legitimacy is wrong in itself—but since structure has purpose, the disregard also has adverse practical consequences. In this case, as suggested earlier, the consequence is to facilitate and encourage judicially uncontrollable delegation.

I respectfully dissent from the Court's decision.

EXERCISE 20:

Consider the following matters in connection with *Mistretta v. United States*:

1. What authority did Congress delegate to the Commission? On a scale of one to ten, with ten being the most capacious, how much power did Congress delegate?

2. What restrictions or limits did Congress place on the Commission's exercise of the delegated authority? Do these restrictions change your answer to Question 1?

3. What is the test that purports to determine whether federal legislation unconstitutionally confers too much discretion upon other branches of government? Did the Court correctly determine that the Act passed the test?

4. When did the Supreme Court last declare federal legislation was unconstitutional for violating the Nondelegation Doctrine? How, other than declaring legislation unconstitutional, has the Court effectuated the concerns underlying that doctrine?

5. After *Mistretta*, what role remains for the Nondelegation Doctrine, if any? Is there any delegation that could or would run afoul of the Nondelegation Doctrine?

6. Is the Court's opinion formalist or functionalist? Explain your answer. What about Justice Scalia's dissent?

7. To the extent the Supreme Court has authorized broad delegation of discretion by Congress, how may exercises of that discretion be controlled? Who exercises that discretion? How is the person exercising that discretion accountable? Are officers like Commissioner Humphrey more or less accountable to Congress than the Secretary of State?

8. To the extent the Supreme Court has authorized broader delegations of discretion than in early congressional practice, should the Court permit Congress innovative means to hold officers accountable for the exercise of that discretion? To the extent those broader delegations are placed in the hands of "principal" officers who, like Commissioner Humphrey, are not subject to unlimited Presidential removal, is the problem of accountability greater or less than delegations to officers like the Secretary of State?

9. In dissent, Justice Scalia argued that the Commission was unconstitutional. With what part of the majority's analysis did he disagree? What delegations, if any, would Justice Scalia allow?

10. In dissent, Justice Scalia contended: "The whole theory of *lawful* congressional 'delegation' is not that Congress is sometimes too busy or too divided and can therefore assign its responsibility of making law to someone else; but rather that a certain degree of discretion, and thus of lawmaking, *inheres* in most executive or judicial action . . . ." Assuming that Justice Scalia accurately described the rationale of the doctrine, which of the following matters, if any, violates the rationale of the Nondelegation Doctrine: the Gramm-Rudman-Hollings Act at issue in *Bowsher v. Synar*; or, (B) the Federal Trade Act at issue in *Humphrey's Executor v. United States*.

11. Justice Scalia argued that judges should not police the *extent* of delegations of discretion because of judicial inability to draw principled lines. Make an argument against that position.

Despite the unbroken track record stretching back to *Schechter*, nondelegation challenges continue to reach the Supreme Court. Proponents of a revitalized Nondelegation Doctrine had high hopes for the following case.

WHITMAN v. AMERICAN TRUCKING ASSOCIATIONS, INC.

531 U.S. 457 (2001)

JUSTICE SCALIA delivered the opinion of the Court.

In a delegation challenge, the constitutional question is whether the statute has delegated legislative power to the agency. Article I, § 1, of the Constitution vests "[a]ll legislative Powers herein granted . . . in a Congress of the United States." This text permits no delegation of those powers, *Loving v. United States*, 517 U.S. 748, 771 (1996); *see id.* at 766–777 (Scalia, J., concurring in part and concurring in judgment), and so we repeatedly have said that when Congress confers decisionmaking authority upon agencies *Congress* must "lay down by legislative act an intelligible principle to which the person or body authorized to [act] is directed to conform." *J.W. Hampton, Jr., & Co. v. United States*, 276 U.S. 394, 409 (1928). We have never suggested that an agency can cure an unlawful delegation of legislative power by adopting in its discretion a limiting construction of the statute. Whether the statute delegates legislative power is a question for the courts, and an agency's voluntary self-denial has no bearing upon the answer.

The scope of discretion § 109(b)(1) allows is in fact well within the outer limits of our nondelegation precedents. In the history of the Court we have found the requisite "intelligible principle" lacking in only two statutes, one of which provided literally no guidance for the exercise of discretion, and the other of which conferred authority to regulate the entire economy on the basis of no more precise a standard than stimulating the economy by assuring "fair competition." *See Panama Refining Co. v. Ryan*, 293 U.S. 388 (1935); *A.L.A. Schechter Poultry Corp. v. United States*, 295 U.S. 495 (1935). We have, on the other hand, upheld the validity of § 11(b)(2) of the Public Utility Holding Company Act of 1935 which gave the Securities and Exchange Commission authority to modify the structure of holding company systems so as to ensure that they are not "unduly or unnecessarily complicate[d]" and do not "unfairly or inequitably distribute voting power among security holders." *American Power & Light Co. v. SEC*, 329 U.S. 90, 104 (1946). In short, we have "almost never felt qualified to second-guess Congress regarding the permissible degree of policy judgment that can be left to those executing or applying the law." *Mistretta v. United States*, 488 U.S. 361, 416 (1989) (Scalia, J., dissenting); *see id.* at 373 (majority opinion).

It is true enough that the degree of agency discretion that is acceptable varies according to the scope of the power congressionally conferred. *See Loving v. United States*, 517 U.S. at 772–73; *United States v. Mazurie*, 419 U.S. 544, 556–57 (1975). While Congress need not provide any direction to the EPA regarding the manner in which it is to define "country elevators," which are to be exempt from new-stationary-source regulations governing grain elevators, *see* 42 U.S.C. § 7411(i), it must provide substantial guidance on setting air standards that affect the entire national economy. But even in sweeping regulatory schemes we have never demanded, as the Court of Appeals did here, that statutes provide a "determinate criterion" for saying "how much [of the regulated harm] is too much." It is therefore not conclusive for delegation purposes that, as respondents argue, ozone and particulate matter are "nonthreshold" pollutants that inflict a continuum of adverse health effects at any airborne concentration greater than zero, and hence require the EPA to make judgments of degree. "[A] certain degree of discretion, and thus of lawmaking, inheres in most executive or judicial action." *Mistretta v. United States*, 488 U.S. at 417 (Scalia, J., dissenting) (emphasis deleted); *see id.* at 378–79 (majority opinion). Section 109(b)(1) of the CAA, which to repeat we interpret as requiring the EPA to set air quality standards at the level that is "requisite"—that is, not lower or higher than is necessary—to protect the public health with an adequate margin of safety, fits comfortably within the scope of discretion permitted by our precedent.

We therefore reverse the judgment of the Court of Appeals.

[The opinion of Justice Thomas, concurring, the opinion of Justice Stevens joined by Justice Souter, concurring in the judgment, and the opinion of Justice Breyer, concurring in the judgment, are omitted.]

EXERCISE 21:

1. The U.S. Supreme Court has never overruled either *Panama Refining Co. v. Ryan*, 293 U.S. 388 (1935), or *A.L.A. Schechter Poultry Corp. v. United States*, 295 U.S. 495 (1935). Nonetheless, the Court has not since those cases found any statute to violate the Nondelegation Doctrine. The cases in this Chapter summarize many of the statutory standards that the Court has determined satisfy the "intelligible principle" test. If the 1935 cases remain good law, they must be distinguishable on some basis. What is that basis? Formulate a test for distinguishing permissible from impermissible legislation.

2. Proponents of the Nondelegation Doctrine have lost their cases before the Supreme Court for approximately 80 years. What accounts for the persistence of Nondelegation Doctrine claims?

2. Executive Discretion and the President's Take-Care Duty

The delegation issue in *Schechter Poultry* and *Whitman* concerns whether the power to fill in legislative gaps that Congress has created for the President—sometimes very large gaps—counts as the executive exercise of "legislative" power. A similar issue is involved when the President *creates* gaps in the law by failing to prosecute all offenders. To what extent is the President required affirmatively to enforce the law? When is presidential non-enforcement so extensive that it amounts to the re-writing of a statute—i.e., the exercise of legislative power?

In 1215, in paragraph 40 of *Magna Charta*, a group of English barons required King John to promise neither to "sell, or deny, or delay right or justice to anyone." In 1689, in the first two articles of the English Bill of Rights following the overthrow of James II, Parliament condemned as illegal "the pretended power of suspending the laws or the execution of laws by regal authority without consent of Parliament" and "the pretended power of dispensing with laws or the execution of laws by regal authority, as it hath been assumed and exercised of late." These requirements were the backdrop of the Take Care Clause in Art. II, § 3, which requires that the President "shall take Care that the Laws be faithfully executed."

We saw in **Chapter 1** that this provision was interpreted in cases like *Myers v. United States* to give the President control over subordinate executive officials. But, does it require the President to enforce the law against everyone to whom it literally applies? The long tradition of prosecutorial discretion acknowledged by both the Court and the dissent in *Morrison v. Olson*, also in **Chapter 1**, suggests that the Take Care clause cannot be taken so strictly. In what respect, then, does the President's power over the law differ from that of the Stuart kings like James II?

The Supreme Court has long acknowledged the existence of prosecutorial discretion in cases like the *Confiscation Cases*, 74 U.S. 454 (1869), where the Court held that the Attorney General had the power not to pursue the confiscation of ships used in support of the rebellion, even though informers stood to receive a portion of those confiscations. The Court has never, however, articulated the precise extent of prosecutorial discretion. It has referred in several opinions to issues related to its control by the President, such as *Morrison v. Olson* and *United States v. Nixon. Nixon* followed an earlier decision by the Fifth Circuit, *United States v. Cox*, which refused to allow a federal district judge, Harold Cox, to use a grand jury to direct the U.S. Attorney to indict and prosecute men whom Judge Cox believed had committed civil contempt. *Cox* was procedurally and doctrinally quite complicated, involving an en banc Fifth Circuit splintered over issues related to the relative powers of the grand jury, the district court, and the U.S. Attorney. We include here only the comments of the judges directly related to prosecutorial discretion and the policies behind it.

UNITED STATES v. COX

342 F.2d 167 (5th Cir. 1965) (en banc)

JONES, CIRCUIT JUDGE:

The judicial power of the United States is vested in the federal courts, and extends to prosecutions for violations of the criminal laws of the United States. The executive power is vested in the President of the United States, who is required to take care that the laws be faithfully executed. The Attorney General is the hand of the President in taking care that the laws of the United States in legal proceedings and in the prosecution of offenses, be faithfully executed. The role of the grand jury is restricted to a finding as to whether or not there is probable cause to believe that an offense has been committed. The discretionary power of the attorney for the United States in determining whether a prosecution shall be commenced or maintained may well depend upon matters of policy wholly apart from any question of probable cause. Although as a member of the bar, the attorney for the United States is an officer of the court, he is nevertheless an executive official of the Government, and it is as an officer of the executive department that he exercises a discretion as to whether or not there shall be a prosecution in a particular case. It follows, as an incident of the constitutional separation of powers, that the courts are not to interfere with the free exercise of the discretionary powers of the attorneys of the United States in their control over criminal prosecutions.

JOHN R. BROWN, CIRCUIT JUDGE (concurring specially):

Responsibility for determining whether a prosecution is to be commenced or maintained must be clearly fixed. The power not to initiate is indeed awesome. But it has to reside somewhere. And the more clearly pinpointed it is, the more the public interest is served through the focus of relentless publicity upon that decision. It may not, with safety, be left to a body whose great virtue is the combination of anonymity, transitory authority, and political unresponsibility.

All must be aware now that there are times when the interests of the nation require that a prosecution be foregone. These instances will most often be in the area of state secrets and national security. With stakes so high, the safety of our country, and hence the security of the world, ought not to be imperiled by leaving the important decision to a body having no definitive political responsibility. And it is hardly realistic to suggest, as do the dissenters, that these factors may be evaluated by the Grand Jury. What will be the source of their information? How extensive will it be? How close will a Grand Jury session approach a presidential cabinet meeting? How will essential government secrets be kept when disclosed to persons none of whom as Grand Jurors will have been subjected to customary security clearance checks?

And even in less sensitive areas, the practical operation of the prosecutorial function makes imperative the need for executive determination. The familiar example is the deliberate choice between those to be prosecuted and those who, often equally guilty, are named as co-conspirators but not as defendants, or others not named who are used as star government witnesses. And in other situations, of which the instant case may well be typical, the executive's purpose to effectuate specific policies thought to be of major importance would be frustrated or encumbered were a Grand Jury given the sole prerogative of determining when a prosecution is to be effectively commenced.

Putting to one side these factors which bear on the delicate nature of governmental decisions, there are technical reasons indigenous to criminal law which are equally compelling. Federal crimes are more and more for violation of highly complex statutes. Federal jurisdiction, indeed, whether the activity constitutes a federal crime, depend on intricate facts, many beyond the knowledge and experience of laymen composing the Grand Jury. The aim of the Grand Jury indictment as the means of protecting the citizen against the initiation of unfounded charges is hardly advanced by a rule that permits the Grand Jury on its own to initiate the prosecution when the conscientious District Attorney knows to a legal certainty that a federal crime cannot be established.

WISDOM, CIRCUIT JUDGE (concurring specially):

The reason for vesting discretion to prosecute in the Executive, acting through the Attorney General is two-fold. First, in the interests of justice and the orderly, efficient administration of the law, some person or agency should be able to prevent an unjust prosecution. The freedom of the petit jury to bring in a verdict of not guilty and the progressive development of the law in the direction of making more meaningful the guarantees of an accused person's constitutional rights give considerable protection to the individual before and after trial. They do not protect against a baseless prosecution. This is a harassment to the accused and an expensive strain on the machinery of justice. The appropriate repository for authority to prevent a baseless prosecution is the chief law-enforcement officer whose duty, unlike the grand jury's duty, is to collect evidence on both sides of a case.

Second, when, within the context of law-enforcement, national policy is involved, because of national security, conduct of foreign policy, or a conflict between two branches of government, the appropriate branch to decide the matter is the executive branch. The executive is charged with carrying out national policy on law-enforcement and, generally speaking, is informed on more levels than the more specialized judicial and legislative branches. In such a situation, a decision not to prosecute is analogous to the exercise of executive privilege.

EXERCISE 22:

1. Is there any difference between the laws being "faithfully executed," as the Take Care Clause requires, and statutes being *completely* executed? Would it even be possible for federal criminal law to be *completely* enforced?

2. Does faithful execution require some degree of fit between executive action and the *goals* and *purposes* of a statute, not just its specific words? How can those goals and purposes be assessed? How are they part of the law, if not expressed in the words enacted by Congress?

3. If the executive branch declines to prosecute a particular offender for what he has done in the past, what is the effect of this decision on the offender's conduct in the future? Is there a difference between the failure to prosecute and the active executive-branch *encouragement* of law violations? Distinguishing encouragement and the giving of a positive benefit from the mere failure to enforce the law can be a difficult issue. After President Obama's Deferred Action for Parents of Americans (DAPA) policy was enjoined on administrative-law grounds in litigation brought by twenty-six states, the Supreme Court granted review and added a Take-Care Clause issue, but ended up dividing 4–4 on the case, leaving the lower-court injunction in place. *United States v. Texas*, 136 S. Ct. 2271 (2016). One of the issues hotly contested in the case was the extent to which the policy gave deportable aliens a benefit beyond merely not enforcing the law against them. If the existence of tangible benefit matters, how much of a benefit should matter? If the President announces a desire that aliens "come out of the shadows," would that be enough of a benefit?

4. Assuming that the President and executive officials do generally have at least *some* discretion about bringing prosecution, is this discretion necessarily boundless? Are there principles that could govern whether some exercises are permissible and others not? Judge Jones in *Cox* refers to "matters of policy" besides the existence of probable cause that would support a prosecution. What sorts of issues might the

Court have in mind? Are there any limits to the sorts of policy issues that might govern the executive branch's exercise of discretion?

5. If the executive branch chooses to prosecute only Democratic violators of a particular law, and not Republicans, would this policy violate the First Amendment according to its text? Would it violate the Take Care Clause? Is the Take Care Clause a plausible textual home for antidiscrimination principles applicable to the executive branch? Does non-discrimination offer an attractive intermediate rule between a total, exceptionless executive obligation to prosecute everyone and a rule allowing the executive branch to prosecute anyone it likes on whatever ground it likes? For a suggestion to this effect, see Nicholas Quinn Rosenkranz, *The Subjects of the Constitution*, 62 STAN. L. REV. 1209, 1272 n.253 (2010) ("[T]he Take Care Clause . . . reflects a principle of nondiscrimination (on the basis of speech and religion, among other things) in the *execution* of the law").

6. Should the Executive be required to explain non-prosecution (or non-investigation) decisions? The Administrative Procedure Act, which does not apply to prosecution decisions, allows agency decisions to be reversed if they are "arbitrary, capricious, or an abuse of discretion," a standard that has been glossed as a requirement that agencies explain themselves adequately. *See Citizens to Preserve Overton Park v. Volpe*, 401 U.S. 402 (1971); Christopher R. Green, *Reverse Broken Windows*, 65 J. LEG. EDUC. 265, 274–76 (2015) (noting proposals for reform by thinkers like the late William Stuntz, in THE COLLAPSE OF AMERICAN CRIMINAL JUSTICE (2011)). The federal government generally explains its prosecutorial priorities in the *U.S. Attorney's Manual*, which is continually updated and available at https://www.justice.gov/usam/united-states-attorneys-manual. State and local prosecutors, however, generally act under no such guidelines, a fact that critics like Stuntz have criticized harshly. *See also* Christopher R. Green, *The Original Sense of the (Equal) Protection Clause: Subsequent Interpretation and Application*, 19 GEO. MASON U. CIV. RTS. L.J. 219, 303–08 (2009) (Equal Protection Clause puts state executives under a duty to supply "protection of the laws" equally).

3. Executive Review and the Duty to Defend

A key question about the relationship of executive and legislative power grows out of the take-care duty. In Volume 1, in *Marbury v. Madison*, we considered the duty and power of judges to declare acts of legislation unconstitutional. What about the President? Does his take-care power/duty extend to all statutes, or only to those that are constitutional? Is "executive review" analogous to "judicial review" ever legitimate? Is it ever mandatory? Is it ever discretionary? Relatedly, when does the President's duty to administer legislation require him to defend such legislation in court against constitutional attack? The following case considered the powers of the President and Congress to defend a law, the Defense of Marriage Act, that the President had decided was unconstitutional, but which he continued to enforce.

UNITED STATES v. WINDSOR

133 S.Ct. 2675 (2013)

JUSTICE KENNEDY delivered the opinion of the Court.

I

Edith Windsor and Thea Spyer met in New York City in 1963 and began a long-term relationship. Spyer died in February 2009, and left her entire estate to Windsor. Because DOMA denies federal recognition to same-sex spouses, Windsor did not qualify for the marital exemption from the federal estate tax.... Windsor paid $363,053 in estate taxes and sought a refund. The Internal Revenue Service denied the refund.

While the tax refund suit was pending, the Attorney General of the United States notified the Speaker of the House of Representatives, pursuant to 28 U.S.C. § 530D, that the Department of Justice would no longer defend the constitutionality of DOMA's § 3. Although "the President . . . instructed the Department not to defend the statute in *Windsor*," he also decided "that Section 3 will continue to be enforced by the Executive Branch" and that the United States had an "interest in providing Congress a full and fair opportunity to participate in the litigation of those cases." The stated rationale for this dual-track procedure (determination of unconstitutionality coupled with ongoing enforcement) was to "recogniz[e] the judiciary as the final arbiter of the constitutional claims raised."

In response to the notice from the Attorney General, the Bipartisan Legal Advisory Group (BLAG) of the House of Representatives voted to intervene in the litigation to defend the constitutionality of § 3 of DOMA.

II

It is appropriate to begin by addressing whether either the Government or BLAG, or both of them, were entitled to appeal to the Court of Appeals and later to seek certiorari and appear as parties here.

The decision of the Executive not to defend the constitutionality of § 3 in court while continuing to deny refunds and to assess deficiencies does introduce a complication. Even though the Executive's current position was announced before the District Court entered its judgment, the Government's agreement with Windsor's position would not have deprived the District Court of jurisdiction to entertain and resolve the refund suit; for her injury (failure to obtain a refund allegedly required by law) was concrete, persisting, and unredressed. The Government's position—agreeing with Windsor's legal contention but refusing to give it effect—meant that there was a justiciable controversy between the parties, despite what the claimant would find to be an inconsistency in that stance. Windsor, the Government, BLAG, and the *amicus* appear to agree upon that point. The disagreement is over the standing of the parties, or aspiring parties, to take an appeal in the Court of Appeals and to appear as parties in further proceedings in this Court.

In this case the United States retains a stake sufficient to support Article III jurisdiction on appeal and in proceedings before this Court. The judgment in question orders the United States to pay Windsor the refund she seeks. That the Executive may welcome this order to pay the refund if it is accompanied by the constitutional ruling it wants does not eliminate the injury to the national Treasury if payment is made, or to the taxpayer if it is not. The judgment orders the United States to pay money that it would not disburse but for the court's order. The Government of the United States has a valid legal argument that it is injured even if the Executive disagrees with § 3 of DOMA, which results in Windsor's liability for the tax. Windsor's ongoing claim for funds that the United States refuses to pay thus establishes a controversy sufficient for Article III jurisdiction. It would be a different case if the Executive had taken the further step of paying Windsor the refund to which she was entitled under the District Court's ruling.

In the case now before the Court the attorneys for BLAG present a substantial argument for the constitutionality of § 3 of DOMA. BLAG's sharp adversarial presentation of the issues satisfies the prudential concerns that otherwise might counsel against hearing an appeal from a decision with which the principal parties agree. [T]he Court need not decide whether BLAG would have standing to challenge the District Court's ruling and its affirmance in the Court of Appeals on BLAG's own authority.

The Court's conclusion that this petition may be heard on the merits does not imply that no difficulties would ensue if this were a common practice in ordinary cases. The Executive's failure to defend the constitutionality of an Act of Congress based on a constitutional theory not yet established in judicial decisions has created a procedural dilemma. On the one hand, as noted, the Government's agreement with Windsor raises questions about the propriety of entertaining a suit in which it seeks affirmance of an order invalidating a federal law and ordering the United States to pay money. On the other hand, if the Executive's agreement with a plaintiff that a law is unconstitutional is enough to preclude judicial review, then the Supreme Court's primary role in determining the constitutionality of a law that has inflicted real injury on a plaintiff who has brought a justiciable legal claim would become only secondary to the President's. This would undermine the clear dictate of the separation-of-powers principle that "when an Act of Congress is alleged to conflict with the Constitution, "[i]t is emphatically the province and duty of the judicial department to say what the law is." Similarly, with respect to the legislative power, when Congress has passed a statute and a President has signed it, it poses grave challenges to the separation of powers for the Executive at a particular moment to be able to nullify Congress' enactment solely on its own initiative and without any determination from the Court.

JUSTICE SCALIA, with whom JUSTICE THOMAS joins, and with whom the CHIEF JUSTICE joins as to Part I, dissenting.

I

A

[T]he plaintiff and the Government agree entirely on what should happen in this lawsuit. They agree that the court below got it right; and they agreed in the court below that the court below that one got it right as well. What, then, are we *doing* here?

The Court says that we have the power to decide this case because if we did not, then our "primary role in determining the constitutionality of a law" (at least one that "has inflicted real injury on a plaintiff") would "become only secondary to the President's." But wait, the reader wonders—Windsor won below, and so *cured* her injury, and the President was glad to see it. True, says the majority, but judicial review must march on regardless, lest we "undermine the clear dictate of the separation-of-powers principle that when an Act of Congress is alleged to conflict with the Constitution, it is emphatically the province and duty of the judicial department to say what the law is."

That is jaw-dropping. It is an assertion of judicial supremacy over the people's Representatives in Congress and the Executive. It envisions a Supreme Court standing (or rather enthroned) at the apex of government, empowered to decide all constitutional questions, always and everywhere "primary" in its role.

This image of the Court would have been unrecognizable to those who wrote and ratified our national charter. They knew well the dangers of "primary" power, and so created branches of government that would be "perfectly coordinate by the terms of their common commission," none of which branches could "pretend to an exclusive or superior right of settling the boundaries between their respective powers." THE FEDERALIST, No. 49. The people did this to protect themselves. They did it to guard their right to self-rule against the black-robed supremacy that today's majority finds so attractive. So it was that Madison could confidently state, with no fear of contradiction, that there was nothing of "greater intrinsic value" or "stamped with the authority of more enlightened patrons of liberty" than a government of separate and coordinate powers. *Id.*, No. 47.

For this reason we are quite forbidden to say what the law is whenever (as today's opinion asserts) "an Act of Congress is alleged to conflict with the Constitution." We can do so only when that allegation will determine the outcome of a lawsuit, and is contradicted by the other party. The "judicial Power" is not, as the majority believes, the power "to say what the law is," giving the Supreme Court the "primary role in determining the constitutionality of laws." The judicial power as Americans have understood it (and their English ancestors before them) is the power to adjudicate, with conclusive effect, disputed government claims (civil or criminal) against private persons, and disputed claims by private persons against the government or other private persons. Sometimes (though not always) the parties before the court disagree not with regard to the facts of their case (or not *only* with regard to the facts) but with regard to the applicable law—in which event (and *only* in which event) it becomes the "province and duty of the judicial department to say what the law is."

[S]ome questions of law will *never* be presented to this Court, because there will never be anyone with standing to bring a lawsuit. *See Schlesinger v. Reservists Comm. to Stop the War*, 418 U.S. 208, 227 (1974); *United States v. Richardson*, 418 U.S. 166, 179 (1974).

That is completely absent here. Windsor's injury was cured by the judgment in her favor. And while, in ordinary circumstances, the United States is injured by a directive to pay a tax refund, this suit is far from ordinary. Whatever injury the United States has suffered will surely not be redressed by the action that it, as a litigant, asks us to take. The final sentence of the Solicitor General's brief on the merits reads: "For the foregoing reasons, the judgment of the court of appeals *should be affirmed*." That will not cure the Government's injury, but carve it into stone. One could spend many fruitless afternoons ransacking our library for any other petitioner's brief seeking an affirmance of the judgment against it.

What the petitioner United States asks us to do in the case before us is exactly what the respondent Windsor asks us to do: not to provide relief from the judgment below but to say that that judgment was correct. And the same was true in the Court of Appeals: Neither party sought to undo the judgment for Windsor, and so that court should have dismissed the appeal (just as we should dismiss) for lack of jurisdiction. Since both parties agreed with the judgment of the District Court for the Southern District of New York, the suit should have ended there. The further proceedings have been a contrivance, having no object in mind except to elevate a District Court judgment that has no precedential effect in other courts, to one that has precedential effect throughout the Second Circuit, and then (in this Court) precedential effect throughout the United States.

We have never before agreed to speak—to "say what the law is"—where there is no controversy before us. In the more than two centuries that this Court has existed as an institution, we have never suggested that we have the power to decide a question when every party agrees with both its nominal opponent *and the court below* on that question's answer. The United States reluctantly conceded that at oral argument.

The closest we have ever come to what the Court blesses today was our opinion in *INS v. Chadha*, 462 U.S. 919 (1983). But in that case, two parties to the litigation disagreed with the position of the United States and with the court below: the House and Senate, which had intervened in the case.

Because *Chadha* concerned the validity of a mode of congressional action—the one-house legislative veto—the House and Senate were threatened with destruction of what they claimed to be one of their institutional powers. The Executive choosing not to defend that power, we permitted the House and Senate to intervene. Nothing like that is present here.

JUSTICE ALITO, with whom JUSTICE THOMAS joins as to Parts II and III, dissenting.

I

I turn first to the question of standing. In my view, the United States clearly is not a proper petitioner in this case. The United States does not ask us to overturn the judgment of the court below or to alter that judgment in any way. Quite to the contrary, the United States argues emphatically in favor of the correctness of that judgment.

Whether the Bipartisan Legal Advisory Group of the House of Representatives (BLAG) has standing to petition is a much more difficult question. In my view, both the Hollingsworth intervenors and BLAG have standing.

A party invoking the Court's authority has a sufficient stake to permit it to appeal when it has " 'suffered an injury in fact' that is caused by 'the conduct complained of' and that 'will be redressed by a favorable decision.' " In the present case, the House of Representatives, which has authorized BLAG to represent its interests in this matter, suffered just such an injury.

In *INS v. Chadha*, 462 U. S. 919 (1983), the Court held that the two Houses of Congress were "proper parties" to file a petition in defense of the constitutionality of the one-house veto statute. Accordingly, the Court granted and decided petitions by both the Senate and the House, in addition to the Executive's petition. That the two Houses had standing to petition is not surprising: The Court of Appeals' decision in *Chadha*, by holding the one-house veto to be unconstitutional, had limited Congress' power to legislate. In discussing Article III standing, the Court suggested that Congress suffered a similar injury whenever federal legislation it had passed was struck down, noting that it had "long held that Congress is the proper party to defend the validity of a statute when an agency of government, as a defendant charged with enforcing the statute, agrees with plaintiffs that the statute is inapplicable or unconstitutional."

The United States attempts to distinguish *Chadha* on the ground that it "involved an unusual statute that vested the House and the Senate themselves each with special procedural rights—namely, the right effectively to veto Executive action." But that is a distinction without a difference: just as the Court of Appeals decision that the Chadha Court affirmed impaired Congress' power by striking down the one-house veto, so the Second Circuit's decision here impairs Congress' legislative power by striking down an Act of Congress.

I appreciate the argument that the Constitution confers on the President alone the authority to defend federal law in litigation, but in my view, as I have explained, that argument is contrary to the Court's holding in *Chadha*, and it is certainly contrary to the *Chadha* Court's endorsement of the principle that "Congress is the proper party to defend the validity of a statute" when the Executive refuses to do so on constitutional grounds. See also 2 U. S. C. § 288h(7) (Senate Legal Counsel shall defend the constitutionality of Acts of Congress when placed in issue). Accordingly, in the narrow category of cases in which a court strikes down an Act of Congress and the Executive declines to defend the Act, Congress both has standing to defend the undefended statute and is a proper party to do so.

EXERCISE 23:

1. Would it have been improper for the IRS simply to give Edith Windsor her refund on the basis of DOMA's unconstitutionality, rather than requiring her to sue?

2. Does the duty to *defend* a law and the duty to *enforce* it require the same amount of evidence of constitutionality? What should the President or other executive official do if the issue is close, so that a statute is *probably* unconstitutional, but not *clearly* so? Is that enough for the official not to enforce the law? If an executive official thinks the law is probably unconstitutional, is it proper for the official to argue to a court that it *is* constitutional? See Christopher R. Green, *Constitutional Theory and the Activismometer: How to Think About Indeterminacy, Restraint, Vagueness, Executive Review, and Precedent*, 54 Santa Clara L. Rev. 403, 452–58 (2014).

3. Is the President required to veto a law that is only partly unconstitutional? Recall **Chapter 2**, Exercise 17, Question 1.

3. If Congress or a part of Congress is takes responsibility for litigating in defense of a statute, is that proper? Keep this question in mind when we discuss congressional exercise of executive power in Section C below. Should the executive branch, instead of delegating authority to BLAG, have picked counsel outside the legislative branch to make arguments in favor of the constitutionality of DOMA?

4. Justice Alito argued that Congress's power to defend the one-house veto in court in *Chadha* was not unique because Congress's self-delegation powers were themselves at issue in the case. Congress had the same interest, Alito argued, in defending the constitutionality of any of laws, including laws like DOMA that do not directly concern Congress as such. Is Alito's argument persuasive?

5. Are lawyers always required to believe arguments they make in court? Should courts allow executive officials simply to identify the *strongest arguments* in favor of the constitutionality of a statute, without endorsing their merit?

6. Justice Scalia notes two cases from 1974 where constitutional provisions might go without judicial enforcement because no plaintiff might ever have standing— *Schlesinger v. Reservists Against the War*, which involved assertions that congressmen were serving in the Reserves contrary to Art. I § 6 cl. 2, and *United States v. Richardson*, which involved assertions that secret spending violates Art. I § 9 cl. 7. In these cases, is executive review more essential than at other times?

7. If executive review is rooted in the oath that all executive officers take, are all executive officers equally obligated to engage in it? What about lower-level-executive-officer review of the constitutionality of higher-level-executive-officer action? What should a clerk at the Social Security Administration do who disagrees with cases approving Social Security under Art. I, § 8, cl. 1 like *Helvering v. Davis*, 301 U.S. 619 (1937) (a case with a non-frivolous dissent)? Cases like *Little v. Barreme*, 6 U.S. (2 Cranch) 170, 179 (1804), allow trespass liability even on those who are merely following the command of the President. Does that imply a power or even duty of lower-level executive officials to disobey the President, if he acts unconstitutionally? The Manual for Courts-Martial, United States ¶ 14.c(d)(2)(a)(i), at IV-20 (2012), provides, "An order requiring the performance of a military duty or act may be inferred to be lawful and it is disobeyed at the peril of the subordinate. This inference does not apply to a patently illegal order, such as one that directs the

commission of a crime." Do all executive officials have to check to make sure the President's decisions on constitutionality are at least not patently wrong?

8. The issue of executive review and the executive duty to defend arises in state-constitutional law as well. This area is one in which a good fify-state survey has been recently conducted. *See* Neal Devins & Saikrishna Bangalore Prakash, *Fifty States, Fifty Attorneys General, and Fifty Approaches to the Duty to Defend*, 124 YALE L.J. 2100 (2015). The state-constitutional issue is even more complicated because state-constitutional executive power is almost always explicitly splintered among the governor, attorney general, and other officials. For a canvass of the issues, see Jordan E. Pratt, *Disregard of Unconstitutional Laws in the Plural State Executive*, 86 MISS. L.J. 1 (2017). Note that the state-constitutional issues regarding the duty to defend will also arise when state officials are challenged regarding issues under the federal constitution. The distribution of California-state-constitutional authority to defend its marriage laws, for instance, was hotly contested in a case decided the same day as *Windsor, Hollingsworth v. Perry*, 133 S. Ct. 2652 (2013) (initiative proponent has no standing to defend opposite-sex-only marriage requirement in federal court if attorney general and governor refuse to defend it).

4. The Line-Item Veto

In addition to limiting the President's ability to legislate on his own, the Court has used separation-of-powers principles to prevent the President from participating in the legislative process in certain ways.

CLINTON v. CITY OF NEW YORK
524 U.S. 417 (1998)

[This case involved a challenge to the Line Item Veto Act. An earlier challenge to the Act was dismissed because it was brought by Senators who opposed the Act who lacked the necessary standing. *See Raines v. Byrd*, 521 U.S. 811 (1997). Two months later, President Clinton "cancelled" provisions in two statutes by following the procedures of the Act. The City of New York and Snake River Potato Growers claimed they were injured by the cancellations.]

JUSTICE STEVENS delivered the opinion of the Court.

On the merits, the District Court held that the cancellations did not conform to the constitutionally mandated procedures.

The Line Item Veto Act gives the President the power to "cancel in whole" three types of provisions that have been signed into law: "(1) any dollar amount of discretionary budget authority; (2) any item of new direct spending; or (3) any limited tax benefit." 2 U.S.C. §691(a). It is undisputed that the New York case involves an "item of new direct spending" and that the Snake River case involves a "limited tax benefit" as those terms are defined in the Act. It is also undisputed that each of those provisions had been signed into law pursuant to Article I, §7, of the Constitution before it was canceled.

The Act requires the President to adhere to precise procedures whenever he exercises his cancellation authority. In identifying items for cancellation he must consider the legislative history, the purposes, and other relevant information about the items. *See* 2 U.S.C. §691(b). He must determine, with respect to each cancellation, that it will "(i) reduce the Federal budget deficit; (ii) not impair any essential Government functions; and (iii) not harm the national interest." §691(a)(3)(A). Moreover, he must transmit a special message to Congress notifying it of each cancellation within five calendar days (excluding Sundays) after the enactment of the canceled provision. *See* §691(a)(3)(B). It is undisputed that the President meticulously followed these procedures in these cases.

A cancellation takes effect upon receipt by Congress of the special message from the President. *See* §691b(a). If, however, a "disapproval bill" pertaining to a special message is enacted into law, the cancellations set forth in that message become "null and void." *Id.* The Act sets forth a detailed expedited procedure for the consideration of a "disapproval bill," *see* §691d, but no such bill was passed for either of the cancellations involved in these cases. A majority vote of both Houses is sufficient to enact a disapproval bill. The Act does not grant the President the authority to cancel a disapproval bill, *see* §691(c), but he does, of course, retain his constitutional authority to veto such a bill.

The effect of a cancellation is plainly stated in §691e, which defines the principal terms used in the Act. With respect to both an item of new direct spending and a limited tax benefit, the cancellation prevents the item "from having legal force or effect." §§691e(4)(B)–(C). Thus, under the plain text of the statute, the two actions of the President that are challenged in these cases prevented one section of the Balanced Budget Act of 1997 and one section of the Taxpayer Relief Act of 1997 "from having legal force or effect." The remaining provisions of those statutes continue to have the same force and effect as they had when signed into law.

In both legal and practical effect, the President has amended two Acts of Congress by repealing a portion of each. "[R]epeal of statutes, no less than enactment, must conform with Art. I." *INS v. Chadha*, 462 U.S. 919, 954 (1983). There is no provision in the Constitution that authorizes the President to enact, to amend, or to repeal statutes. Both Article I and Article II assign responsibilities to the President that directly relate to the lawmaking process, but neither addresses the issue presented by these cases.

There are important differences between the President's "return" of a bill pursuant to Article I, §7, and the exercise of the President's cancellation authority pursuant to the Line Item Veto Act. The constitutional return takes place *before* the bill becomes law; the statutory cancellation occurs *after* the bill becomes law. The constitutional return is of the entire bill; the statutory cancellation is of only a part. Although the Constitution expressly authorizes the President to play a role in the process of enacting statutes, it is silent on the subject of unilateral Presidential action that either repeals or amends parts of duly enacted statutes.

There are powerful reasons for construing constitutional silence on this profoundly important issue as equivalent to an express prohibition. The procedures governing the enactment of statutes set forth in the text of Article I were the product of the great debates and compromises that produced the Constitution itself. Familiar historical materials provide abundant support for the conclusion that the power to enact statutes may only "be exercised in accord with a single, finely wrought and exhaustively considered, procedure." *Chadha*, 462 U.S. at 951. Our first President understood the text of the Presentment Clause as requiring that he either "approve all the parts of a Bill, or reject it in toto."[30] What has emerged in these cases from the President's exercise of his statutory cancellation powers, however, are truncated versions of two bills that passed both Houses of Congress. They are not the product of the "finely wrought" procedure that the Framers designed.

V

The Government advances two related arguments to support its position that despite the unambiguous provisions of the Act, cancellations do not amend or repeal properly enacted statutes in violation of the Presentment Clause. First, relying primarily on *Field v. Clark*, 143 U.S. 649 (1892), the Government contends that the cancellations were merely exercises of discretionary authority granted to the President by the Balanced Budget Act and the Taxpayer Relief Act read in light of the previously enacted Line Item Veto Act. Second, the Government submits that the substance of the authority to cancel tax and spending items "is, in practical effect, no more and no less than the power to 'decline to spend' specified sums of money, or to 'decline to implement' specified tax measures." Neither argument is persuasive.

In *Field v. Clark*, the Court upheld the constitutionality of the Tariff Act of 1890. That statute contained a "free list" of almost 300 specific articles that were exempted from import duties "unless otherwise specially provided for in this act." 143 U.S. at 602. Section 3 was a special provision that directed the President to suspend that exemption for sugar, molasses, coffee, tea, and hides "whenever, and so often" as he should be satisfied that any country producing and exporting those products imposed duties on the agricultural products of the United States that he deemed to be "reciprocally unequal and unreasonable . . . ." The section then specified the duties to be imposed on those products during any such suspension. The Court provided this explanation for its conclusion that § 3 had not delegated legislative power to the President:

> Nothing involving the expediency or the just operation of such legislation
> was left to the determination of the President. [W]hen he ascertained the

---

30. 33 Writings of George Washington 96 (J. Fitzpatrick ed. 1940); *see also* W. Taft, The Presidency: Its Duties, Its Powers, Its Opportunities and Its Limitations 11 (1916) (stating that the President "has no power to veto part of a bill and let the rest become a law"); *cf.* 1 W. Blackstone, Commentaries *154 ("The crown cannot begin of itself any alterations in the present established law; but it may approve or disapprove of the alterations suggested and consented to by the two houses").

fact that duties and exactions, reciprocally unequal and unreasonable, were imposed upon the agricultural or other products of the United States by a country producing and exporting sugar, molasses, coffee, tea or hides, it became his duty to issue a proclamation declaring the suspension, as to that country, which Congress had determined should occur. He had no discretion in the premises except in respect to the duration of the suspension so ordered. But that related only to the enforcement of the policy established by Congress. As the suspension was absolutely required when the President ascertained the existence of a particular fact, it cannot be said that in ascertaining that fact and in issuing his proclamation, in obedience to the legislative will, he exercised the function of making laws. It was a part of the law itself as it left the hands of Congress that the provisions, full and complete in themselves, permitting the free introduction of sugars, molasses, coffee, tea and hides, from particular countries, should be suspended, in a given contingency, and that in case of such suspensions certain duties should be imposed.

Id. at 693.

This passage identifies three critical differences between the power to suspend the exemption from import duties and the power to cancel portions of a duly enacted statute. First, the exercise of the suspension power was contingent upon a condition that did not exist when the Tariff Act was passed: the imposition of "reciprocally unequal and unreasonable" import duties by other countries. In contrast, the exercise of the cancellation power within five days after the enactment of the Balanced Budget and Tax Reform Acts necessarily was based on the same conditions that Congress evaluated when it passed those statutes. Second, under the Tariff Act, when the President determined that the contingency had arisen, he had a duty to suspend; in contrast, while it is true that the President was required by the Act to make three determinations before he canceled a provision, *see* 2 U.S.C. § 691(a)(A), those determinations did not qualify his discretion to cancel or not to cancel. Finally, whenever the President suspended an exemption under the Tariff Act, he was executing the policy that Congress had embodied in the statute. In contrast, whenever the President cancels an item of new direct spending or a limited tax benefit he is rejecting the policy judgment made by Congress and relying on his own policy judgment. Thus, the conclusion in *Field v. Clark* that the suspensions mandated by the Tariff Act were not exercises of legislative power does not undermine our opinion that cancellations pursuant to the Line Item Veto Act are the functional equivalent of partial repeals of Acts of Congress that fail to satisfy Article I, § 7.

The cited statutes all relate to foreign trade, and this Court has recognized that in the foreign affairs arena, the President has "a degree of discretion and freedom from statutory restriction which would not be admissible were domestic affairs alone involved." *United States v. Curtiss-Wright Export Corp.*, 299 U.S. 304, 320 (1936).

Neither are we persuaded by the Government's contention that the President's authority to cancel new direct spending and tax benefit items is no greater than his traditional authority to decline to spend appropriated funds. The Government has reviewed in some detail the series of statutes in which Congress has given the Executive broad discretion over the expenditure of appropriated funds. For example, the First Congress appropriated "sum[s] not exceeding" specified amounts to be spent on various Government operations. *See, e.g.,* Act of Sept. 29, 1789, ch. 23, § 1, 1 Stat. 95; Act of Mar. 26, 1790, ch. 4, § 1, 1 Stat. 104; Act of Feb. 11, 1791, ch. 6, 1 Stat. 190. In those statutes, as in later years, the President was given wide discretion with respect to both the amounts to be spent and how the money would be allocated among different functions. It is argued that the Line Item Veto Act merely confers comparable discretionary authority over the expenditure of appropriated funds. The critical difference between this statute and all of its predecessors, however, is that unlike any of them, this Act gives the President the unilateral power to change the text of duly enacted statutes. None of the Act's predecessors could even arguably have been construed to authorize such a change.

VI

[O]ur decision rests on the narrow ground that the procedures authorized by the Line Item Veto Act are not authorized by the Constitution. The Balanced Budget Act of 1997 is a 500-page document that became "Public Law 105-33" after three procedural steps were taken: (1) a bill containing its exact text was approved by a majority of the Members of the House of Representatives; (2) the Senate approved precisely the same text; and (3) that text was signed into law by the President. If there is to be a new procedure in which the President will play a different role in determining the final text of what may "become a law," such change must come not by legislation but through the amendment procedures set forth in Article V of the Constitution.

The judgment of the District Court is affirmed.

JUSTICE KENNEDY, concurring.

A Nation cannot plunder its own treasury without putting its Constitution and its survival in peril. The statute before us, then, is of first importance, for it seems undeniable the Act will tend to restrain persistent excessive spending. Nevertheless, for the reasons given by Justice Stevens in the opinion for the Court, the statute must be found invalid. Failure of political will does not justify unconstitutional remedies.

I write to respond to my colleague Justice Breyer, who observes that the statute does not threaten the liberties of individual citizens, a point on which I disagree. Separation of powers was designed to implement a fundamental insight: Concentration of power in the hands of a single branch is a threat to liberty. The Federalist states the axiom in these explicit terms: "The accumulation of all powers, legislative, executive, and judiciary, in the same hands . . . may justly be pronounced the very definition of tyranny." THE FEDERALIST No. 47. [The Founders] used the principles of separation of powers and federalism to secure liberty in the fundamental political sense of the term, quite in addition to the idea of freedom from intrusive governmental acts. The idea and the promise were that when the people delegate some degree of control to a remote central authority, one branch of government ought not possess the power to shape their destiny without a sufficient check from the other two. In this vision, liberty demands limits on the ability of any one branch to influence basic political decisions.

The principal object of the statute, it is true, was not to enhance the President's power to reward one group and punish another, to help one set of taxpayers and hurt another, to favor one State and ignore another. Yet these are its undeniable effects. The law establishes a new mechanism which gives the President the sole ability to hurt a group that is a visible target, in order to disfavor the group or to extract further concessions from Congress. The law is the functional equivalent of a line item veto and enhances the President's powers beyond what the Framers would have endorsed.

It is no answer, of course, to say that Congress surrendered its authority by its own hand; nor does it suffice to point out that a new statute, signed by the President or enacted over his veto, could restore to Congress the power it now seeks to relinquish. That a congressional cession of power is voluntary does not make it innocuous. The Constitution is a compact enduring for more than our time, and one Congress cannot yield up its own powers, much less those of other Congresses to follow. *See Freytag v. Commissioner*, 501 U.S. 868, 880 (1991); *cf. Chadha*, 462 U.S. at 942 n. 13. Abdication of responsibility is not part of the constitutional design.

The Constitution is not bereft of controls over improvident spending. Federalism is one safeguard, for political accountability is easier to enforce within the States than nationwide. The other principal mechanism, of course, is control of the political branches by an informed and responsible electorate. Whether or not federalism and control by the electorate are adequate for the problem at hand, they are two of the structures the Framers designed for the problem the statute strives to confront. The fact that these mechanisms, plus the proper functioning of the separation of powers itself, are not employed, or that they prove insufficient, cannot validate an otherwise unconstitutional device. With these observations, I join the opinion of the Court.

JUSTICE SCALIA, with whom JUSTICE O'CONNOR joins, and with whom JUSTICE BREYER joins as to Part III, concurring in part and dissenting in part.

III

The Presentment Clause requires, in relevant part, that "[e]very Bill which shall have passed the House of Representatives and the Senate, shall, before it become a Law, be presented to the President of the United States; If he approve he shall sign it, but if not he shall return it." U.S. Const., Art. I, § 7, cl. 2. There is no question that enactment of the Balanced Budget Act complied with these requirements: the House and Senate passed the bill, and the President signed it into law. It was only *after* the requirements of the Presentment Clause had been satisfied that the President exercised his authority under the Line Item Veto Act to cancel the spending item. Thus, the Court's problem with the Act is not that it authorizes the President to veto parts of a bill and sign others into law, but rather that it authorizes him to "cancel"—prevent from "having legal force or effect"—certain parts of duly enacted statutes.   ·

Article I, § 7, of the Constitution obviously prevents the President from canceling a law that Congress has not authorized him to cancel. Such action cannot possibly be considered part of his execution of the law, and if it is legislative action, as the Court observes, "repeal of statutes, no less than enactment, must conform with Art. I." But that is not this case. It was certainly arguable, as an original matter, that Art. I, § 7, also prevents the President from canceling a law which itself *authorizes* the President to cancel it. But as the Court acknowledges, that argument has long since been made and rejected. In 1809, Congress passed a law authorizing the President to cancel trade restrictions against Great Britain and France if either revoked edicts directed at the United States. Joseph Story regarded the conferral of that authority as entirely unremarkable in *The Orono*, 18 F. Cas. 830 (No. 10,585) (C.C.D. Mass. 1812). The Tariff Act of 1890 authorized the President to "suspend, by proclamation to that effect" certain of its provisions if he determined that other countries were imposing "reciprocally unequal and unreasonable" duties. This Court upheld the constitutionality of that Act in *Field v. Clark*, 143 U.S. 649 (1892), reciting the history since 1798 of statutes conferring upon the President the power to, *inter alia*, "discontinue the prohibitions and restraints hereby enacted and declared," *id.* at 684, "suspend the operation of the aforesaid act," *id.* at 685, and "declare the provisions of this act to be inoperative," *id.* at 688.

As much as the Court goes on about Art. I, § 7, therefore, that provision does not demand the result the Court reaches. It no more categorically prohibits the Executive *reduction* of congressional dispositions in the course of implementing statutes that authorize such reduction, than it categorically prohibits the Executive *augmentation* of congressional dispositions in the course of implementing statutes that authorize such augmentation—generally known as substantive rulemaking. There are, to be sure, limits upon the former just as there are limits upon the latter—and I am prepared to acknowledge that the limits upon the former may be much more severe. Those limits are established, however, not by some categorical prohibition of Art. I, § 7, which our cases conclusively disprove, but by what has come to be known as the doctrine of unconstitutional delegation of legislative authority: When authorized Executive reduction or augmentation is allowed to go too far, it usurps the nondelegable function of Congress and violates the separation of powers.

It is this doctrine, and not the Presentment Clause, that was discussed in the *Field* opinion, and it is this doctrine, and not the Presentment Clause, that is the issue presented by the statute before us here. That is why the Court is correct to distinguish prior authorizations of Executive cancellation, such as the one involved in *Field*, on the ground that they were contingent upon an Executive finding of fact, and on the ground that they related to the field of foreign affairs, an area where the President has a special "degree of discretion and freedom." These distinctions have nothing to do with whether the details of Art. I, § 7, have been complied with, but everything to do with whether the authorizations went too far by transferring to the Executive a degree of political, lawmaking power that our traditions demand be retained by the Legislative Branch.

I turn, then, to the crux of the matter: whether Congress's authorizing the President to cancel an item of spending gives him a power that our history and traditions show must reside exclusively in the Legislative Branch.

Insofar as the degree of political, "lawmaking" power conferred upon the Executive is concerned, there is not a dime's worth of difference between Congress's authorizing the President to *cancel* a spending item, and Congress's authorizing money to be spent on a particular item at the President's discretion. And the latter has been done since the founding of the Nation. From 1789–1791, the First Congress made lump-sum appropriations for the entire Government—"sum[s] not exceeding" specified amounts for broad purposes. Act of Sept. 29, 1789, ch. 23, 1 Stat. 95; Act of Mar. 26, 1790, ch. 4, § 1, 1 Stat. 104; Act of Feb. 11, 1791, ch. 6, 1 Stat. 190. From a very early date Congress also made permissive individual appropriations, leaving the decision whether to spend the money to the President's unfettered discretion.

Certain Presidents have claimed Executive authority to withhold appropriated funds even *absent* an express conferral of discretion to do so. In 1876, for example, President Grant reported to Congress that he would not spend money appropriated for certain harbor and river improvements because "[u]nder no circumstances [would he] allow expenditures upon works not clearly national," and in his view, the appropriations were for "works of purely private or local interest, in no sense national," 4 Cong. Rec. 5628.

The short of the matter is this: Had the Line Item Veto Act authorized the President to "decline to spend" any item of spending contained in the Balanced Budget Act of 1997, there is not the slightest doubt that authorization would have been constitutional. What the Line Item Veto Act does instead—authorizing the President to "cancel" an item of spending—is technically different. But the technical difference does *not* relate to the technicalities of the Presentment Clause, which have been fully complied with; and the doctrine of unconstitutional delegation, which *is* at issue here, is preeminently *not* a doctrine of technicalities. The title of the Line Item Veto Act, which was perhaps designed to simplify for public comprehension, or perhaps merely to comply with the terms of a campaign pledge, has succeeded in faking out the Supreme Court. The President's action it authorizes in fact is not a line-item veto and thus does not offend Art. I, § 7; and insofar as the substance of that action is concerned, it is no different from what Congress has permitted the President to do since the formation of the Union.

For the foregoing reasons, I respectfully dissent.

JUSTICE BREYER, with whom JUSTICE O'CONNOR and JUSTICE SCALIA join as to Part III, dissenting.

I

In my view the Line Item Veto Act (Act) does not violate any specific textual constitutional command, nor does it violate any implicit separation-of-powers principle. Consequently, I believe that the Act is constitutional.

III

The Court believes that the Act violates the literal text of the Constitution. A simple syllogism captures its basic reasoning:

> Major Premise: The Constitution sets forth an exclusive method for enacting, repealing, or amending laws.

> Minor Premise: The Act authorizes the President to "repea[l] or amen[d]" laws in a different way, namely by announcing a cancellation of a portion of a previously enacted law.

> Conclusion: The Act is inconsistent with the Constitution.

I find this syllogism unconvincing, however, because its Minor Premise is faulty. When the President "canceled" the two appropriation measures now before us, he did not *repeal* any law nor did he *amend* any law. He simply *followed* the law, leaving the statutes, as they are literally written, intact.

To understand why one cannot say, *literally speaking*, that the President has repealed or amended any law, imagine how the provisions of law before us might have been, but were not, written. Imagine that the canceled New York health care tax provision at issue here had instead said the following:

> Section One. Taxes . . . that were collected by the State of New York from a health care provider before June 1, 1997, and for which a waiver of the provisions [requiring payment] have been sought . . . are deemed to be permissible health care related taxes . . . *provided however that the President may prevent the just-mentioned provision from having legal force or effect if he determines x, y, and z.* (Assume x, y and z to be the same determinations required by the Line Item Veto Act).

Whatever a person might say, or think, about the constitutionality of this imaginary law, there is one thing the English language would prevent one from saying. One could not say that a President who "prevent[s]" the deeming language from "having legal force or effect," *see* 2 U.S.C. §691e(4)(B), has either *repealed* or *amended* this particular hypothetical statute. Rather, the President has *followed* that law to the letter. He has exercised the power it explicitly delegates to him. He has executed the law, not repealed it.

It could make no significant difference to this linguistic point were the italicized proviso to appear, not as part of what I have called Section One, but, instead, at the bottom of the statute page, say, referenced by an asterisk, with a statement that it applies to every spending provision in the Act next to which a similar asterisk appears. And that being so, it could make no difference if that proviso appeared, instead, in a different, earlier enacted law, along with legal language that makes it applicable to every future spending provision picked out according to a specified formula.

But, of course, this last mentioned possibility is this very case. The earlier law, namely, the Line Item Veto Act, says that "the President may . . . prevent such [future] budget authority from having legal force or effect." 2 U.S.C. §§ 691(a), 691e(4)(B). For that reason, one cannot dispose of this case through a purely literal analysis as the majority does. Literally speaking, the President has not "repealed" or "amended" anything. He has simply *executed* a power conferred upon him by Congress, which power is contained in laws that were enacted in compliance with the exclusive method set forth in the Constitution. *See Field v. Clark*, 143 U.S. 649, 693 (1892) (President's power to raise tariff rates *"was a part of the law itself, as it left the hands of Congress"* (emphasis added)).

Nor can one dismiss this literal compliance as some kind of formal quibble, as if it were somehow "obvious" that what the President has done "amounts to," "comes close to," or is "analogous to" the repeal or amendment of a previously enacted law. That is because the power the Act grants the President (to render designated appropriations items without "legal force or effect") also "amounts to," "comes close to," or is "analogous to" a different legal animal, the delegation of a power to choose one legal path as opposed to another, such as a power to appoint.

IV

Because I disagree with the Court's holding of literal violation, I must consider whether the Act nonetheless violates separation-of-powers principles—principles that arise out of the Constitution's vesting of the "executive Power" in "a President," U.S. Const., Art. II, § 1, and "[a]ll legislative Powers" in "a Congress," Art. I, § 1. There are three relevant separation-of-powers questions here: (1) Has Congress given the President the wrong kind of power, *i.e.*, "non-Executive" power? (2) Has Congress given the President the power to "encroach" upon Congress' own constitutionally reserved territory? (3) Has Congress given the President too much power, violating the doctrine of "nondelegation?"

A

Viewed conceptually, the power the Act conveys is the right kind of power. It is "executive." As explained above, an exercise of that power "executes" the Act. Conceptually speaking, it closely resembles the kind of delegated authority—to spend or not to spend appropriations, to change or not to change tariff rates—that Congress has frequently granted the President, any differences being differences in degree, not kind.

The fact that one could also characterize this kind of power as "legislative," say, if Congress itself (by amending the appropriations bill) prevented a provision from taking effect, is beside the point. This Court has frequently found that the exercise of a particular power, such as the power to make rules of broad applicability or to adjudicate claims, can fall within the constitutional purview of more than one branch of

Government. *See Wayman v. Southard*, 23 U.S. 1, 43 (1825) (Marshall, C.J.) ("Congress may certainly delegate to others, powers which the legislature may rightfully exercise itself"). The Court does not "carry out the distinction between legislative and executive action with mathematical precision" or "divide the branches into watertight compartments," for, as others have said, the Constitution "blend[s]" as well as "separat[es]" powers in order to create a workable government.

B

The Act does not undermine what this Court has often described as the principal function of the separation of powers, which is to maintain the tripartite structure of the Federal Government—and thereby protect individual liberty—by providing a "safeguard against the encroachment or aggrandizement of one branch at the expense of the other." *Buckley v. Valeo*, 424 U.S. 1, 122 (1976) (per curiam); *Mistretta v. United States*, 488 U.S. at 380–382.

In contrast to these cases, one cannot say that the Act "encroaches" upon Congress' power, when Congress retained the power to insert, by simple majority, into any future appropriations bill, into any section of any such bill, or into any phrase of any section, a provision that says the Act will not apply. *See* 2 U.S.C. § 691f(c)(1); *Raines v. Byrd*, 521 U.S. 811, 824 (1997) (Congress can "exempt a given appropriations bill (or a given provision in an appropriations bill) from the Act"). Congress also retained the power to "disapprov[e]," and thereby reinstate, any of the President's cancellations. *See* 2 U.S.C. § 691b(a). And it is Congress that drafts and enacts the appropriations statutes that are subject to the Act in the first place—and thereby defines the outer limits of the President's cancellation authority. Thus *this* Act is not the sort of delegation "without . . . sufficient check" that concerns Justice Kennedy. Indeed, the President acts only in response to, and on the terms set by, the Congress.

Nor can one say that the Act's basic substantive objective is constitutionally improper, for the earliest Congresses could and often did, confer on the President this sort of discretionary authority over spending. Nor can one say the Act's grant of power "aggrandizes" the Presidential office. The grant is limited to the context of the budget. It is limited to the power to spend, or not to spend, particular appropriated items, and the power to permit, or not to permit, specific limited exemptions from generally applicable tax law from taking effect.

C

The "nondelegation" doctrine represents an added constitutional check upon Congress' authority to delegate power to the Executive Branch. And it raises a more serious constitutional obstacle here. The Constitution permits Congress to "see[k] assistance from another branch" of Government, the "extent and character" of that assistance to be fixed "according to common sense and the inherent necessities of the governmental co-ordination." *J.W. Hampton & Co. v. United States*, 276 U.S. 394, 406 (Taft, C.J.). But there are limits on the way in which Congress can obtain such assistance; it "cannot delegate any part of its legislative power except under the limitation of a prescribed standard." Or, in Chief Justice Taft's more familiar words, the

Constitution permits only those delegations where Congress "shall lay down by legislative act an *intelligible principle* to which the person or body authorized to [act] is directed to conform." *J.W. Hampton*, 276 U.S. at 409 (emphasis added).

The Act before us seeks to create such a principle in three ways. The first is procedural. The Act tells the President that, in "identifying dollar amounts [or] . . . items . . . for cancellation" (which I take to refer to his selection of the amounts or items he will "prevent from having legal force or effect"), he is to "consider" [certain specified things]. The second is purposive. The clear purpose behind the Act, confirmed by its legislative history, is to promote "greater fiscal accountability" and to "eliminate wasteful federal spending and . . . special tax breaks." The third is substantive. The President must determine that, to "prevent" the item or amount "from having legal force or effect" will "reduce the Federal budget deficit; . . . not impair any essential Government functions; and . . . not harm the national interest." 2 U.S.C. § 691(a)(A).

The resulting standards are broad. But this Court has upheld standards that are equally broad, or broader. *See, e.g., National Broadcasting Co. v. United States*, 319 U.S. 190, 225–26 (1943) (upholding delegation to Federal Communications Commission to regulate broadcast licensing as "public interest, convenience, or necessity" require); *FPC v. Hope Natural Gas Co.*, 320 U.S. 591, 600–03 (1944) (upholding delegation to Federal Power Commission to determine "just and reasonable" rates).

Indeed, the Court has only twice in its history found that a congressional delegation of power violated the "nondelegation" doctrine. One such case, *Panama Refining Co. v. Ryan*, 293 U.S. 388 (1935), was in a sense a special case, for it was discovered in the midst of the case that the particular exercise of the power at issue, the promulgation of a Petroleum Code under the National Industrial Recovery Act, did not contain any legally operative sentence. *Id.* at 412–413. The other case, *A.L.A. Schechter Poultry Corp. v. United States*, 295 U.S. 495 (1935), involved a delegation through the National Industrial Recovery Act that contained not simply a broad standard ("fair competition"), but also the conferral of power on private parties to promulgate rules applying that standard to virtually all of American industry, *id.* at 521– 525. The case before us does not involve any such "roving commission," nor does it involve delegation to private parties, nor does it bring all of American industry within its scope.

[I]nsofar as monetary expenditure (but not "tax expenditure") is at issue, the President acts in an area where history helps to justify the discretionary power that Congress has delegated, and where history may inform his exercise of the Act's delegated authority. Congress has frequently delegated the President the authority to spend, or not to spend, particular sums of money.

V

Consequently, with respect, I dissent.

EXERCISE 24:

In light of *Clinton v. City of New York*, consider the following questions:

1. The majority of the Court asserted that President Clinton's actions had the "legal and practical effect" of "repealing a portion" of the statutes at issue. Is that true?

2. How, if at all, did the procedure followed by President Clinton differ from the procedure specified by Congress? How, if at all, did the procedure followed by President Clinton differ from the procedure historically employed to "veto" legislation?

3. The majority of the Court asserted that "constitutional silence" should be construed "as equivalent to an express prohibition" of enactment of legislation in any manner other than the one specified by the Constitution. Is that a fair inference? If so, should constitutional silence regarding removal of a non-judicial officer from office by means other than impeachment be construed to prohibit alternative means of removal? Why or why not?

4. The majority of the Court based its conclusion, in part, on the fact that President Washington "understood the text of the Presentment Clause as requiring that he either 'approve all the parts of a Bill, or reject it in toto.'" Could the text of the Presentment Clause support any alternative construction? Why or why not? How much weight, if any, should have been given, in 1998, to President Washington's views and historical practice? Why?

5. The majority of the Court distinguished on three bases numerous precedents authorizing limited "delegation" to the Executive. One basis of distinction suggested by the Court was that "the suspension power [at issue in *Field v. Clark*] was contingent upon a condition that did not exist" when the statute was enacted. A second basis of distinction suggested by the Court was that "when the President determined that the contingency had arisen, he had a duty to suspend" under the statute at issue in *Field v. Clark*, rather than retaining "discretion" whether to act. Assume that on April 5, 1952, Congress enacted a statute providing that "the President may seize control of the means of production of any commodities for up to one year upon certifying that (a) a nation-wide disruption of production was imminent and (b) each such commodity was essential to national defense." Could President Truman have relied upon that statute to seize the steel mills on April 9, or would the statute be unconstitutional because the crisis existed at the time Congress legislated? Would the statute have been unconstitutional because it did not mandate seizure whenever the President certified the two conditions were satisfied?

6. The third basis for distinguishing precedent identified by the majority of the Court was that "whenever the President suspended an exemption [under the statute at issue in *Field v. Clark*], he was executing the policy that Congress had embodied in the statute." Is it not equally true that President Clinton was executing the policy that Congress embodied in the Line Item Veto Act? Is there some reason for

distinguishing between the policy of Congress in the Line Item Veto Act and the policy of Congress in the statutes as to which President Clinton asserted "cancellation" authority? If so, would a different result follow if, instead of enacting the Line Item Veto Act, Congress had written its provisions directly into the Balanced Budget Act of 1997 and the Taxpayer Relief Act of 1997? Why or why not?

7. A possible fourth basis for distinguishing precedent identified by the majority of the Court is that the statutes cited by the government "all relate to foreign trade" as distinguished from "domestic affairs alone." Is that distinction pertinent to analysis under the Presentment Clause? Why or why not?

8. The majority of the Court asserted that it was irrelevant "that Congress intended" to convey discretion upon the President absent its "amending the Constitution." Why is the view of Congress in 1996 that such a procedure was constitutionally permissible "of no moment" but the views of President Washington were persuasive in eliminating a constitutional power in the executive to make partial vetoes?

9. The majority of the Court identified "three procedural steps" which are "explicitly require[d]" by the Constitution so that "[i]f one paragraph of [the text of the bill] had been omitted at any one of those three stages, Public Law 105-33 would not have been validly enacted" and was "surely not a document that may 'become a law'" under the Constitution. How are those statements consistent with the scope of judicial review expressed in *Field v. Clark*? In light of the extensive discussion of that precedent in the majority's opinion, albeit on a different issue, is it reasonable to believe the Court overlooked the matter? Did Congress and the President make a mistake in enacting and operating under the Line Item Veto Act instead of simply conspiring to omit from published law specific sections that the President identified?

10. What rationale did Justice Kennedy provide for judicial enforcement of separation of powers vested in Congress and the President? What other structural provisions of the Constitution did he assert were subject to judicial enforcement on the same rationale?

11. How did Justice Kennedy's rationale support his conclusion that Congress may not voluntarily surrender its own powers to the Executive?

12. Other than prohibiting a transfer of power from Congress to the Executive, what other intra-governmental power transfer did Justice Kennedy find implicit in the design of the Line Item Veto Act? Are such transfers consistent with, or in opposition to, democratic theory? Did the Line Item Veto Act actually make any such transfer?

13. What constitutionally-permissible mechanisms did Justice Kennedy identify for control of federal spending?

14. What kind of power does the dissent think is at stake in making budgetary decisions generally? What kind of power was exercised by the president in this case? Does it make sense that exactly the same power can be legislative in one context but executive in another? Keep this issue in mind when we discuss *Chadha* below.

C. EXCLUDING CONGRESS FROM LAW-EXECUTION: THE LEGISLATIVE VETO AND ITS KIN

Our central concern up to now has been executive power as such. The flip side of a ban on executive legislation, however, is a ban on legislative law-administration. It is unsurprising that this principle has become part of American constitutional law as well. The Framers crafted a detailed set of requirements for Congress to pass legislation. This stemmed from their concern that Congress was the branch most likely to absorb power and subjugate the other branches. In the following case, which struck down a large number of "legislative veto" provisions in a single day, the Supreme Court made clear that Article I's legislative steps were the only method by which Congress, or components of Congress, may exercise power over the content of the law.

INS v. CHADHA

462 U.S. 919 (1983)

CHIEF JUSTICE BURGER delivered the opinion of the Court.

[These cases] present a challenge to the constitutionality of the provision in § 244(c)(2) of the Immigration and Nationality Act authorizing one House of Congress, by resolution, to invalidate the decision of the Executive Branch, pursuant to authority delegated by Congress to the Attorney General of the United States, to allow a particular deportable alien to remain in the United States.

I

Chadha is an East Indian who was born in Kenya and holds a British passport. He was lawfully admitted to the United States in 1966 on a nonimmigrant student visa. His visa expired on June 30, 1972. On October 11, 1973, the District Director of the Immigration and Naturalization Service ordered Chadha to show cause why he should not be deported for having "remained in the United States for a longer time than permitted." Pursuant to § 242(b) of the Immigration and Nationality Act (Act), 8 U.S.C. § 1252(b), a deportation hearing was held before an Immigration Judge on January 11, 1974. Chadha conceded that he was deportable for overstaying his visa and the hearing was adjourned to enable him to file an application for suspension of deportation under § 244(a)(1) of the Act. Section 244(a)(1), at the time in question, provided:

> As hereinafter prescribed in this section, the Attorney General may, in his discretion, suspend deportation and adjust the status to that of an alien lawfully admitted for permanent residence, in the case of an alien who applies to the Attorney General for suspension of deportation and—

> (1) is deportable under any law of the United States except the provisions specified in paragraph (2) of this subsection; has been physically present in the United States for a continuous period of not less than seven years immediately preceding the date of such application, and proves that during all of

such period he was and is a person of good moral character; and is a person whose deportation would, in the opinion of the Attorney General, result in extreme hardship to the alien or to his spouse, parent, or child, who is a citizen of the United States or an alien lawfully admitted for permanent residence.[1]

After Chadha submitted his application for suspension of deportation, the deportation hearing was resumed.

Pursuant to § 244(c)(1) of the Act, the Immigration Judge suspended Chadha's deportation and a report of the suspension was transmitted to Congress. Section 244(c)(1) provides:

> Upon application by any alien who is found by the Attorney General to meet the requirements of subsection (a) of this section the Attorney General may in his discretion suspend deportation of such alien. If the deportation of any alien is suspended under the provisions of this subsection, a complete and detailed statement of the facts and pertinent provisions of law in the case shall be reported to the Congress with the reasons for such suspension.

Once the Attorney General's recommendation for suspension of Chadha's deportation was conveyed to Congress, Congress had the power under § 244(c)(2) of the Act to veto[2] the Attorney General's determination that Chadha should not be deported. Section 244(c)(2) provides:

> In the case of an alien specified in paragraph (1) of subsection (a) of this subsection—
>
> if either the Senate or the House of Representatives passes a resolution stating in substance that it does not favor the suspension of such deportation, the Attorney General shall thereupon deport such alien.

On December 12, 1975, Representative Eilberg, Chairman of the Judiciary Subcommittee on Immigration, Citizenship, and International Law, introduced a resolution opposing "the granting of permanent residence in the United States to [six] aliens," including Chadha. The resolution had not been printed and was not made available to other members of the House [other than the Committee on the Judiciary] prior to or at the time it was voted on. The resolution was passed without debate or recorded vote. Since the House action was pursuant to § 244(c)(2), the resolution was not treated as an Art. I legislative act; it was not submitted to the Senate or presented to the President for his action.

---

1. Congress delegated the major responsibilities for enforcement of the Immigration and Nationality Act to the Attorney General. 8 U.S.C. § 1103(a). The Attorney General discharges his responsibilities through the Immigration and Naturalization Service (INS), a division of the Department of Justice. *Id.*

2. In constitutional terms, "veto" is used to describe the President's power under Art. I, § 7, of the Constitution. It appears, however, that congressional devices of the type authorized by § 244(c)(2) have come to be commonly referred to as a "veto." We refer to the congressional "resolution" authorized by § 244(c)(2) as a "one-House veto" of the Attorney General's decision to allow a particular deportable alien to remain in the United States.

[After the veto by the House, INS reopened Chadha's case and he was ordered to be deported. Chadha argued to INS and on administrative appeal that §244(c)(2) was unconstitutional. Chadha sought judicial review of that administrative action in the U.S. Court of Appeals for the Ninth Circuit. That court held the House action to be unconstitutional.]

III

A

We turn now to the question whether action of one House of Congress under §244(c)(2) violates strictures of the Constitution. We begin, of course, with the presumption that the challenged statute is valid. Its wisdom is not the concern of the courts; if a challenged action does not violate the Constitution, it must be sustained: "Once the meaning of an enactment is discerned and its constitutionality determined, the judicial process comes to an end. We do not sit as a committee of review, nor are we vested with the power of veto." *TVA v. Hill*, 437 U.S. 153, 194–95 (1978).

By the same token, the fact that a given law or procedure is efficient, convenient, and useful in facilitating functions of government, standing alone, will not save it if it is contrary to the Constitution. Convenience and efficiency are not the primary objectives—or the hallmarks—of democratic government and our inquiry is sharpened rather than blunted by the fact that congressional veto provisions are appearing with increasing frequency in statutes which delegate authority to executive and independent agencies.

Explicit and unambiguous provisions of the Constitution prescribe and define the respective functions of the Congress and of the Executive in the legislative process. Since the precise terms of those familiar provisions are critical to the resolution of these cases, we set them out verbatim. Article I provides:

> "All legislative Powers herein granted shall be vested in a Congress of the United States, which shall consist of a Senate *and* House of Representatives." Art. I, § 1 (emphasis added).

> "Every Bill which shall have passed the House of Representatives *and* the Senate, *shall*, before it becomes a law, be presented to the President of the United States . . . ." Art. I, § 7, cl. 2 (emphasis added).

> "*Every* Order, Resolution, or Vote to which the Concurrence of the Senate and the House of Representatives may be necessary (except on a question of Adjournment) *shall be* presented to the President of the United States; and before the Same shall take Effect, *shall be* approved by him, or being disapproved by him, *shall be* repassed by two thirds of the Senate and House of Representatives, according to the Rules and Limitations prescribed in the Case of a Bill." Art. I, § 7, cl. 3 (emphasis added).

These provisions of Art. I are integral parts of the constitutional design for the separation of powers. We have recently noted that "[t]he principle of separation of powers was not simply an abstract generalization in the minds of the Framers: it was woven into the document that they drafted in Philadelphia in the summer of 1787." *Buckley v. Valeo*, 424 U.S. at 124. Just as we relied on the textual provision of Art. II, § 2, cl. 2, to vindicate the principle of separation of powers in *Buckley*, we see that the purposes underlying the Presentment Clauses, Art. I, § 7, cls. 2, 3, and the bicameral requirement of Art. I, § 1, and § 7, cl. 2, guide our resolution of the important question presented in these cases. The very structure of the Articles delegating and separating powers under Arts. I, II, and III exemplifies the concept of separation of powers, and we now turn to Art. I.

B. *The Presentment Clauses*

The records of the Constitutional Convention reveal that the requirement that all legislation be presented to the President before becoming law was uniformly accepted by the Framers. Presentment to the President and the Presidential veto were considered so imperative the draftsmen took special pains to assure that these requirements could not be circumvented. During the final debate on Art. I, § 7, cl. 2, James Madison expressed concern that it might easily be evaded by the simple expedient of calling a proposed law a "resolution" or "vote" rather than a "bill." 2 MAX FARRAND, THE RECORDS OF THE FEDERAL CONVENTION OF 1787F pp. 301–02 (1911). As a consequence, Art. I, § 7, cl. 3, was added. 2 MAX FARRAND, *supra*, at 304–05.

The decision to provide the President with a limited and qualified power to nullify proposed legislation by veto was based on the profound conviction of the Framers that the powers conferred on Congress were the powers to be most carefully circumscribed. The President's role in the lawmaking process also reflects the Framers' careful efforts to check whatever propensity a particular Congress might have to enact oppressive, improvident, or ill-considered measures. The Court also has observed that the Presentment Clauses serve the important purpose of assuring that a "national" perspective is grafted on the legislative process.

C. *Bicameralism*

The bicameral requirement of Art. I, §§ 1, 7, was of scarcely less concern to the Framers than was the Presidential veto. By providing that no law could take effect without the concurrence of the prescribed majority of the Members of both Houses, the Framers reemphasized their belief, already remarked upon in connection with the Presentment Clauses, that legislation should not be enacted unless it has been carefully and fully considered by the Nation's elected officials. In the Constitutional Convention debates on the need for a bicameral legislature, James Wilson, later to become a Justice of this Court, commented:

> Despotism comes on mankind in different shapes, sometimes in an Executive, sometimes in a military, one. Is there danger of a Legislative despotism? Theory & practice both proclaim it. If the Legislative authority be not restrained, there can be neither liberty nor stability; and it can only be restrained by dividing it within itself, into distinct and independent branches.

In a single house there is no check, but the inadequate one, of the virtue & good sense of those who compose it.

2 Max Farrand, *supra*, at 254.

Hamilton argued that a Congress comprised of a single House was antithetical to the very purposes of the Constitution. Were the Nation to adopt a Constitution providing for only one legislative organ, he warned:

[W]e shall finally accumulate, in a single body, all the most important prerogatives of sovereignty, and thus entail upon our posterity one of the most execrable forms of government that human infatuation ever contrived. Thus we should create in reality that very tyranny which the adversaries of the new Constitution either are, or affect to be, solicitous to avert.

The Federalist No. 82.

These observations are consistent with what many of the Framers expressed, none more cogently than Madison in pointing up the need to divide and disperse power in order to protect liberty:

In republican government, the legislative authority necessarily predominates. The remedy for this inconveniency is to divide the legislature into different branches; and to render them, by different modes of election and different principles of action, as little connected with each other as the nature of their common functions and their common dependence on the society will admit.

The Federalist No. 51.

However familiar, it is useful to recall that apart from their fear that special interests could be favored at the expense of public needs, the Framers were also concerned, although not of one mind, over the apprehensions of the smaller states. Those states feared a commonality of interest among the larger states would work to their disadvantage; representatives of the larger states, on the other hand, were skeptical of a legislature that could pass laws favoring a minority of the people. *See* 1 Max Farrand, *supra*, at 176–77, 484–91.

We see therefore that the Framers were actually conscious that the bicameral requirement and the Presentment Clauses would serve essential constitutional functions. The President's participation in the legislative process was to protect the Executive Branch from Congress and to protect the whole people from improvident laws. The division of the Congress into two distinctive bodies assures that the legislative power would be exercised only after opportunity for full study and debate in separate settings. The President's unilateral veto power, in turn, was limited by the power of two-thirds of both Houses of Congress to overrule a veto thereby precluding final arbitrary action of one person. *See id.* at 99–104. It emerges clearly that the prescription for legislative action in Art. I, §§ 1, 7, represents the Framers' decision that the legislative power of the Federal Government be exercised in accord with a single, finely wrought and exhaustively considered, procedure.

IV

The Constitution sought to divide the delegated powers of the new Federal Government into three defined categories, Legislative, Executive, and Judicial, to assure, as nearly as possible, that each branch of government would confine itself to its assigned responsibility. The hydraulic pressure inherent within each of the separate Branches to exceed the outer limits of its power, even to accomplish desirable objectives, must be resisted.

Although not "hermetically" sealed from one another, *Buckley v. Valeo*, 424 U.S. at 121, the powers delegated to the three Branches are functionally identifiable. When any Branch acts, it is presumptively exercising the power the Constitution has delegated to it. When the Executive acts, he presumptively acts in an executive or administrative capacity as defined in Art. II. And when, as here, one House of Congress purports to act, it is presumptively acting within its assigned sphere.

Beginning with this presumption, we must nevertheless establish that the challenged action under § 244(c)(2) is of the kind to which the procedural requirements of Art. I, § 7, apply. Not every action taken by either House is subject to the bicameralism and presentment requirements of Art. I.

Examination of the action taken here by one House pursuant to § 244(c)(2) reveals that it was essentially legislative in purpose and effect. In purporting to exercise power defined in Art. I, § 8, cl. 4, to "establish an uniform Rule of Naturalization," the House took action that had the purpose and effect of altering the legal rights, duties, and relations of persons, including the Attorney General, Executive Branch officials and Chadha, all outside the Legislative Branch. Section 244(c)(2) purports to authorize one House of Congress to require the Attorney General to deport an individual alien whose deportation otherwise would be canceled under § 244. The one-House veto operated in these cases to overrule the Attorney General and mandate Chadha's deportation; absent the House action, Chadha would remain in the United States. Congress has *acted* and its action has altered Chadha's status.

The legislative character of the one-House veto in these cases is confirmed by the character of the congressional action it supplants. Neither the House of Representatives nor the Senate contends that, absent the veto provision in § 244(c)(2), either of them, or both of them acting together, could effectively require the Attorney General to deport an alien once the Attorney General, in the exercise of legislatively delegated authority,[16] had determined the alien should remain in the United States. Without

---

16. Congress protests that affirming the Court of Appeals in these cases will sanction "lawmaking by the Attorney General . . . ." When the Attorney General performs his duties pursuant to § 244, he does not exercise "legislative" power. The bicameral process is not necessary as a check on the Executive's administration of the laws because his administrative activity cannot reach beyond the limits of the statute that created it—a statute duly enacted pursuant to Art. I, §§ 1, 7. The constitutionality of the Attorney General's execution of the authority delegated to him by § 244 involves only a question of delegation doctrine. It is clear, therefore, that the Attorney General acts in his presumptively Art. II capacity when he administers the Immigration and Nationality Act.

the challenged provision in § 244(c)(2), this could have been achieved, if at all, only by legislation requiring deportation. Similarly, a veto by one House of Congress under § 244(c)(2) cannot be justified as an attempt at amending the standards set out in § 244(a)(1), or as a repeal of § 244 as applied to Chadha. Amendment and repeal of statutes, no less than enactment, must conform with Art. I.

Finally, we see that when the Framers intended to authorize either House of Congress to act alone and outside of its prescribed bicameral legislative role, they narrowly and precisely defined the procedure for such action. There are four provisions in the Constitution,[20] explicit and unambiguous, by which one House may act alone with the unreviewable force of law, not subject to the President's veto:

(a) The House of Representatives alone was given the power to initiate impeachments. Art. I, § 2, cl. 5;

(b) The Senate alone was given the power to conduct trials following impeachment on charges initiated by the House and to convict following trial. Art. I, § 3, cl. 6;

(c) The Senate alone was given final unreviewable power to approve or to disapprove Presidential appointments. Art. II, § 2, cl. 2;

(d) The Senate alone was given unreviewable power to ratify treaties negotiated by the President. Art. II, § 2, cl. 2.

Clearly, when the Draftsmen sought to confer special powers on one House, independent of the other House, or of the President, they did so in explicit, unambiguous terms.[21] These carefully defined exceptions from presentment and bicameralism underscore the difference between legislative functions of Congress and other unilateral but important and binding one-House acts provided for in the Constitution. These exceptions are narrow, explicit, and separately justified; none of them authorize the action challenged here. On the contrary, they provide further support for the conclusion that congressional authority is not to be implied and for the conclusion that the veto provided for in § 244(c)(2) is not authorized by the constitutional design of the powers of the Legislative Branch.

Executive action under legislatively delegated authority that might resemble "legislative" action in some respects is not subject to the approval of both Houses of Congress and the President for the reason that the Constitution does not so require. That kind of Executive action is always subject to check by the terms of the legislation that authorized it; and if that authority is exceeded it is open to judicial review as well as the power of Congress to modify or revoke the authority entirely. A one-House veto is clearly legislative in both character and effect and is not so checked; the need for the check provided by Art. I, §§ 1, 7, is therefore clear. Congress' authority to delegate portions of its power to administrative agencies provides no support for the argument that Congress can constitutionally control administration of the laws by way of a congressional veto.

20. *See also* U.S. Const., Art. II, § 1, & Amend. XII.

21. An exception from the Presentment Clauses was ratified in *Hollingsworth v. Virginia*, 3 U.S. 378 (1798). There the Court held Presidential approval was unnecessary for a proposed constitutional amendment which had passed both Houses of Congress by the requisite two-thirds majority. *See* U.S. CONST. ART. v.

Since it is clear that the action by the House under §244(c)(2) was not within any of the express constitutional exceptions authorizing one House to act alone, and equally clear that it was an exercise of legislative power, that action was subject to the standards prescribed in Art. I. The bicameral requirement, the Presentment Clauses, the President's veto, and Congress' power to override a veto were intended to erect enduring checks on each Branch and to protect the people from the improvident exercise of power by mandating certain prescribed steps. To preserve those checks, and maintain the separation of powers, the carefully defined limits on the power of each Branch must not be eroded. To accomplish what has been attempted by one House of Congress in this case requires action in conformity with the express procedures of the Constitution's prescription for legislative action: passage by a majority of both Houses and presentment to the President.

The choices we discern as having been made in the Constitutional Convention impose burdens on governmental processes that often seem clumsy, inefficient, even unworkable, but those hard choices were consciously made by men who had lived under a form of government that permitted arbitrary governmental acts to go unchecked. There is no support in the Constitution or decisions of this Court for the proposition that the cumbersomeness and delays often encountered in complying with explicit constitutional standards may be avoided, either by Congress or by the President. *See Youngstown Sheet & Tube Co. v. Sawyer*, 343 U.S. 579 (1952). With all the obvious flaws of delay, untidiness, and potential for abuse, we have not yet found a better way to preserve freedom than by making the exercise of power subject to the carefully crafted restraints spelled out in the Constitution.

V

We hold that the congressional veto provision in §244(c)(2) is severable from the Act and that it is unconstitutional. Accordingly, the judgment of the Court of Appeals is affirmed.

Justice Powell, concurring in the judgment. [Opinion omitted.]

Justice White, dissenting.

Today the Court not only invalidates §244(c)(2) of the Immigration and Nationality Act, but also sounds the death knell for nearly 200 other statutory provisions in which Congress has reserved a "legislative veto." For this reason, the Court's decision is of surpassing importance. And it is for this reason that the Court would have been well advised to decide the cases, if possible, on the narrower grounds of separation of powers, leaving for full consideration the constitutionality of other congressional review statutes operating on such varied matters as war powers and agency rulemaking, some of which concern the independent regulatory agencies.

The prominence of the legislative veto mechanism in our contemporary political system and its importance to Congress can hardly be overstated. It has become a central means by which Congress secures accountability of executive and independent agencies. Without the legislative veto, Congress is faced with a Hobson's choice: either to refrain from delegating the necessary authority, leaving itself with a hopeless task of writing laws with the requisite specificity to cover endless special circumstances across the entire policy landscape, or in the alternative, to abdicate its lawmaking function to the Executive Branch and independent agencies. To choose the former leaves major national problems unresolved; to opt for the latter risks unaccountable policymaking by those not elected to fill that role. Accordingly, over the past five decades, the legislative veto has been placed in nearly 200 statutes. The device is known in every field of governmental concern.

I

[Congress employed the first legislative veto in 1929, at the invitation of President Hoover, in the context of delegating authority to the Executive to reorganize the growing federal administrative state. In 1939 and thereafter, it was employed in various other contexts. The Roosevelt administration proposed legislation that included such provisions and argued that such provisions were constitutional. Later, Presidents Kennedy and Johnson proposed legislation that included legislative veto provisions and both took actions to defend its constitutionality. The record of the Nixon administration on the constitutionality of such procedures was mixed.]

Even this brief review suffices to demonstrate that the legislative veto is more than "efficient, convenient, and useful." It is an important if not indispensable political invention that allows the President and Congress to resolve major constitutional and policy differences, assures the accountability of independent regulatory agencies, and preserves Congress' control over lawmaking. Perhaps there are other means of accommodation and accountability, but the increasing reliance of Congress upon the legislative veto suggests that the alternatives to which Congress must now turn are not entirely satisfactory.[10]

The history of the legislative veto also makes clear that it has not been a sword with which Congress has struck out to aggrandize itself at the expense of the other branches — the concerns of Madison and Hamilton. Rather, the veto has been a means of defense, a reservation of the ultimate authority necessary if Congress is to fulfill its designated role under Art. I as the Nation's lawmaker. While the President has often objected to particular legislative vetoes, generally those left in the hands of congressional Committees, the Executive has more often agreed to legislative review as the price for a broad delegation of authority. To be sure, the President may have

---

10. While Congress could write certain statutes with greater specificity, it is unlikely that this is a realistic or even desirable substitute for the legislative veto. The controversial nature of many issues would prevent Congress from reaching agreement on many major problems if specificity were required in their enactments. Oversight hearings and congressional investigations have their purpose, but unless Congress is to be rendered a think tank or debating society, they are no substitute for the exercise of actual authority. Finally, the passage of corrective legislation after agency regulations take effect or Executive Branch officials have acted entails the drawbacks endemic to a retroactive response.

preferred unrestricted power, but that could be precisely why Congress thought it essential to retain a check on the exercise of delegated authority.

II

If the legislative veto were as plainly unconstitutional as the Court strives to suggest, its broad ruling today would be more comprehensible. But, the constitutionality of the legislative veto is anything but clear-cut. The issue divides scholars, courts, Attorneys General, and the two other branches of the National Government. If the veto devices so flagrantly disregard the requirements of Art. I as the Court today suggests, I find it incomprehensible that Congress, whose Members are bound by oath to uphold the Constitution, would have placed these mechanisms in nearly 200 separate laws over a period of 50 years.

The reality of the situation is that the constitutional question posed today is one of immense difficulty over which the Executive and Legislative Branches—as well as scholars and judges—have understandably disagreed. That disagreement stems from the silence of the Constitution on the precise question: The Constitution does not directly authorize or prohibit the legislative veto. Thus, our task should be to determine whether the legislative veto is consistent with the purposes of Art. I and the principles of separation of powers which are reflected in that Article and throughout the Constitution. We should not find the lack of a specific constitutional authorization for the legislative veto surprising, and I would not infer disapproval of the mechanism from its absence. From the summer of 1787 to the present the Government of the United States has become an endeavor far beyond the contemplation of the Framers. Only within the last half century has the complexity and size of the Federal Government's responsibilities grown so greatly that the Congress must rely on the legislative veto as the most effective if not the only means to insure its role as the Nation's lawmaker. But the wisdom of the Framers was to anticipate that the Nation would grow and new problems of governance would require different solutions. Accordingly, our Federal Government was intentionally chartered with the flexibility to respond to contemporary needs without losing sight of fundamental democratic principles. This was the spirit in which Justice Jackson penned his influential concurrence in the *Steel Seizure Case*.

III

The power to exercise a legislative veto is not the power to write new law without bicameral approval or Presidential consideration. The veto must be authorized by statute and may only negative what an Executive department or independent agency has proposed. On its face, the legislative veto no more allows one House of Congress to make law than does the Presidential veto confer such power upon the President.

B

The Court heeded this counsel in approving the modern administrative state. The Court's holding today that all legislative-type action must be enacted through the lawmaking process ignores that legislative authority is routinely delegated to the

Executive Branch, to the independent regulatory agencies, and to private individuals and groups. "The rise of administrative bodies probably has been the most significant legal trend of the last century . . . . They have become a veritable fourth branch of the Government, which has deranged our three-branch legal theories . . . ." *FTC v. Ruberoid Co.*, 343 U.S. 470, 487 (1952) (Jackson, J. dissenting).

This Court's decisions sanctioning such delegations make clear that Art. I does not require all action with the effect of legislation to be passed as a law. Theoretically, agencies and officials were asked only to "fill up the details," and the rule was that "Congress cannot delegate any part of its legislative power except under the limitation of a prescribed standard." *United States v. Chicago, M., St. P. & P.R. Co.*, 282 U.S. 311, 324 (1931). In practice, however, restrictions on the scope of the power that could be delegated diminished and all but disappeared. In only two instances did the Court find an unconstitutional delegation. *Panama Refining Co. v. Ryan*, 293 U.S. 388 (1935); *A.L.A. Schechter Poultry Corp. v. United States*, 295 U.S. 495 (1935).

The wisdom and the constitutionality of these broad delegations are matters that still have not been put to rest. But for present purposes, these cases establish by virtue of congressional delegation, legislative power can be exercised by independent agencies and Executive departments without the passage of new legislation. For some time, the sheer amount of law—the substantive rules that regulate private conduct and direct the operation of government—made by the agencies has far outnumbered the lawmaking engaged in by Congress through the traditional process. There is no question but that agency rulemaking is lawmaking in any functional or realistic sense of the term. In sum, they have the force of law.

If Congress may delegate lawmaking power to independent and Executive agencies, it is most difficult to understand Art. I as prohibiting Congress from also reserving a check on legislative power for itself. Absent the veto, the agencies receiving delegations of legislative or quasi-legislative power may issue regulations having the force of law without bicameral approval and without the President's signature. It is thus not apparent why reservation of a veto over the exercise of that legislative power must be subject to a more exacting test. In both cases, it is enough that the initial statutory authorization comply with the Art. I requirements.

If the effective functioning of a complex modern government requires the delegation of vast authority which, by virtue of its breadth, is legislative or "quasi-legislative" in character, I cannot accept that Art. I—which is, after all, the source of the nondelegation doctrine—should forbid Congress to qualify that grant with a legislative veto.[21]

---

21. The Court also argues that the legislative character of the challenged action of one House is confirmed by the fact that "when the Framers intended to authorize either House of Congress to act alone and outside of its prescribed bicameral legislative role, they narrowly and precisely defined the procedure for such action." Leaving aside again the above-refuted premise that all action with a legislative character requires passage in a law, the short answer is that all of these carefully defined exceptions to the presentment and bicameralism strictures do not involve action of the Congress

C

The Court also takes no account of perhaps the most relevant consideration: However resolutions of disapproval under § 244(c)(2) are formally characterized, in reality, a departure from the status quo occurs only upon the concurrence of opinion among the House, Senate, and President. Reservations of legislative authority to be exercised by Congress should be upheld if the exercise of such reserved authority is consistent with the distribution of and limits upon legislative power that Art. I provides.

1

The history of the Immigration and Nationality Act makes clear that § 244(c)(2) did not alter the division of the actual authority between Congress and the Executive. At all times, whether through private bills, or through affirmative concurrent resolutions, or through the present one-House veto, a permanent change in a deportable alien's status could be accomplished only with the agreement of the Attorney General, the House, and the Senate.

2

The central concern of the presentment and bicameralism requirements of Art. I is that when a departure from the legal status quo is undertaken, it is done with the approval of the President and both Houses of Congress. This interest is fully satisfied by the operation of § 244(c)(2). The President's approval is found in the Attorney General's action in recommending to Congress that the deportation order for a given alien be suspended. The House and the Senate indicate their approval of the Executive's action by not passing a resolution of disapproval within the statutory period. Thus, a change in the legal status quo—the deportability of the alien—is consummated only with the approval of each of the three relevant actors. The disagreement of any one of the three maintains the alien's pre-existing status.

The very construction of the Presentment Clauses which the Executive Branch now rejects was the basis upon which the Executive branch defended the constitutionality of the Reorganization Act. When the Department of Justice advised the Senate on the constitutionality of congressional review in reorganization legislation in 1949, it stated: "In this procedure there is no question involved of the Congress taking legislative action beyond its initial passage of the Reorganization Act."

IV

It is true that the purpose of separating the authority of the Government is to prevent unnecessary and dangerous concentration of power in one branch. For that reason, the Framers saw fit to divide and balance the powers of Government so that each branch would be checked by the others. Virtually every part of our constitutional system bears the mark of this judgment.

---

pursuant to a duly enacted statute. Indeed, for the most part these powers—those of impeachment, review of appointments, and treaty ratification—are not legislative powers at all.

But the history of the separation-of-powers doctrine is also a history of accommodation and practicality. Section 244(c)(2) survives this test. The legislative veto provision does not "preven[t] the Executive Branch from accomplishing its constitutionally assigned functions."

In comparison to private bills, which must be initiated in the Congress and which allow a Presidential veto to be overridden by a two-thirds majority in both Houses of Congress, § 244 augments rather than reduces the Executive Branch's authority. So understood, congressional review does not undermine, as the Court of Appeals thought, the "weight and dignity" that attends the decisions of the Executive Branch.

Nor does § 244 infringe on the judicial power. Section 244 makes clear that Congress has reserved its own judgment as part of the statutory process. Congressional action does not substitute for judicial review of the Attorney General's decisions. The Act provides for judicial review of the refusal of the Attorney General to suspend a deportation and to transmit a recommendation to Congress.

V

Today's decision strikes down in one fell swoop provisions in more laws enacted by Congress than the Court has cumulatively invalidated in its history. I fear it will now be more difficult to "insur[e] that the fundamental policy decisions in our society will be made not by an appointed official but by the body immediately responsible to the people," *Arizona v. California*, 373 U.S. 546, 626 (1963) (Harlan, J., dissenting in part). I must dissent.

JUSTICE REHNQUIST, with whom JUSTICE WHITE joins, dissenting. [Opinion omitted.]

EXERCISE 25:

Consider the following questions in connection with *INS v. Chadha*:

1. Articulate an argument that the Supreme Court should have declined to hear this case as a "political question" under *Baker v. Carr*, 369 U.S. 186 (1962), covered in Volume 1.

2. Describe how the majority utilized textual, structural, historical, and traditional arguments to support its conclusion that the one-house legislative veto violated Article I.

3. Is Chief Justice Burger's opinion formalist or functionalist? Explain your answer. What about Justice White's dissent?

4. The Court asserted that "[c]onvenience and efficiency are not the primary objectives . . . of democratic government." Is that true? If so, should innovation be available so as to minimize the inconvenience and inefficiency inherent in the system? The Court asserted that the fact a law "is efficient, convenient, and useful" is not sufficient to justify a departure from the constitutional design. Throughout the remainder of the course, consider whether the Court (or another coordinate branch of government) seeks to justify a departure from the Constitution on such a basis.

5. The Court asserted that the first legislative veto provision was enacted in 1932. From 1789 until 1932—a period of 143 years—Congress did not employ the device. (Justice White, in dissent, asserted the legislative veto was first used in 1929.) What structural changes, if any, prompted the introduction and rapid expansion of the device?

6. The Court interpreted the procedure described in Article I, Section 7, of the Constitution as the exclusive method—rather than merely one (and, perhaps, the preferred) manner—for enactment of legislation. Does the text of the Constitution support that conclusion? Have we examined other examples of procedures explicit in the Constitution that the Court has held did not imply an absence of alternative procedures? Or, has the Court consistently viewed one express procedure to constitute the exclusive permissible means?

7. The Court asserted that each house of Congress may take some actions that are not "subject to the bicameralism and presentment requirements." What are examples of such actions? What is the test formulated by the Court to ascertain which actions are subject to the bicameralism and presentment requirements?

8. The Court identified four examples where the Constitution expressly permits one house of Congress to act alone. Are those the only such examples?

9. If the decision whether to admit an alien is the exercise of legislative power, as the Court says, why is the Attorney General allowed to exercise such power? What if the decision is the exercise of judicial power? If, on the other hand, it is executive power, is there a simpler way to reach the same result?

10. In dissent, Justice White asserted that the Court's decision "sound[ed] the death knell for nearly 200 other statutory provisions." Is that true or does the Court's reasoning provide potential grounds to distinguish among various forms of legislative vetoes? Justice White asserted that, in view of that impact, "the Court would have been well-advised to decide the case, if possible, on the narrower grounds of separation of powers." Was a narrower rationale available to the Court?

11. In dissent, Justice White asserted that, without a legislative veto, Congress confronts the dilemma of selecting between (a) "writing laws with the requisite specificity to cover endless special circumstances across the entire policy landscape" and which would leave "major national problems unresolved," or (b) "abdicat[ing] its lawmaking function to the executive branch and independent agencies" which would "risk[] unaccountable policymaking by those not elected to fill that role." Does Congress really face such a dilemma or are there other alternatives aside from a legislative veto?

12. In dissent, Justice White asserted that Presidents often signed legislation which contained legislative veto provisions. Should that make a difference in evaluating whether the practice is constitutional? Why or why not? Justice White further asserted that Presidents often signed legislation containing such provisions "as the price for a broad delegation of authority." To the extent the Executive thus obtained some

authority in exchange for agreeing to limitation of that authority through the legislative veto, should such an exchange make a difference in evaluating whether the legislative vetoes are constitutional? (If, in fact, the "broad delegation of authority" was to an "independent regulatory agency," did the Executive gain anything in exchange for agreeing to the legislative veto?)

13. In dissent, Justice White quoted Justice Jackson, from 1952, for the proposition that the rise of the modern administrative state introduced "a veritable fourth branch of the Government, which has deranged our three-branch legal theories." To the extent the constitutional text, its structure, the drafting and ratification history, and early precedents were all premised upon "three-branch legal theories," upon what basis can the judiciary determine whether actions of Congress and/or the Executive comply with the Constitution? What are the constraints, if any, on the judiciary in declaring the appropriate separation of powers once "three-branch legal theories" are discarded as obsolete?

14. In dissent, Justice White asserted "that agency rulemaking is lawmaking in any functional or realistic sense of the term." If so, is there any reason to prohibit Congress, in legislation complying with bicameralism and presentment requirements, from delegating legislative power to a single house of Congress acting alone? If that would be permissible, could Congress so delegate legislative power to the appropriate committee of a single house of Congress? If that would be permissible, could Congress so delegate legislative power to the chair of the appropriate committee of a single house of Congress? If Congress could so delegate legislative power to one house alone, could it so authorize not only a "legislative veto" reacting to executive activity (or the activity of an independent agency) but affirmative legislation without any trigger from executive activity?

15. In dissent, Justice White asserted that upholding the legislative veto before the Court would not necessarily justify legislative vetoes over other forms of executive action. Do you agree? Justice White identified, for example, the "inherently executive function" of "initiating prosecutions." Do you agree that the example constitutes an "inherently executive function"? If so, do you agree that separation of powers principles would prohibit Congress from intruding (or authorizing anyone else to intrude) on the executive's decision whether to initiate prosecutions?

16. In dissent, Justice White asserted that the legislative veto was a "necessary check on the unavoidably expanding power of the agencies." Do you agree that the expanding power of federal agencies is "unavoidabl[e]"? If so, why? If not, who is capable of avoiding such expansions of power?

17. Without a legislative veto, how could Congressman Eilberg (or his Committee or the House of Representatives) have obtained (or encouraged) the deportation of Chadha? How could he (or they) more broadly supervise the Attorney General's exercise of discretionary authority?

18. Many state courts have considered the legislative veto under their own constitutions. Most agree with *Chadha*, see, e.g., *Alexander v. State*, 441 So. 2d 1329 (Miss. 1983), but some do not, see, e.g., *Mead v. Arnell*, 791 P. 2d 410, 417–18 (Idaho 1990) (following the approach in Justice White's dissent, and quoting it at length); see also *Blank v. Department of Corrections*, 611 N.W. 2d 103 (Mich. 2000) (splintered court with several rationales). Several states have adopted new constitutional provisions explicitly providing for legislative vetoes, most recently Idaho in 2016, allowing the legislature to invalidate agency actions without the possibility of a gubernatorial veto. For a survey of state approaches, see *Legislative Review of Administrative Regulations: Structures and Procedures*, in BOOK OF THE STATES 2015, at 132–35, available at http://knowledgecenter.csg.org/kc/system/files/3.25%202015.pdf. Does the removal of a governor's veto in such cases improve or worsen the separation of legislative and executive power?

19. Would Chadha necessarily invalidate a scheme involving a two-house veto, or quasi-legislative agency action? Two weeks after the *Chadha* decision was announced, the Court summarily affirmed other cases including one that invalidated a two-house legislative veto provision and two others that invalidated legislative vetoes of agency rulemaking (that is, *quasi*-legislative action) rather than adjudication (that is, *quasi*-judicial action).[3] *Process Gas Consumers Group v. Consumer Energy Council*, 463 U.S. 1216 (1983) (veto of agency rulemaking); *United States Senate v. Federal Trade Commission*, 463 U.S. 1216 (1983) (two-house veto provision with no presentment); *see* id. at 1217–19 (Justice White dissenting from these summary dispositions). Should the Court have considered these cases in more detail?

20. Reading *Chadha* through the lens of those summary affirmances, one might conclude that legislative veto provisions are relics of an earlier age, now condemned. In fact, it has been found that Congress included 500 legislative veto provisions in statutes codified between 1983 and 2005,[4] or more than twice the number of such provisions cumulatively enacted in the decades prior to *Chadha*. After *Chadha*, how should the President react when presented with a bill that includes a legislative veto provision? If the President favors the substance of the bill, is there any method for him to disapprove the legislative veto provision while signing the bill into law? For an examination of these matters, see Anthony M. Bottenfield, *Congressional Creativity: The Post-Chadha Struggle for Agency Control in the Era of Presidential Signing Statements*, 112 PENN. ST. L. REV. 1125 (2008).

21. To the extent the *Chadha* Court relied on an *expresio unius* argument based on explicit textual provisions permitting Congress (or one house thereof) to act

---

3. Justice White explained in his dissent that *Process Gas Consumers Group* arose in the context of rulemaking (specifically, ratemaking) by the Federal Energy Regulatory Commission. 463 U.S. at 1217–18. His description of *United States Senate v. Federal Trade Commission* also indicated that rulemaking was involved in that case as well.

4. *See* LOUIS FISHER & NEAL DEVINS, POLITICAL DYNAMICS OF CONSTITUTIONAL LAW 121 (4th ed. 2006).

outside of the framework of bicameralism and presentment, to what extent is that line of reasoning undermined by judicial precedent recognizing that (1) presentment was not required for a proposed constitutional amendment[5] and (2) that neither bicameralism nor presentment were required for legislative investigations and oversight[6] of the Executive? For an argument that these exceptions "illustrate that there is a category of congressional powers not mentioned in the text in addition to the power to pass statutes" that invalidates reliance on the *expresio unius* rationale, see E. Donald Elliott, INS v. Chadha: *The Administrative Constitution, The Constitution, and the Legislative Veto*, 1983 SUP. CT. REV. 125, 139–44 (1983). For a defense of the holding in *Chadha* based on "a more complete rationale" connected "to the purposes of bicameralism and presentment," see Harold H. Bruff, *The Incompatibility Principle*, 59 ADMIN. L. REV. 225, 246–48 (2007).

If the Court in *Chadha* had concluded that the alien-admission decision at issue there was an exercise of executive power, it could have reached its conclusion in a more straightforward way: that legislators are not to possess executive power. Three years later, the Court used this method to strike down a very similar sort of congressional self-delegation to the one in *Chadha*, holding that congressionally-controlled offers may not execute federal law.

BOWSHER v. SYNAR

478 U.S. 714 (1986)

CHIEF JUSTICE BURGER delivered the opinion of the Court.

The question presented by these appeals is whether the assignment by Congress to the Comptroller General of the United States of certain functions under the Balanced Budget and Emergency Deficit Control Act of 1985 violates the doctrine of separation of powers.

---

5. *See Hollingsworth v. Virginia*, 3 U.S. 378 (1798) (holding that the Eleventh Amendment was adopted in accordance with the Constitution despite the objection that Congress did not submit the proposal to the President prior to sending it to states for ratification), discussed in *Chadha*, 462 U.S. at 955 n. 21.

6. *See McGrain v. Daugherty*, 273 U.S. 135, 173 (1927) (stating "that the two houses of Congress, in their separate relations, possess not only such powers as are expressly granted to them by the Constitution, but such auxiliary powers as are necessary and appropriate to make the express powers effective" and concluding that the Senate may authorize a committee to subpoena the appearance of a private citizen to testify in an investigation into "various charges of misfeasance and nonfeasance in the Department of Justice" and, upon failure to appear, find the individual in contempt and issue a warrant for the Sergeant at Arms to seize the individual and bring him before the Senate and hold him in jail until the individual testified); *Barenblatt v. United States*, 360 U.S. 109, 111 (1959) (sustaining misdemeanor judicial conviction for contempt of Congress resulting in a $250 fine and six-month prison sentence to a private individual who, on bases addressing the Committee's jurisdiction including separation of powers violations, refused to answer questions before a subcommittee of the House Un-American Activities Committee relating to his past or then-present membership in the Communist Party).

I

A

On December 12, 1985, the President signed into law the Balanced Budget and Emergency Deficit Control Act of 1985, popularly known as the "Gramm-Rudman-Hollings Act." The purpose of the Act is to eliminate the federal budget deficit. To that end, the Act sets a "maximum deficit amount" for federal spending for each of fiscal years 1986 through 1991. The size of that maximum deficit amount progressively reduces to zero in fiscal year 1991. If in any fiscal year the federal budget deficit exceeds the maximum deficit amount by more than a specified sum, the Act requires across-the-board cuts in federal spending to reach the targeted deficit level.

These "automatic" reductions are accomplished through a rather complicated procedure, spelled out in § 251, the so-called "reporting provisions" of the Act. Each year, the Directors of the Office of Management and Budget (OMB) and the Congressional Budget Office (CBO) independently estimate the amount of the federal budget deficit for the upcoming fiscal year. If that deficit exceeds the maximum targeted deficit amount for that fiscal year by more than a specified amount, the Directors of OMB and CBO independently calculate, on a program-by-program basis, the budget reductions necessary to ensure that the deficit does not exceed the maximum deficit amount. The Act then requires the Directors to report jointly their deficit estimates and budget reduction calculations to the Comptroller General.

The Comptroller General, after reviewing the Directors' reports, then reports his conclusions to the President. § 251(b). The President in turn must issue a "sequestration" order mandating the spending reductions specified by the Comptroller General. § 252. There follows a period during which Congress may by legislation reduce spending to obviate, in whole or in part, the need for the sequestration order. If such reductions are not enacted, the sequestration order becomes effective and the spending reductions included in that order are made.

[The Act contained a "fall back" provision in the event the reporting procedures were invalidated. Under this alternative procedure, the report prepared by the Directors of the OMB and CBO would be submitted to a congressional committee, which would prepare a joint resolution to be presented to Congress for consideration under special, expedited rules that preclude amendments. If both Houses passed the resolution and the President signed it, it would serve "as the basis for a Presidential sequestration order."]

B

Within hours of the President' signing of the Act,[31] Congressman Synar, who had voted against the Act, filed a complaint seeking declaratory relief that the Act was unconstitutional. Eleven other Members later joined Congressman Synar's suit. A

---

31. In his signing statement, the President expressed his view that the Act was constitutionally defective because of the Comptroller General's ability to exercise supervisory authority over the President.

virtually identical lawsuit was also filed by the National Treasury Employee's Union. The Union alleged that its members had been injured as a result of the Act's automatic spending reduction provisions, which have suspended certain cost-of-living benefit increases to the Union's members.

[A three-judge District Court concluded that the parties had standing to bring the suit and, on the merits, rejected certain arguments. The District Court held] that the role of the Comptroller General in the deficit reduction process violated the constitutionally imposed separation of powers. The court first explained that the Comptroller General exercises executive functions under the Act. The District Court therefore held that

> since the powers conferred upon the Comptroller General as part of the automatic deficit reduction process are executive powers, which cannot constitutionally be exercised by an officer removable by Congress, those powers cannot be exercised and therefore the automatic deficit reduction process to which they are central cannot be implemented.

III

We noted recently that "[t]he Constitution sought to divide the delegated powers of the new Federal Government into three defined categories, Legislative, Executive, and Judicial." *INS v. Chadha*, 462 U.S. 919, 951 (1983). The declared purpose of separating and dividing the powers of the government, of course, was to "diffus[e] power to better secure liberty." *Youngstown Sheet & Tube Co. v. Sawyer*, 343 U.S. 579, 635 (1952) (Jackson, J., concurring). Justice Jackson's words echo the famous warning of Montesquieu, quoted by James Madison in The Federalist No. 47, that "'there can be no liberty where the legislative and executive powers are united in the same person, or body of magistrates' . . . . "

The Constitution does not contemplate an active role for Congress in the supervision of officers charged with the execution of the laws it enacts. The President appoints "Officers of the United States" with the "Advice and Consent of the Senate." Art. II, § 2. Once the appointment has been made and confirmed, however, the Constitution explicitly provides for removal of Officers of the United States by Congress only upon impeachment by the House of Representatives and conviction by the Senate. An impeachment by the House and trial by the Senate can rest only on "Treason, Bribery or other high crimes and Misdemeanors." Art. II, § 4. A direct congressional role in the removal of officers charged with the execution of the laws beyond this limited one is inconsistent with separation of powers.

This was made clear in the First Congress in 1789. When Congress considered an amendment to a bill establishing the Department of Foreign Affairs, the debate centered around whether the Congress "should recognize and declare the power of the President under the Constitution to remove the Secretary of Foreign Affairs without the advice and consent of the Senate." *Myers*, 272 U.S. at 114. James Madison urged rejection of a congressional role in the removal of Executive Branch officers, other than by impeachment, saying in debate:

Perhaps there was no argument urged with more success, or more plausibly grounded against the Constitution, under which we are now deliberating, than that founded on the mingling of the Executive and Legislative branches of the Government in one body. It has been objected, that the Senate have too much of the Executive power even, by having a control over the President in the appointment to office. Now, shall we extend this conne[ction] between the Legislative and Executive departments, which will strengthen the objection, and diminish the responsibility we have in the head of the Executive?

1 Annals of Cong. 380 (1789). Madison's position ultimately prevailed, and a congressional role in the removal process was rejected. This "Decision of 1789" provides "contemporaneous and weighty evidence" of the Constitution's meaning since many of the Members of the First Congress "had taken part in framing that instrument." *Marsh v. Chambers*, 463 U.S. 783 (1983).

This Court first directly addressed this issue in *Myers v. United States*, 272 U.S. 52 (1926). Chief Justice Taft, writing for the Court, declared the statute unconstitutional on the ground that for Congress to "draw to itself, or to either branch of it, the power to remove or the right to participate in the exercise of that power . . . would be . . . to infringe the constitutional principle of the separation of governmental powers." *Id.* at 161.

A decade later, in *Humphrey's Executor v. United States*, 295 U.S. 602 (1935), relied upon heavily by appellants, a Federal Trade Commissioner who had been removed by the President sought backpay. *Humphrey's Executor* involved an issue not presented either in the *Myers* case or in this case—*i.e.*, the power of Congress to limit the President's powers of removal of a Federal Trade Commissioner. 295 U.S. at 630. The Court distinguished *Myers*, reaffirming its holding that congressional participation in the removal of executive officers is unconstitutional.

In light of these precedents, we conclude that Congress cannot reserve for itself the power of removal of an officer charged with the execution of the laws except by impeachment. To permit the execution of the laws to be vested in an officer answerable only to Congress would, in practical terms, reserve in Congress control over the execution of the laws. As the District Court observed: "Once an officer is appointed, it is only the authority that can remove him, and not the authority that appointed him, that he must fear and, in the performance of his functions, obey." The structure of the Constitution does not permit Congress to execute the laws; it follows that Congress cannot grant to an officer under its control what it does not possess.

Congress could simply remove, or threaten to remove, an officer for executing the laws in any fashion found to be unsatisfactory to Congress. This kind of congressional control over the execution of the laws is unconstitutionally impermissible.

The dangers of congressional usurpation of Executive Branch functions have long been recognized. "[T]he debates of the Constitutional Convention, and the Federalist Papers, are replete with expressions of fear that the Legislative Branch of the

National Government will aggrandize itself at the expense of the other two branches." *Buckley v. Valeo*, 424 U.S. 1, 129 (1976). Indeed, we also have observed only recently that "[t]he hydraulic pressure inherent within each of the separate Branches to exceed the outer limits of its power, even to accomplish desirable objectives, must be resisted." *INS v. Chadha*, 462 U.S. 919, 951 (1983). With these principles in mind, we turn to consideration of whether the Comptroller General is controlled by Congress.

IV

Appellants urge that the Comptroller General performs his duties independently and is not subservient to Congress. We agree with the District Court that this contention does not bear close scrutiny.

The critical factor lies in the provisions of the statute defining the Comptroller General's office relating to removability. Although the Comptroller General is nominated by the President from a list of three individuals recommended by the Speaker of the House of Representatives and the President *pro tempore* of the Senate, and confirmed by the Senate, he is removable only at the initiative of Congress. He may be removed not only by impeachment but also by joint resolution of Congress "at any time" resting on any of the following bases:

> (i) permanent disability; (ii) inefficiency; (iii) neglect of duty; (iv) malfeasance; or (v) a felony or conduct involving moral turpitude.

31 U.S.C. §703(e)(1)B.[7] This provision was included, as one Congressman explained in urging the passage of the Act, because Congress "felt that [the Comptroller General] should be brought under the sole control of Congress, so that Congress at any moment when it found he was inefficient and was not carrying on the duties of his office as he should and as the Congress expected, could remove him without the long, tedious process of a trial by impeachment." 61 Cong. Rec. 1081 (1921).

The removal provision was an important part of the legislative scheme, as a number of Congressman recognized. Representative Hawley commented: "[H]e is our officer, in a measure, getting information for us. If he does not do his work properly, we, as practically his employers, ought to be able to discharge him from his office." 58 Cong. Rec. 7136 (1919). Representative Sisson observed that the removal provisions would give "[t]he Congress of the United States . . . absolute control of the man's destiny in office." 61 Cong. Rec. 987 (1921). The ultimate design was to "give the legislative branch of the Government control of the audit, not through the power of appointment, but through the power of removal." 58 Cong. Rec. 7211 (1919) (Rep. Temple).

Justice White contends: "The statute does not permit anyone to remove the Comptroller at will; removal is permitted only for specified cause, with the existence of cause to be determined by Congress following a hearing. Any removal under the

---

7. Although the President could veto such a joint resolution, the veto could be overridden by a two-thirds vote of both Houses of Congress. Thus, the Comptroller General could be removed in the face of Presidential opposition.

statute would presumably be subject to post-termination judicial review to ensure that a hearing had in fact been held and that the finding of cause for removal was not arbitrary." [T]he dissent's assessment of the statute fails to recognize the breadth of the grounds for removal. The statute permits removal for "inefficiency," "neglect of duty," or "malfeasance." These terms are very broad and, as interpreted by Congress, could sustain removal of a Comptroller General for any number of actual or perceived transgressions of the legislative will. The Constitutional Convention chose to permit impeachment of executive officers only for "Treason, Bribery, or other high Crimes and Misdemeanors." It rejected language that would have permitted impeachment for "maladministration," with Madison arguing that "[s]o vague a term will be equivalent to a tenure during pleasure of the Senate." 2 MAX FARRAND, RECORDS OF THE FEDERAL CONVENTION OF 1787, p. 550 (1911).

We need not decide whether "inefficiency" or "malfeasance" are terms as broad as "maladministration" in order to reject the dissent's position that removing the Comptroller General requires "a feat of bipartisanship more difficult than that required to impeach and convict." Surely no one would seriously suggest that judicial independence would be strengthened by allowing removal of federal judges only by a joint resolution finding "inefficiency," "neglect of duty," or "malfeasance."

Justice White, however, assures us that "[r]ealistic consideration" of the "practical result of the removal provision" reveals that the Comptroller General is unlikely to be removed by Congress. The separated powers of our Government cannot be permitted to turn on judicial assessment of whether an officer exercising executive power is on good terms with Congress. The Framers recognized that, in the long term, structural protections against abuse of power were critical to preserving liberty. In constitutional terms, the removal powers over the Comptroller General's office dictate that he will be subservient to Congress.

It is clear that Congress has consistently viewed the Comptroller General as an officer of the Legislative Branch. Over the years, Comptrollers General have also viewed themselves as part of the Legislative Branch.

Against this background, we see no escape from the conclusion that, because Congress has retained removal authority over the Comptroller General, he may not be entrusted with executive powers. The remaining question is whether the Comptroller General has been assigned such powers in the [Gramm-Rudman-Hollings Act].

V

The primary responsibility of the Comptroller General under the instant Act is the preparation of a "report." The report must specify the reductions, if any, necessary to reduce the deficit to the target for the appropriate fiscal year. The reductions must be set forth on a program-by-program basis.

In preparing the report, the Comptroller General is to have "due regard" for the estimates and reductions set forth in a joint report submitted to him by the Director of CBO and the Director of OMB, the President's fiscal and budgetary adviser.

However, the Act plainly contemplates that the Comptroller General will exercise his independent judgment and evaluation with respect to those estimates. The Act also provides that the Comptroller General's report "shall explain fully any differences between the contents of such report and the report of the Directors." § 251(b)(2).

Appellants suggest that the duties assigned to the Comptroller General in the Act are essentially ministerial and mechanical so that their performance does not constitute "execution of the law" in a meaningful sense. On the contrary, we view these functions as plainly entailing execution of the law in constitutional terms. Interpreting a law enacted by Congress to implement the legislative mandate is the very essence of "execution" of the law. Under § 251, the Comptroller General must exercise judgment concerning facts that affect the application of the Act. He must also interpret the provisions of the Act to determine precisely what budgetary calculations are required. Decisions of that kind are typically made by officers charged with executing the statute.

The executive nature of the Comptroller General's functions under the Act is revealed in § 252(a)(3) which gives the Comptroller General the ultimate authority to determine the budget cuts to be made. Indeed, the Comptroller General commands the President himself to carry out, without the slightest variation (with exceptions not relevant to the constitutional issues presented), the directive of the Comptroller General as to the budget reductions.

Congress of course initially determined the content of the [Act]; and undoubtedly the content of the Act determines the nature of the executive duty. However, once Congress makes its choice in enacting legislation, its participation ends. Congress can thereafter control the execution of its enactment only indirectly—by passing new legislation. By placing the responsibility for execution of the [Act] in the hands of an officer who is subject to removal only by itself, Congress in effect has retained control over the execution of the Act and has intruded into the executive function. The Constitution does not permit such intrusion.

VII

No one can doubt that Congress and the President are confronted with fiscal and economic problems of unprecedented magnitude, but "the fact that a given law or procedure is efficient, convenient, and useful in facilitating functions of government, standing alone, will not save it if it is contrary to the Constitution . . . ." *Chadha*, 462 U.S. at 944.

We conclude that the District Court correctly held that the powers vested in the Comptroller General under § 251 violate the command of the Constitution that the Congress play no direct role in the execution of the laws. Accordingly, the judgment and order of the District Court are affirmed.

Our judgment is stayed for a period not to exceed 60 days to permit Congress to implement the fallback provisions.

JUSTICE STEVENS with whom JUSTICE MARSHALL joins, concurring in the judgment.

I agree with the Court that the "Gramm-Rudman-Hollings" Act contains a constitutional infirmity so severe that the flawed provision may not stand. I disagree with the Court, however, on the reasons why the Constitution prohibits the Comptroller General from exercising the powers assigned to him by § 251(b) and § 251(c)(2) of the Act. [T]he Comptroller General must be characterized as an agent of Congress because of his longstanding statutory responsibilities; that the powers assigned to him under the Gramm-Rudman-Hollings Act require him to make policy that will bind the Nation; and that, when Congress, or a component or an agent of Congress, seeks to make policy that will bind the Nation, it must follow the procedures mandated by Article I of the Constitution—through passage by both houses and presentment to the President.

JUSTICE WHITE, dissenting.

I

It is evident (and nothing in the Court's opinion is to the contrary) that the powers exercised by the Comptroller General under the Gramm-Rudman-Hollings Act are not such that vesting them in an officer not subject to removal at will by the President would itself improperly interfere with Presidential powers. Determining the level of spending by the Federal Government is not by nature a function central either to the exercise of the President's enumerated powers or to his general duty to ensure the execution of the laws; rather, appropriating funds is a peculiarly legislative function, and one expressly committed to Congress by Art. I, § 9. In enacting Gramm-Rudman-Hollings, Congress has chosen to exercise this legislative power to establish the level of federal spending by providing a detailed set of criteria for reducing expenditures below the level of appropriations in the event that certain conditions are met. Delegating the execution of this legislation—that is, the power to apply the Act's criteria and make the required calculations—to an officer independent of the President's will does not deprive the President of any power that he would otherwise have or that is essential to the performance of the duties of his office. Rather, the result of such a delegation, from the standpoint of the President, is no different from the result of more traditional forms of appropriation: under either system, the level of funds available to the Executive Branch to carry out its duties is not within the President's discretionary control. To be sure, if the budget-cutting mechanism required the responsible officer to exercise a great deal of policymaking discretion, one might argue that having created such broad discretion Congress had some obligation based upon Art. II to vest it in the Chief Executive or his agents. In Gramm-Rudman-Hollings, however, Congress has done no such thing; instead, it has created a precise and articulated set of criteria designed to minimize the degree of policy choice exercised by the officer executing the statute and to ensure that the relative spending priorities established by Congress in the appropriations it passes into law remain unaltered. Given that the exercise of policy choice by the officer executing the statute would be inimical to Congress' goal in enacting "automatic" budget-cutting measures, it is eminently reasonable and proper for Congress to vest the budget-cutting authority in an officer who is to the greatest degree possible nonpartisan and independent of the President and his political agenda and who therefore may be relied upon not to allow his calculations to be colored by political considerations. Such a delegation deprives the President of no authority that is rightfully his.

II

If, as the Court seems to agree, the assignment of "executive" powers under Gramm-Rudman-Hollings to an officer not removable at will by the President would not in itself represent a violation of the constitutional scheme of separated powers, the question remains whether, as the Court concludes, the fact that the officer to whom Congress has delegated the authority to implement the Act is removable by a joint resolution of Congress should require invalidation of the Act. I have no quarrel with the proposition that the powers exercised by the Comptroller under the Act may be characterized as "executive" in that they involve the interpretation and carrying out of the Act's mandate. I can also accept the general proposition that although Congress has considerable authority in designating the officers who are to execute legislation, the constitutional scheme of separated powers does prevent Congress from reserving an executive role for itself or for its "agents." I cannot accept, however, that the exercise of authority by an officer removable for cause by a joint resolution of Congress is analogous to the impermissible execution of the law by Congress itself, nor would I hold that the congressional role in the removal process renders the Comptroller an "agent" of the Congress, incapable of receiving "executive" power.

Because the Comptroller is not an appointee of Congress but an officer of the United States appointed by the President with the advice and consent of the Senate, *Buckley* neither requires that he be characterized as an agent of the Congress nor in any other way calls into question his capacity to exercise "executive" authority. *See* 424 U.S. at 128 n. 165.

The deficiencies in the Court's reasoning are apparent. First, the Court badly mischaracterizes the removal provision when it suggests that it allows Congress to remove the Comptroller for "executing the laws in any fashion found to be unsatisfactory;" in fact, Congress may remove the Comptroller only for one or more of five specified reasons. Second, and more to the point, the Court overlooks or deliberately ignores [the provision that] Congress may remove the Comptroller only through a joint resolution, which by definition must be passed by both Houses and signed by the President. *See United States v. California*, 332 U.S. 19, 28 (1947). In other words, a removal of the Comptroller under the statute *satisfies the requirements of bicameralism and presentment.*

[T]he question is whether there is a genuine threat of "encroachment or aggrandizement of one branch at the expense of the other." *Buckley v. Valeo*, 424 U.S. at 122. Common sense indicates that the existence of the removal provision poses no such threat to the principle of separation of powers.

The statute does not permit anyone to remove the Comptroller at will; removal is permitted only for specified cause, with the existence of cause to be determined by Congress following a hearing. Any removal under the statute would presumably be subject to post-termination judicial review to ensure that a hearing had in fact been held and that the finding of cause for removal was not arbitrary. Indeed, similarly qualified grants of removal power are generally deemed to protect the officers to whom they apply and to establish their independence from the domination of the possessor of the removal power. *See Humphrey's Executor*, 295 U.S. at 625–26, 629–30. Removal authority limited in such a manner is more properly viewed as motivating adherence to a substantive standard established by law than as inducing subservience to the particular institution that enforces that standard.

More importantly, the substantial role played by the President in the process of removal through joint resolution reduces to utter insignificance the possibility that the threat of removal will induce subservience to Congress. The requirement of Presidential approval obviates the possibility that the Comptroller will perceive himself as so completely at the mercy of Congress that he will function as its tool. If the Comptroller's conduct in office is not so unsatisfactory to the President as to convince the latter that removal is required under the statutory standard, Congress will have no independent power to coerce the Comptroller unless it can muster a two-thirds majority in both Houses—a feat of bipartisanship more difficult than required to impeach and convict.

The practical result of the removal provision is not to render the Comptroller unduly dependent upon or subservient to Congress, but to render him one of the most independent officers in the entire federal establishment. Those who have studied the office agree that the procedural and substantive limits on the power of Congress and the President to remove the Comptroller make dislodging him against his will practically impossible.

Realistic consideration of the nature of the Comptroller General's relation to Congress thus reveals that the threat to separation of powers conjured up by the majority is wholly chimerical. The power over removal retained by the Congress is not a power that is exercised outside the legislative process as established by the Constitution, nor does it appear likely that it is a power that adds significantly to the influence Congress may exert over executive officers through other, undoubtedly constitutional exercises of legislative power.

The majority's contrary conclusion rests on the rigid dogma that, outside of the impeachment process, any "direct congressional role in the removal of officers charged with the execution of the laws is inconsistent with separation of powers." Reliance on such an unyielding principle to strike down a statute posing no real danger of aggrandizement of congressional power is extremely misguided and insensitive to our constitutional role.

JUSTICE BLACKMUN, dissenting. [Opinion omitted.]

EXERCISE 26:

Consider the following questions in regard to *Bowsher v. Synar*:

1. Did Congress control the Comptroller General? How likely was it that, as a practical matter, Congress could or would have removed the Comptroller General?

2. Did the Comptroller General "execute[]" the laws?

3. Which functions, if any, vested in the Comptroller General could be exercised without significant constitutional problems?

4. Which functions, if any, vested in the Comptroller General were "executive" functions that could be exercised only by one or more "Officers of the United States"?

5. With respect to the issues presented in *Bowsher v. Synar*, what interpretation of the Constitution is suggested by practical policy and political considerations? What weight does the Court give to such matters?

6. In *Bowsher*, the Act called for the Comptroller General to review the independent calculations of OMB and CBO to formulate his own conclusion which he then reported to the President. If, instead, the calculations of OMB and CBO were reported directly to the President to provide information with which the President could prepare a "sequestration" order, would the process have been constitutional? Why or why not? Would it have made a difference if, before the presidential sequestration order became effective, there was a period during which Congress could legislate to reduce spending so as to obviate, in whole or in part, the need for the sequestration order? Why or why not?

7. Assume that Congress followed the approach of Question 6 and provided that any presidential sequestration order would not become effective for thirty days after notice of the order was communicated to Congress. Assume further that the Act provided that the two houses of Congress, by majority vote within the thirty day period, could disallow the application of the sequestration order to any specific agency or program. Would that process have been constitutional? Why or why not?

8. The first suit challenging the constitutionality of the Gramm-Rudman-Hollings Act was filed by Congressman Synar (which eleven other members of Congress then joined). If that was the only suit filed, how should the Court have ruled? Why?

9. With regard to the role of the Comptroller General under the Act, the Supreme Court considered whether there was any textual support for a constitutional role for Congress in the removal of officers outside of the impeachment process. Is there any less textual support for congressional removal than there is for presidential removal?

10. Throughout *Bowsher v. Synar*, did the Court fairly characterize *Myers* and *Humphrey's Executor*, two of its important precedents on removal of officers?

11. The Court observed that the Budget and Accounting Act of 1921 (on the course website) created the office of "Comptroller General" and provided criteria for his removal from office. Section 303 of that statute specified that the officer, who would

be nominated by the President and confirmed by the Senate, would serve a single term of fifteen years. At the time it was enacted, would this statute have been understood to limit the President's power to remove the officer during the fifteen year term? Why or why not? Assuming the statute was so understood, did Congress have authority, in 1921, to provide this officer with tenure in office that would limit Presidential removal? Why or why not?

12. In dissent, Justice White asserted that the *Bowsher* Court recognized "the legitimacy of legislation vesting 'executive' authority in officers independent of the President." Did the Court do so? If so, did the Court reserve some portion of that power for the President, consistent with Justice White's suggestion that there "are undoubtedly executive functions that, regardless of the enactments of Congress, must be performed by officers subject to removal at will by the President"? What are the characteristics of such functions that distinguish them from functions that can be vested by Congress in officers who are not subject to removal at will by the President?

13. In dissent, Justice White asserted that the core executive functions (addressed in the immediately preceding question) were not at issue in the case and that the functions vested in the Comptroller General were not such as "would in itself improperly interfere with Presidential powers." Does the majority reject the test as well as the conclusion? That is, does the majority of the Court suggest that it is simply the wrong question to ask: "Whether placing the duties at issue in an officer not removable at will by the President improperly interferes with the President's duties?" Or do they agree with that question but reach a different answer?

14. Which of the opinions utilized a formalist methodology and which utilized a functionalist?

15. In dissent, Justice White accused the majority of the *Bowsher* Court of adhering to "rigid dogma" and a "distressingly formalistic view of separation of powers." Which approach—that of the majority or Justice White in dissent—produces the most appropriate role for the judiciary?

16. After *Clinton v. City of New York* and *Bowsher v. Synar*, what alternatives remain for Congress in seeking to facilitate balancing the budget short of a constitutional amendment?

17. Recall that in *Myers v. United States*, Congress had not simply insulated the postmaster from presidential removal, but had insisted on Senate consent for that removal. Even given *Humphrey's Executor*, is this procedure consistent with *Chadha* and *Bowsher*? See *Morrison*, 487 U.S. at 694 (distinguishing the removal situation there and in *Humphrey's Executor*—a simple tenure protection, rather than insertion of Congress into the removal process—from the one in both *Myers* and *Chadha*).

In the course of their work, Professors Calabresi and Yoo address the various historical episodes referenced in **Chapters 1** and **3**, including: President Truman's seizure of the steel mills, *see* STEVEN G. CALABRESI AND CHRISTOPHER S. YOO, THE

Unitary Executive: Presidential Power from Washington to Bush 315–16 (2008); and President Reagan's opposition to the role assigned to the Comptroller General, *see id.* at 379.

TABLE OF CASES

INDEX